Jay and I truly cherish our 50-year relat
and Harvey shared a commitment and dedication to public service in West Virginia
and Kentucky. Their lives continued on parallel paths as Harvey ran for mayor of
Louisville and Jay ran for governor of West Virginia. We treasure our friendship.
Harvey has had a fascinating life by being truly devoted to others. He is a unique
individual with a fascinating life story. Harvey has led and exemplary life from
which we can all learn. Jay and I highly recommend this intriguing book.

—SHARON PERCY ROCKEFELLER
President and CEO of WETA

When one looks up in the dictionary the term "public servant" Harvey Sloane's name
is the example given. From a commitment to medical patients who lacked access and
financial support, to neighborhoods throughout Louisville and Jefferson County who
needed basic support for social services and infrastructure support, Harvey Sloane was
their advocate. His energy, genuineness and vision for making the Louisville
community as good as it could possibly be, made a positive difference in the lives of
over 700,000 citizens of Harvey's adopted hometown. The quality of life for all
Louisvillians throughout the 70's and 80's was positively impacted by Harvey's
decisiveness, leadership and quality of life values that excited and energized Louisville
as never before. The strength of his personality and love of community that he
exhibited daily turned Louisville into a vibrant and destination community!

—JERRY ABRAMSON
Former Mayor of Louisville and Former Lieutenant Governor of Kentucky

Harvey Sloane, whom I have know for many years, is a great humanitarian, doctor,
and devoted family man. He cares tremendously about people and the human race.
His work throughout his life is even deeper with the immense respect he shows his
colleagues, his constituents, his patients, and his family. This book clearly depicts a
man who has lived a good, full, and fulfilling life.

—MARTHA STEWART
Businesswoman, Writer, and TV personality

Riding the Rails is a wonderfully told story of public service at its best. Sloane's many
adventures—from the halls of power in Kentucky to perhaps the grimmest place in
Siberia—offer valuable lessons to anyone interested in the greater good. It could
hardly be more timely.

—PHIL ROOSEVELT
Editorial Director, Magazine, Barron's

Harvey Sloane has written a truly engaging book about a life of breathtaking variety—physician, mayor, candidate, administrator, public health innovator, globe-trotter, activist (a dozen times over)—and a skillful story teller with an apparently limitless and unfailingly vivid memory. If you want to know what it is like to be the mayor of a major American city (Louisville), a dedicated physician saving and enhancing lives around the world, a good man sometimes fired for doing the right thing—but more often recognized for a life of energetic public service—read this book.

— RICHARD PERLE
Political and foreign policy advisor to President George W. Bush,
President Ronald Reagan, and Senator Henry "Scoop" Jackson

Harvey Sloane is an American treasure—a true progressive public servant who dedicated his life to helping the underserved and giving voice to the voiceless. In his fascinating memoir, Sloane recounts his many adventures (from riding the rails and hitchhiking across country) and friendships (with heroes like Muhammed Ali and Harry Caudill), to bringing health care to Appalachia, and as Louisville's two-time mayor who helped integrate the public schools and modernize the city. His storied career, which in its later chapters takes us on a grueling Senate campaign battle against Mitch McConnell, and to Washington, DC where he serves as the city's public health commissioner, has the common denominator of a man acting on principle, with purpose, who made a lasting positive impact. Sloane's is a meaningful life well-lived, and a reminder of how rare it is these days that politicians act as public servants who actually honor the interests of their constituents rather than their personal interest in remaining in power.

— CLARA BINGHAM
Author of Witness to the Revolution: Radicals, Resisters, Vets, Hippies, and the Year America
Lost its Mind and Found its Soul

This is the untold story of a man who followed his calling to change the world and lived a life of undaunted accomplishment. A riveting read that's uplifting at the same time. Harvey Sloane is an inspiration.

— TINA BROWN
Author and journalist

As time passes, the Sloane era in Louisville shines brighter, and his accomplishments seem more enduring. It was my pleasure to observe those yeasty times and to be a part of what surely were among Louisville's "golden days." Harvey Sloane's engaging memoir brings them all back, and what a pleasure to relive them! Or at least most of them.

— KEITH L. RUNYON
Retired editorial page editor, The Courier-Journal.

If you want to understand a life dedicated to public service, read Harvey Sloane's book. He shows us how to serve others in every conceivable way, and how to live nobly, honestly, compassionately, and selflessly. In this age of ego and selfishness, Harvey Sloane gives us a meaningful alternative.

—JOHN YARMUTH
Former U.S. House Representative (KY 3rd District)

Harvey Sloane brings out the best in the American experience: Diligent in his medical skills, dedicated to serving those most in need, patient but persistent in democratic ideals and workmanship, open to fresh knowledge and circumstances, and always teaming with those who share these values. Citizens in Appalachia, DC and Russia have benefited directly from his care. Others throughout the world have benefited from his example and his passion. His call is for all citizens to use their talents, their time and their passion on behalf of their fellow citizens – particularly those of modest means. The rewards are not always immediate or recognizable. But they are real and represent the best of humanity.

—JOHNNY ALLEM
Political Consultant, former DC Deputy Commissioner of Mental Health, and national advocate for Addiction Recovery

Harvey was a truly great Mayor, but his greatest contribution to Louisville is overlooked by many, including Harvey himself. His novel neighborhood walks allowed ordinary people to voice their concerns and problems directly to the Mayor. He reinforced this approach by creating a city department devoted to neighborhoods, fostering organizations and educating residents about the resources of City government. This truly nurtured "power to the people."

—A. WALLACE "SKIP" GRAFTON
Louisville Attorney

An unsanitized adventure tale of a man of privilege who has dedicated his life to improving the lives of the most forlorn and most forgotten. Dr. Harvey Sloane is a citizen of the world who has shown the world the best of America. This memoir is not without humor, but definitely not for the faint of heart. It should be on the reading list of every 14 year old who hopes to do something really important and every 84 year old who failed to. Dr. Sloane is both Dr. Johnson and his own Boswell.

—DAVID LEWIS GOODMAN

Meeting Dr. Harvey Sloane in November 2016 when he asked me to assemble past and present Board Members and Staff who had served during his tenure as the founding CEO of the Neighborhood Health Center was for me like meeting a head of state. As the newly minted CEO, meeting "the legend" was an unexpected dream come true. Dr. Sloane's vision for providing affordable and accessible health care for the most vulnerable and in need and accomplishing that goal in the west end of Louisville Kentucky in 1968 changed the health care landscape for all Kentuckians. The Kentucky Health Center Network (a 501c3 organization composed of only the federally funded health centers in Kentucky) stated that "As of December 31, 2020, KHCN member organizations had more than 2 million patient encounters at nearly 400 clinic sites, including school-based and mobile clinics." The momentum that the founding of the federally funded Neighborhood Health Center in the Park DuValle area of Louisville began has only continued to grow and serve and save lives of patients throughout Kentucky and surrounding states. I knew bits and pieces of that part of the history, but *Riding the Rails* opened my eyes to the full legacy of service exemplified by the life of Dr. Sloane. Louisville native and friend of Dr. Sloane, Muhammad Ali, is quoted as saying "Service to others is the rent you pay for your room here on earth." If service is truly the rent, then Dr. Sloane must be renting an estate. *Riding the Rails* will bring insights into the character, compassion, commitment, perseverance, joys, sorrows, successes, and challenges of a man not only immersed in the health center movement, but also in making the world a better place for all peoples to thrive and grow. This is a "don't miss it" read which will challenge your view of how you too can help change the world.

—ELIZABETH ANN HAGAN-GRIGSBY
Former Chief Executive Officer, Park DuValle Community Health Center, Inc.

I met Dr. Harvey Sloane in 1968. He had a vision of a Health Center in West Louisville. In June 1967, the Office of Economic Opportunity accepted the application and allotted the funds. The Municipal Housing Authority and the city administration designated two buildings in the Cotter Homes housing projects for use of the health center: one of the first in Kentucky. The residents were so happy to have a Health Center! We had to ride a bus if you could afford one or catch a cab to the nearest medical facility miles away. With Dr. Sloane's guidance and a 25-member board made up of community residents, doctors, lawyers, and pastors, we had a Health Center! Dr. Sloane launched the first professional emergency service in Louisville, in addition to patient services including adult, pediatric and dental care, we provided social services and transportation service. The patients were proud of the work Dr. Sloane was doing at Park DuValle. To know Dr. Sloane is an honor and privilege.

—BARBARA MITCHELL, *Original Board Member,*
Park DuValle Community Health Center, Inc.

To Peter,
a fellow traveler
of life.   Harvey

RIDING THE RAILS

My Unexpected Adventures
In Medicine, City Hall and Public Service

HARVEY I. SLOANE

Published through Opus Self-Publishing Services
Located at:
Politics and Prose Bookstore
5015 Connecticut Ave. NW
Washington, D.C. 20008
www.politics-prose.com / / (202) 364-1919

Dedicated to the next generation:
Sloane and Charlie Davenport
Fox and Winslow Sloane

"Ask not what your country can do for you
–ask what you can do for your country."
—PRESIDENT JOHN F. KENNEDY
Inaugural address, January 20, 1961

"We didn't know what we couldn't do."
—LOU BYRON, *Louisville City Government employee and friend*

CONTENTS

Foreword

by Peter D. Hart
(leading pollster and public policy expert,
founder of Hart Research Associates)

I once bumped into Muhammad Ali, the world's heavyweight champion, on the streets of New York, and I mentioned to him our mutual friend, Harvey Sloane. Ali's response put it best: "Harvey Sloane is a good man." Those six words encapsulate what has been a lifetime of devoted public service, both in Sloane's capacity as a medical doctor attending to the health of individuals, and in the various elected, appointed and volunteer positions that he has jumped into over the years in pursuit of what seems to be an insatiable desire to improve the lives of people everywhere, both individually and collectively. As someone who has worked with Harvey on thirteen political campaigns over the years, I can emphatically second Ali: Harvey Sloane is indeed a good man. Over the decades Sloane has held a dizzying series of titles, among them medical doctor, public health officer in Appalachia, volunteer physician in Vietnam, director of Louisville's first community medical center, Mayor of Louisville, KY, County Judge/Executive of Jefferson County, KY, Health Commissioner for Washington D.C. and global health ambassador to Russia and Siberia on a special mission to deal with the health crises of HIV and TB. In this fascinating account of Sloane's unusual journey, one watches as an adventurous young man who spends his college summers hopping trains and hitch-hiking around the country matures into a dedicated doctor and public servant who takes on the toughest political challenges and jumps on planes to the most remote regions of the globe. In the process, one learns what a wild and daring and passionate adventure it can be to be a good man.

George Harvey Ingalls Sloane was born to a family of financial, educational, and social privilege. He was educated at St. Paul's School in New Hampshire, Yale University, Case Western Reserve medical school and the Cleveland Clinic. But it was never the advantages he was born to that shaped Sloane's life. On the contrary, it was his restless curiosity about the world beyond his own privileged domain, his enormous capacity for empathy and his passion to always do his best to help those in need that created the defining arc of Harvey Sloane's life. At an early age, deeply moved by the story told in John Steinbeck's *Grapes of Wrath*, this well-to-do Ivy Leaguer struck out— by rail and by thumb and by motorcycle—to see and learn more about his country. What he saw wound up inspiring him, again and again over the years in one role after another, to turn away from the privilege of his circumstances and instead embrace the privilege of serving those who were less privileged.

Perhaps one of the most unique characteristics of Sloane's lifelong devotion to public service has been that he has always met and served people on their turf, not his own. In every chapter of his life—whether in Appalachia or in Vietnam or in the neighborhoods of Louisville or in the steppes of Russia—Sloane has traveled to wherever constituents and patients who needed his help could be found. After his post-medical-school internship at the Cleveland Clinic, the young Sloane joined the Public Health Program and moved to eastern Kentucky to work on President Kennedy's newly created Appalachian Health Care project. When that two-year program was over, he joined the American Medical Association exchange program and headed out to Vietnam. After Vietnam, haunted by the poverty and poor health care he had seen in Kentucky, Sloane moved to Louisville, KY and, against all odds, founded the Park DuValle Community Health Center—one of the first of its kind, and one that is still going strong 54 years later.

Even when he moved into the political sphere, Sloane's values remained the same and his concern for those in need remained a priority. For the most part, politicians break into two categories: the "ME" candidates and the "WE" candidates. Harvey Sloane has always been a "WE" candidate. As Mayor of Louisville, in a departure from previous administrations, he focused intensely on the various neighborhoods of the city, with a particular concern for leveling the playing field in the lower income neighborhoods. Working with others in the community, he saved the city's transit system and set up Louisville's first emergency medical service. When he ran for Governor of Kentucky, he chose to "walk the state" not as a political gimmick but because that was where Harvey Sloane was most comfortable—in the community, with the people. He liked people and was intensely interested in learning their stories. Sloane has never been a politician in the traditional sense of the word—he is not crafty or cunning, but open and truthful, and he always see things in very human terms versus governmental terms. Politics, like the performing arts, can be an ego driven profession. Candidates can be compassionate and empathic but many merely mouth the words. In a world of "givers and takers," Harvey has always been a 100% giver. Although he never did grab the brass ring to become Governor or United States Senator for Kentucky, in the annals of history he will undeniably be seen as a major player in changing how government served the people there.

One of the joys of reading this book is the anecdotes that surface as Sloane recounts his efforts to improve the various communities and countries in which he has served. His stories are both entertaining and inspiring. His memories of riding the rails and hitch-hiking across the country as a youth are wild and sometimes hair-raising tales; his experiences guiding a city through the racial shoals of school busing are perhaps even more courageous, and they triggered a transformative change for Louisville and Jefferson County. As we follow Sloane—a perennially rail-thin, truth-telling non-politician—as he tilts against the insider groups of political, business, and special interest types that governed so many big cities back in the 1970s and 80s (and still do today), we receive a fascinating lesson in history, as well as a cautionary tale for our present and future. The backdrop for Sloane's 1973 Mayoral race was a nation that was consumed by Vietnam physically and psychologically, and by Watergate and the Nixon impeachment-resignation domestically. America was looking for a fresh group of leaders with a fresh approach. In urban southern cities from Louisville to Raleigh to Miami, the credentials of longevity were being replaced by the credentials of accessibility. The times were changing. From the White House to the Congress to the State House to the Court House, voters were opening up to a whole new generation of leaders including women, minorities and non-politicians. The rule of the "party machine" was being replaced by the appeal of the younger independent candidates with experiences outside of politics. And Harvey Sloane broke all the old molds. He epitomized the kind of candidate the public was looking to elect to make a difference in the quality of their lives. Reading about the various forces in play in this era from our past, one can't help wishing that today, with the unprecedented levels of disinformation and disagreement and unrest that pervade politics, there could be more Harvey Sloanes running for office.

More than anything, perhaps, one hopes that this book will be read by and serve as an inspiration for younger generations. Our country needs honest, caring, fearless individuals who are ready for the kind of grand adventure Harvey Sloane has been on all his life—the adventure of embracing risks, jumping into the fray and taking action to try to make things better for people everywhere. In his poem "The Road Not Taken" the poet, Robert Frost writes about two roads diverging in the woods and concludes: "I took the one less traveled by, and that has made all the difference." Harvey Sloane is a man who has always taken the road less traveled—whether it be by riding the rails across America or by exploring unpaved arteries on four continents around the globe—and by doing so he has always made a difference. In 1961, Frost recited another of his poems—"The Gift Outright"—at the presidential inauguration during which newly elected President John F Kennedy urged a nation to engage with the words: "Ask not what your country can do for you—ask what you can do for your country." Harvey Sloane, a young medical student at the time, happened to be in the audience that day. The young medical student not only heard JFK's words—he accepted the challenge. Pursuing opportunities to help others has been the road Harvey Sloane has chosen throughout his life. And with every step, he has made the world a better place.

November 1974

"By the way, where's the mayor?" Muhammad Ali asked. A crowd had come to the Louisville airport to welcome the famous boxer, and a bunch of us were squeezed into the back of a giant limousine with him. The car—a long, white Cadillac, replete with sunroof, two telephones and a television set—had been sent specially for the occasion by a Kentucky state senator who knew the champ.

"Where's the Mayor?" Ali asked again. My wife Kathy, who was sitting next to Ali in the back seat, pointed to me as I crouched on a jump-seat in the way back of the crowded car. Ali turned to look at me and grinned: "Oh, you're a hippie mayor," he said. "The mayor I remember was bald and old." That's exactly how the great man would describe me to reporters later that day: "Man, we got a hippie mayor."

Just days earlier Ali had knocked George Foreman out in the eighth round of their highly touted "Rumble in the Jungle" match in Zaire. After his victory, Ali had given his hometown a shout-out, proclaiming "Louisville is the greatest!" As the newly elected 38-year-old Mayor of that same town, I had wired Ali my congratulations and agreement. "One reason we are [the greatest] is because of native sons like you," I wrote. "We hope you will come back home to Louisville and give us the chance to show our pride."

A few days after I sent that wire, one Eugene Dibble, identifying himself as Ali's financial consultant, telegrammed me to say that the champ would be arriving in Louisville the following Friday—an arrival date that gave us just five days to organize a fitting homecoming welcome for the famous athlete. To compound the pressure, that five-day span would be punctuated on Tuesday by Election Day, with a referendum I had been pushing on the ballot. For me, Tuesday's final vote on the referendum would mark the culmination of a year-long, hard-fought campaign in which I and County Judge Todd Hollenbach had been trying to convince Louisville and county-wide voters to raise their own taxes in order to save the city's bus system.

As it turned out, those five days would make a fittingly chaotic close to my first year in office as Mayor of Louisville, putting the capstone on a challenging twelve months that had included the worst tornado in the city's history, a wildcat garbage-collectors' strike and an intense campaign to establish the city's first emergency medical service. Surprisingly to many, we won the referendum on the tax hike on Tuesday, and on Friday Muhammad Ali landed in a gleaming white private jet. "The greatest come from Louisville," he proclaimed to the crowd that met him at the airport.

By 1974 Ali had fought his way almost all the way back to the upper tiers of professional boxing, and with his October 30th "Rumble in the Jungle" triumph over reigning champion George Foreman, he was back on top. When he arrived in Louisville that November day in 1974, Ali was electric—a powerful mix of charisma, banter and sheer force of personality. He clearly delighted in the (mostly black) crowds that greeted him first at the Belvedere, the public park and event space overlooking the Ohio River, and then at his old high school, Central High School. Ali had not been back in the decade since he had converted to Islam and fought being drafted into the army, and this crisp, glorious fall afternoon was a raucous display of mutual love between man and city. He stood up through the roof of the limo as he was driven through town, waving at the adoring crowds lining the streets.

When I announced at the Belvedere that we planned to change the name of one of our best-known downtown streets, Armory Place, to Muhammad Ali Place, the crowd went wild. Little did I anticipate the antagonism toward Ali that still smoldered in many white areas of town and the suburbs. The complaints started coming in days later: "You mean you're going to rename Armory Place, where the munitions for our boys in Bataan were during the Second World War, after this draft dodger?" With opposition building, Ali graciously told us to cool it. (Walnut Street was eventually renamed Muhammad Ali Boulevard in 1978, and the Louisville Airport was named after him in 2019.)

That lingering racial animus wove itself all through the region and the times. It found expression in numerous ways, some as blatant as segregated hospitals, others as quiet as whispers about whether blacks could dance ballet. It was the background noise of a region often unwillingly going through a wrenching experience of social reckoning and reconciliation. And it was a smoldering set of tensions which would threaten to engulf the city the following summer when a federal judge ordered Louisville to bus its black students into surrounding Jefferson County and bring white kids into the urban schools. We were the first city to have cross urban-suburban busing and the experience rent the fabric of our community.

Little did I realize that my November 1974 meeting with the living legend Ali would prove the start of a lifelong friendship. He would campaign with me; I would officiate at his wedding to his fourth wife, Lonnie, in my home. And at his end I had the privilege of being one of his honorary pallbearers. Inscribed on his tombstone at Louisville's Cave Hill Cemetery is the epitaph: "Service to others is the rent you pay for your room in Heaven."

My friendship with Ali was just one of many unexpected and notable developments in the often-unpredictable adventure of my life—an ongoing quest that has been largely a personal odyssey of public service. In many ways an unplanned venture, my journey through the years has taken me from cloistered privilege in the Virginia suburbs outside of Washington, D.C. to the back-breaking work of laying pipe in the Gulf of Mexico; from serving as a physician on President Kennedy's Appalachian Healthcare Project and in Vietnam, to a long-shot campaign to become Louisville's mayor; from a career in Kentucky politics when the state and region were changing culturally and politically to the head-spinning mess of Washington, D.C. city government to the public health disaster of post-Soviet Russia.

Most of all, my story is about a life that has been committed to making a difference through public service. The late Justice Oliver Wendell Holmes once said that "as life is action and passion, it is required of a man that he should share in the passion and action of his time, at peril of being judged not to have lived well."

I hope that you will judge me as having lived well—and that my story will inspire others to share in the action and passion of *their* time.

RIDING THE RAILS

My Unexpected Adventures
In Medicine, City Hall and Public Service

HARVEY I. SLOANE

CHAPTER ONE

Early Influences—
From Home To Eternity

I grew up on a farm near Warrenton, Virginia, about 50 miles west of Washington, D.C. My early life was happy and relatively prosperous even though I was born in the gloomy days of the Great Depression, in 1936. But my clearest early memory was my mother waking me at 5 am one 1946 morning with shattering news: "Ingalls, your father's gone to heaven."

Ingalls was my mother's maiden name, and it was her nickname for me. I was 10 years old and could not make sense of my shattered world. I didn't even yet understand the *concept* of heaven.

I was an only child as neither of my parents had children from their respective first marriages. Mother had me by way of a Caesarean section when she was 36. *Her* mother, Katherine Ingalls, insisted that she go to New York, to the old Doctors' Hospital (which has since been torn down) for the birth. Except for some cousins—who weren't nearby—I didn't grow up with any family my age. Perhaps that is one of the reasons Mother sent me to Aiken Prep School in Aiken, South Carolina when I was eleven.

It was certainly why my father had been my best friend and playmate. He had enlisted in the army at age 26, first serving on the

U.S.-Mexican border and then in World War I, before becoming a New York stockbroker and a prominent horseman—his first wife, Isabel Dodge Sloane, owned Cavalcade, winner of the 1934 Kentucky Derby. But heart problems sidelined him at a relatively young age. George "Tod" Sloane was a man of warmth and gentleness and he enjoyed other people immensely. But after a pair of heart attacks other adults treated him as an invalid. So he would read to me for hours and we would play Chinese checkers and cards. We hunted quail and golfed. When he needed exercise, I walked with him. It was an enjoyable life of quiet privilege.

My relationship with my mother was more complicated. Katherine Ingalls Sloane, or Kay as she was called, was a woman with whom to be reckoned: She had strong opinions on just about everything and was active in politics throughout her life. She had, for example, been a leader of the women's Prohibition-repeal movement in Virginia. Her grandfather was Melville Ingalls, who had been chairman of the Big Four railroad. She was the first female delegate from Virginia to a presidential nominating convention, traveling to Chicago to support Franklin Roosevelt in 1932. I knew how to say FDR before I learned A-B-C! She had no sisters (she had two brothers) but had one very close friend, Fern Culver, who lived in Canada; I called her Aunt Fern.

Mother was fearless and generous, sometimes dangerously so. One of the causes to which she was dedicated was helping former prisoners assimilate back into society. In the early 1930s Mother arranged to spend a weekend hosting a newly released prisoner at a female friend's Warrenton home. My father called Mother on the night before she was supposed to do this, explaining the economic devastation of the market crash. "People are jumping out of windows," he said, and pleaded with her to join him in New York City. "Kay, I need you very badly," he said.

Mother got on a train in Washington and went up to New York. When she called her friend on Monday, she learned that her friend had been murdered by the released prisoner. My mother never told me this story. I don't know why exactly she didn't: It might have been because it was such a horrific story, or she might have felt some guilt in not staying with her friend. If the prisoner had killed both of them, our family, particularly me, would have never arrived. I didn't learn this story until years later when Aunt Fern told my wife, Kathy.

During the war, Mother was head of the War Bonds for Virginia, going around the state to sell as many bonds as possible. She was allotted three things during these days of rationing: a car, unlimited fuel and a driver. She chose "Aunt" Fern Culver, her longtime friend, to be that driver. Of course, Canada was in the midst of that war, too, so it was easy for Aunt Fern to come over to be her driver. The two of them drove around Virginia, and in the end they sold more bonds than anyone else in Virginia.

After my father's death, what I wanted most was to be close to Mother, but she pushed me away. She didn't want me tucked away alone on a farm, bereft of masculine influence. So she hired a young man a few years older, Sid Lovett, to keep me company over the following summer. He was 18 and I was 11 but we started a lifelong friendship—but not without some tough love: At one point he admonished me not to be such a "spoiled brat," that I was growing up with too much luxury and expected to always live that way. The remark stung but imparted an enduring lesson for me: I needed to explore life outside my upbringing. Seventy years later, addressing St. Paul's students on a Zoom call, he quipped, "I think that remark may have sparked Sloane to great achievements." Sid remained my oldest friend to the day he died, on October 5, 2021. I proudly spoke of our 74-year friendship at his recent funeral services.

Mother eventually banished me to the Aiken Prep boarding school in South Carolina and, later, to St. Paul's in New Hampshire for high school. (My father had enrolled me at St. Paul's when I was born, for the cost of $25.) And she didn't even keep the farm, selling it in 1948 and moving into Washington, D.C., where she built a place on Whitehaven Street with her third husband, Edwin Graves, a World War II submarine commander who had been captain of the U.S. rowing team which won gold at the 1920 Olympic games in Antwerp. He was a staff officer in Newfoundland at the time of the Atlantic charter, the first meeting between Roosevelt and Prime Minister Churchill.

My mother's aloofness affected me profoundly. From a very young age, I was bereft of family and largely unmoored from any sense of home. It set me on a course of restless independence. Instinctively, I tried to escape the privilege into which I had been born and discover how the rest of this magnificent country lived.

*   *   *

There was one element of my upbringing and my heritage that was so much a part of me that I could not have disentangled myself from it even if I wanted to—something I carry in my heart to this day. In the 1890s, before William Howard Taft became president, he took a delegation from Cincinnati up to visit a small community along the

St. Lawrence about 100 miles above Quebec City, then called Murray Bay. (It has in recent times reverted to its original moniker, La Malbaie—so named by the explorer Samuel Champlain when his ship ran aground there in 1608). Many in the delegation really liked the community and built summer houses. My ancestors, the McKaggs, Taft relations, built our summer house there in 1897. Our house was called the Spinney and from it we would often travel inland to Eternity, a fish and game camp on Petite Lac St. Jean which my family joined when I was three. We would get into a canoe and paddle down the lake seven miles. In later years we had a motorboat. The camp was a solidly built log cabin which had no power but did have running water from the stream. It had a beautiful main room where you ate and you huddled around the great hearth. All the kids loved to sleep in that big room. It was a source of great joy to me, and to my mother and father as long as they lived.

One year, when I was quite young, before my father died, my family was at Eternity when a man flew in on a seaplane and landed on the lake nearby. He came over and said: "Does anyone want to go up? We will have a little flyby to see the lakes at Eternity." I said yes, and Aunt Fern did also. My mother wasn't feeling well so she did not join us. We took off and he started to dip and swing this way and that way, I think showing off. I said to Aunt Fern: "I really feel sick, do you?" She said: "No, I just feel terribly scared, and you can't be sick and scared at the same time." I thought for a moment and asked Aunt Fern: "Would you teach me how to be scared?"

This admission—that I didn't quite know how to be scared—pretty much summarizes the attitude I have taken toward all the adventures I have encountered in life, whether it be climbing mountains, going down rivers, riding the rails or running for elected office.

Mother was quite fit and a good fisherwoman. She and I went with Jean-Marie Menier, an experienced local woodsman and fishing guide and a kind man, for overnight fishing at Lac à la Catin, at the end of a 10-mile portage along trail that goes up a mountain. It is a challenging trip. We got there finally, fished and were having dinner by the fire. Mother had gotten her boots quite wet because we had to go across streams and sometimes you slipped. She took her boots off and laid them by the fire and then we went to bed in our tent. When we awoke the soles were totally burned off. "I will walk down in my slippers," Mother said, without great ado. And that's what she did, over the logs and the stones and forward on the difficult trail.

I have had a few camp adventures of my own over the years, not all of them ending well. One year I went up there with a friend from Cleveland, Harvey Brown. We had decided to take a canoe trip down from our camp at Lac St. Jean, and then walk the 12-mile portage to the La Malbaie River, which eventually empties into the St. Lawrence.

After the canoe trip down the lake and the long portage, we finally got to the La Malbaie river and launched our canoe. What I didn't realize at that time—this was around the mid-'60s—was that they still floated logs down the river to the pulp paper mill near La Malbaie. They would dam up a couple of places along the river, and then they would open the locks. This would flush out the logs from the shore that hadn't gone down in the previous run. It also created a rather sizable torrent rushing down the river.

We got into our canoe with our fishing rods, looking forward to catching and eating a lot of fish that night. We heard a roar from behind us, and then came a six-foot wave of water. They had lifted the locks to get the wood logs off the side of the shore. In seconds it engulfed us and turned our canoe over. A log hit Harvey's temple and knocked his thick glasses off, and we just made it to shore. Our canoe went over the shoot which was about a mile down. We had lost our fishing gear and our camping equipment had floated away.

So, there we were in the latter part of the afternoon. We bushwhacked back to the trail where we had gotten into the river. We were wet and didn't have any matches. And, of course, Harvey could hardly see anything, so I had to lead him around. Finally, when night came, we tried to go to sleep. This was in June and the black flies were just vicious, and of course all our fly repellent had gone down the river. We spent the night trying to cuddle up and get a little sleep. What buzzing in our ears! Anyway, we lived through the night. The next day was beautiful and the sun was out. We marched down the trail—and I didn't go on any more trips for quite a while.

Jean-Marie was an extraordinary man. He was of medium height, strong as an ox. When he paddled against another guide, Belley in a race across the lake, they paddled with such strength and speed that they literally lifted the boats out of the water. Jean-Marie loved the woods and knew everything about them. If our canoe got a hole in it, he would get the sap from a tree and patch it up. He really just fumed when people abused the woods.

Jean-Marie and his family—and he had many children—lived in a small town of Saint-Félix d'Otis, 100 miles away from La Malbaie. In the winter he would take off for a month to trap game and live in the snow, staying at various rudimentary camps. He and I had a real kinship. He taught me everything I know about the woods. He didn't speak any English, but I spoke reasonable French—and together we had some wonderful times.

Our cabin is still there, and my family and I still go up on occasion. We don't go up there as often, and it has gotten tough to carry a canoe.

*   *   *

There are some special places in this world that seem to forge friendships on a deeper, more profound level. La Malbaie and Eternity have always been such places for me. They have remained mainstays for me, for my own family as it developed, and for the friends we have gathered throughout life. My wife Kathy and I have taken our kids and grandchildren up there almost every year, and they love it. The Parti Quebecois, the Quebec nationalist party, came in and broke up the clubs in 1976. And they were not wrong: It was not right that club members had sole access to 200 lakes. And sadly, over the years everyone has fished out these lakes. Now, however, they are re-stocking the lakes and they are limiting the number of fish that can be taken out. The area in general remains very pristine and beautiful.

One of my oldest and most special friends who has shared adventures in Canada with me is Peter Taft. Peter and I met at Yale when we were both inducted into Scroll and Key. Other lifelong friendships from Scroll and Key were Oliver Henkel, Ben Eppes, Anson Beard, David Greenway, Paul Semonin, Bobby Zarem, Sam Schoonmaker, and Scott Sullivan. We were sitting next to each other one day, and we started talking about Canada. Peter said that his family went up to a place called La Malbaie. I said, "Oh, we do too.

And we fish in a place called Eternity." Peter, who was the grandson of President Taft, would always go up with his family in July and we would always go up in August—so we had never met up there. We finally went there together for the first time after Peter's father, Charlie Taft, died. We swam the lakes together (he was captain of the Yale swim team) and we carried canoes up the mountains on trips together.

Peter, a successful attorney, continues to visit La Malbaie each summer (with his wife Diana). There is a group of four of us in La Malbaie most summers who were born the same year and have celebrated many milestone birthdays together with our families. The group also includes my close friend from St. Paul's and Yale, Reeve Schley (and his wife Georgie), who is a successful painter with a substantial body of work in watercolor and oil. Philippe de Montebello, the former long-time director of the Metropolitan Museum of Art in New York completes our birthday group (with his wife Edith). Unhappily the COVID-19 pandemic prevented us from celebrating in 2020. But we made it in 2021.

Other friends who have shared good times with us at Eternity and La Malbaie include the former NBC News anchor Tom Brokaw and his wife Meredith, CBS anchor Dan Rather and his wife Jean. John and Judy Bross are a wonderful couple who helped revive the local Murray Bay protestant church. We were saddened by John's death in 2020, and appreciate Judy's continued devotion to collecting and sharing stories of La Malbaie's history and culture. I also appreciate that she helped me in preparing this manuscript.

One of our most enduring friendships that was definitely strengthened by shared time in Canada has been with Tom and Pam

Wicker. Tom, who died in 2011, was one of the most wonderful people I ever met. A North Carolina native, he rose in the journalism ranks and eventually became The New York Times' Washington Bureau Chief. He was as deep a liberal as I ever met, particularly on civil rights. One of his great books, 1975's *A Time To Die*, was about the 1971 Attica prison riot in upstate New York. The prisoners, living under horrid conditions, and tortured by the New York prison authorities, rebelled and took 38 hostages. They asked for Tom, among others, to come up and mediate with the state about their grievances. He did that and presented potential agreements with the state and they suggested that Nelson Rockefeller, then New York's Republican governor, go to the prison. His advisers told him not to go and he did not, which proved to be a fateful mistake. Police stormed the prison, killing 10 hostages and 29 inmates.

Tom and Pam came up with us in the late 1970s and fell in love with the lake. When President Taft's son (and Peter's father) Charlie Taft sold the camp he had built, the Wickers acquired it. Even after Tom's death Pam continues to come up each summer for a month. Kathy and I spent a night with her at her camp in 2021. For a woman in her late 70s and early 80s coming up was courageous. She renovated the cabin so that it could withstand the heavy winds that come blasting down the lake.

The Spinney in La Malbaie has sheltered multiple generations of my family, including my mother and father, my wife Kathy and me, and our children and grandchildren. In the 2000s our daughter Abigail was married there in the small Murray Bay Protestant church. It was wonderful to ride in a horse and carriage with her down to the church. In 2007 my son Patrick proposed to his wife-to-be Erin. They took a canoe out to the narrows of the lake at Eternity in the moonlight. When he knelt down in the middle of the canoe, two large owls immediately flew out of a nearby tree, blessing the union.

Over the years I have greatly enjoyed my trips to Quebec, Canada, and have developed a great respect for the citizens of my adopted country. I find French Canadians to be very friendly to Americans in general, and if you can speak French they are even more responsive. One issue that French Canadians—who were the original settlers of Canada—get really worked up about is their language and culture, which they are constantly fearful will be overcome by the English-speaking provinces of Canada. French Canadians have even had two referenda proposing the secession of the Province of Quebec from Canada. The first referendum in 1982 was defeated, with 60% voting against it and 40% voting in favor. The second referendum in 1995 was barely defeated, with 50.6% voting against it and 49.4% voting in favor. Alec Patterson, a leading attorney from Montreal who is a friend from La Malbaie, worked closely with Canadian Prime Minister Jean Chretien to defeat the referendum. In my opinion such a secession would have had severe implications and a negative impact, and I hope it never happens.

I admire the way that Canadian government has addressed two issues in particular: gun control and health care. Although the French Canadians have a lot of guns and they do a lot of hunting, every firearm must be registered. This is strictly enforced, and there are very few shooting deaths in Canada compared to The United States. The other social value that I admire in Canada is their National Health Service. Every citizen can receive medical service at no charge, and every family is covered. Bankruptcy from health care expenses simply

doesn't exist, and I have found the quality of Canadian medicine—
from personal experiences in our family—to be very good. If only the
U.S. could look to its neighbor—and biggest trading partner—for
guidance on these issues.

CHAPTER TWO

Charting My Course—
Thumb, Rail and Bike

When I told my mother in the spring of 1954 that I needed to see the world and planned to do it by hitchhiking, she was not pleased. It wasn't the traveling she minded, just the hitchhiking. So she made me a proposition: She would pay my way wherever I wanted to go as long as I took the train or, short of that, the bus. I said absolutely not, and we spent the next several days arguing.

She was still pleading for the bus when she stopped the car on the outskirts of Washington D.C. on Route 1 heading south toward Richmond. My St. Paul's classmate and fellow recent graduate Sam Sylvester and I both climbed out and threw our knapsacks on the ground. I told Mother I'd send a postcard every week or so. She said she'd worry anyhow. I told her there was no need. Stalemated, she said goodbye, told us to be careful and drove off.

Sam and I had never hitchhiked before and while we weren't about to let on, we both felt awkward. I tried to look worldly, but was self-conscious of even my thumb, certain there was a right way to hold it of which I was unaware. We stood there for 20 minutes without luck when a car began to slow and pull off, onto the shoulder.

It was Mother, back to make one last pitch for the bus. I was furious, ready to take off walking if I had to. I shouted at her and Sam joined me. She had no chance, she realized, and she finally gave up.

I was fortunate my rebellion took the form it did. I would spend the next five summers hitchhiking or jumping freight trains to get where I needed to go, and those summers were among the most important times of my life. Each summer, I would leave home with no more than $75, intent on paying my own way with honest labor and on accepting whatever adventure came along. Calling home for more money wasn't an option. My experiences, starting that summer just before my first year at Yale, gave me the self-confidence to face life's challenges. I didn't know what I could not do.

*   *   *

Many today see the 1950s as a golden age, but it was a bland period of quiet conformity for the nation. I felt like I was gliding down a preplanned trail—prep school, boarding school, Yale—from which I yearned to escape. I started my travels motivated by a fear of being swallowed up in the gray flannel morass of the times and I longed for a sense of mission, common purpose and social challenge—qualities that the nation as a whole seemed to lack. I longed for an independence that was not the freedom many assume comes from wealth, but one that derives from following one's own course. What I found was the satisfaction not of having set myself apart but of having made my own place.

John Steinbeck's *The Grapes of Wrath* had deeply influenced me at St. Paul's: It described an existence utterly alien to me, that was playing out in my own country. It made me see that my own worldview was terribly narrow. It communicated such a sense of despair—in people who had nothing but their land and were watching it die—that it inspired me to explore the country. In my pampered upbringing, I had not conceived of, let alone seen, such a side of life. By the time I graduated from St. Paul's my world seemed a comfortable and confined cocoon, my friends and I pampered and pretentious. To climb into life, I reasoned, I would first have to leave comfort behind and live on society's margins, give up the East and go to the frontiers.

In the 1950s hitchhiking was much more commonplace. The great transcontinental highway system that President Dwight Eisenhower called for was still in its preliminary stage, and the police were also a lot more lenient since most of the roads were two lanes. There was some concern about security, which was why my mother was against it, but I never had a bad experience in my five years of hitchhiking, including three cross-country trips. People, usually men, were interested in talking and getting my story. It was much more common to be picked up by a solo driver than to be picked up by a car that had more than one occupant.

Truckers were the most interesting drivers I encountered. Hitchhiking on trucks was more difficult because many companies prohibited truck drivers from picking up hikers. On a couple of occasions, I met drivers at truck stops and asked them to give me a lift. Many were accommodating, especially after meeting me in person rather than seeing me from a distance on the side of the road.

One driver eagerly talked about his life on the road and his dislike of erratic drivers, particularly at night. We were in eastern Colorado, where the land was rolling but not mountainous, following a car of teenagers who would slow on an incline and then speed up going down the other side. A truck that slowed down going up the hill had to downshift a number of times (some had eight gears) but when he reached the top of the hill and the car with the teenagers accelerated, he couldn't catch them and pass. After this happened a number of times, he turned off his lights and slowed down so the teens didn't see him. They probably thought he had turned off the road.

Then the trucker sped up and climbed the next hill going at a good speed. The car had reached the top of the hill and was not going particularly fast. The trucker, going at a good speed, was able to accelerate significantly going down it so he was directly behind the car. He passed the car and when he was parallel to it on the downhill, fishtailed his rear end to hit the car, causing it to veer off the road. "Why did you do that?" I yelled at him. "You could have killed those kids!" He responded: "That serves them right. they had been messing with me for over an hour and that will be the last time they will do that." I got off at the next town and went to a junkyard to sleep in a car.

That first summer on the road with Sam was glorious. We hitchhiked to New Orleans, worked at a lumber company owned by a classmate Cochie Rathborn, and headed west again on Route 66. We hooked up with a used-car hustler in Amarillo, Texas who paid us $3 a day to drive one car and tow another to Portland non-stop. We lived off the Salvation Army, or "Sally" as we called it, joining the sullen shuffle to afternoon religious services and being rousted at 4am to start looking for work. We bought a cheap 1945 motorcycle, sideswiped a parked car at a Lake Tahoe hotel, and spent two weeks washing dishes for nothing to pay for the manager's silence. We camped out. We spent stormy nights holed up in junkyard wrecks. We worked and we lived on 40 cents a day.

In Oregon, we picked strawberries with Native Americans on Mt. Hood, and felt the vise that squeezes migrants. The rate for a crate of berries—six cartons to a crate—was 25 cents. To make anything at all meant long days and few breaks. It was not actually active work, which made it worse: just one berry after another, one bush after another, one row after another. You squatted all day, your body cramped, your mind rebelled. And there was nothing to relieve the frustration—no bursts of exertion, no time to relax, no room for anger or sloppiness. The "strawboss" checked every berry and threw out any that were bruised, rejected any whose stems hadn't been plucked. About the best anybody could do was two crates an hour—50 cents. Even then it was not enough on which to support a family, so the fields were full of men, women and children—whole clans toiling together so they could get by.

The migrants had a kind of strength, decency and mutual concern that was alien to the competitiveness and exclusiveness of my background. Despite the differences between us, they accepted and helped me, teaching me how to pick and how to stay out of trouble with the straw boss. I was proud to be working with them, and I gloried in the camaraderie of the fields. I admired them and disliked the world that gave me so much and them so little. The sympathies born in those fields were the same ones that later led me to spend my nights working at the New Haven Hope Mission and to decide on a career of service.

In Southern California, we picked celery with Mexican migrants. It paid better than strawberries, 78 cents an hour, but in return the workers had to live in the shacks and eat the food the grower provided—at a cost of a quarter of the day's wages, deducted before you were paid. The shacks were miserable, furnished only with tables and bunk beds. Each night 30-50 people jammed into each one.

At the end of the summer, Sam and I motorcycled home, trading places every hour because the ride on the luggage rack of the spring-less rear end pounded your kidneys. We had 75 cents for meals between the two of us each day but the only thing I missed during the summer was milk, and I dreamed of it during that 10-day return. When we got home, I figured that if milk would be good, cream would be better and proceeded to down four pints—which I promptly threw up.

Sam took off for New England and I rode the motorcycle up to La Malbaie. I-95 had not been built yet, so I had to take a series of local roads. I started having stomachaches so bad that I had to stop and curl up alongside the road. However, they improved once I got to Canada and ate some regular meals.

The pains returned after I started at Yale so when I returned to Washington at Thanksgiving, my mother insisted that I go to see the family physician, Dr. Leigh Martin, at Johns Hopkins. He took x-rays and diagnosed me with a peptic ulcer, or more specifically a duodenal ulcer, which meant that it was situated in my small intestines. He knew my background and specifically my relationship with my mother. At the end of the visit, he said if I don't get this straightened out "You'll end up as James Forestall did."

Forestall had been a successful financier who joined the New Deal, and at the end of World War II became Secretary of the Navy and then, after the war, President Harry Truman's Secretary of Defense. But he "resigned" in 1949 after finding out that Truman planned to replace him (Forestal had secretly sided with Truman's opponent, Tom Dewey, during the 1948 election) and subsequently fell into a deep depression. That May he jumped from a 16th floor window at Bethesda Naval Hospital, killing himself. I guess Dr. Martin was saying that if I didn't get things worked out with my mother the inner conflict would drive me to suicide.

*   *   *

Yale seemed a paltry place when I arrived as a freshman that fall, and I doubted it could teach me anything of value. I was bored, resentful, and full of myself. To be honest, I led a double life throughout my college years. I put in my time at Yale and in Washington. I played squash, became captain of the team that won the collegiate playoffs in 1958, attended classes and went to Christmas season coming-out parties. But my heart and my imagination were always far off. I would spend hours in the library just looking through atlases and yearning to be gone. Studying seemed so remote that I often couldn't do it at all. I would head to the New Haven railroad yards and spend my nights hopping boxcars, riding them back and forth as freights were being "humped"—a process in which the engine takes about four or five cars at a time, pushes or drags them to where there is a switch in the track and then connects them with the rest of the train. During my vacations, I would go to whatever wilderness I could reach by whatever means I could get there—by thumb, by rail or by motorbike.

Near the end of that first fall semester at Yale I had to return home to Washington, to rest and follow a very bland diet in an effort to heal my duodenal ulcer. After a week or so I was feeling fine, but with the upcoming Christmas holidays I knew there would be a lot of debutante cotillion parties at the Sulgrave Club that my mother would really want me to go to. This Washington tradition of boys and girls meeting at elegant dances was not something I looked forward to—you had to get all dressed up and your manners had to be perfect. While attending one Cotillion the previous year I had spilled some champagne down the front of the dress of the woman that organized the events, Mrs. Shippen, which hadn't endeared me to her. With Christmas fast approaching, I began thinking about ways to get out of town. A former teacher I admired had recently retired to Spokane, WA, and when he suggested I come visit him over Christmas, I jumped at the opportunity.

The first obstacle was how to get to the West Coast. While perusing an automobile magazine, I came across an ad looking for someone to drive a '52 Plymouth from Chicago to Tacoma, Washington. The driver would get $3 a day plus gas. Bingo. I took a bus to Chicago and went to the address listed in the ad. The 52 Plymouth seemed to be in pretty good shape, except that the front tires were a little bald and the steering wheel had a 50s "Neckers'" knob—a spinning knob on the steering that allowed the driver to navigate with his left hand, leaving his right arm and hand free to attend to the girl sitting beside him.

As I left Chicago it was starting to snow, and by the time I headed toward Indiana to get on a major road west I was in a full-blown blizzard. At one point I got stuck behind a semi-truck that was going about 20 miles an hour, and I thought to myself: it's going to take me a week to get to Spokane at this pace—so I pulled into the left lane to pass. The road was slushy, and as the car swerved to the left I tried to bring it back to the right—but the cuff of my coat caught on the Neckers' knob, and the next thing I knew the car was lying on its right side in a ditch by the side of the road. As I crawled out of the car through the one door that was accessible, Elvis Presley singing "Rock Around the Clock" was blasting from the radio. A snowplow was passing by, and the driver yelled out, "Do you want me to turn you right side up?" I said "Absolutely! Thanks!"

I resumed my trip, which was uneventful until I picked up an army private hitch-hiking back to his camp in California. When we got to the Rocky Mountains my passenger said, "I know a shortcut." He pointed to a narrow road that went along the side of a mountain, tilting toward the mountain and away from the gorge below. The road had started to freeze and there was about an inch of black ice, and the car (with its slightly bald tires) was slipping and sliding wildly as we tried to ascend. The army private said, "OK I'll get out and push you around the curves." He got out, climbed up on the embankment, put his hands on the side of the car and damned if he didn't push the car around the slippery curves all the way up the mountain.

After dropping my hitchhiker at a spot where he could head to San Francisco, I headed north to Tacoma. I finally reached the city on Christmas Eve. It was a foggy night and there were dim lights on the main street as I came in, and I didn't see a Buick with no taillights stopped at a light which was turning from yellow to red—I missed a full-on collision with the Buick, but the right front side of the Plymouth hot pretty banged up.

My next stop was the police station. The Plymouth, having now weathered two accidents, had to be towed—the right front bumper and fender were pretty well finished, as was the door that had landed on its side in the ditch in Indiana. When the police captain saw that I had no money to pay for damages to the car and heard that I was trying to get to Spokane for Christmas Eve, he must have decided the best thing would be to get me out of town before I did any more damage. "OK," he said, "I'll give you $25 for a train ticket."

I finally got to Spokane about 9 pm Christmas Eve, and my former teacher and I had a good hearty Christmas dinner. He lived in a very modest one-bedroom house, and after dinner he invited me to spend the night in his big double bed. I was so exhausted I fell asleep immediately. However, sometime during the night I felt a cold hand settling on my shoulder. I literally jumped out of bed as if an electric current had shocked me. I caught the first bus I could back to Washington and, chastened by all my recent misadventures, dutifully went to the remaining parties my mother was so anxious for me to attend.

My first year at Yale might have turned out badly but for a stroke of fortune: Sid Lovett Sr., the father of my old friend whom my mother had years earlier employed as my summer companion, was the master of Pierson College, the residential college to which I was assigned at the University (he had previously been the school chaplain). He knew how to roll with the punches, never pushing anything to a crisis. My mother hated my motorcycle, going so far as to call Uncle Sid, as we called him, to tell him that I had one, which was illegal at Yale. I was furious with her and when he confronted me, I got my hackles up. "Uncle Sid, she ratted on me," I complained. "There's just no choice. Either I keep the motorcycle, or I leave." My one concession was that I wouldn't ride it in New Haven. He let the whole thing drop.

Despite Uncle Sid's light touch, I still felt smothered in Yale's cosseted, ivy walls. Toward the end of that first year, I decided I couldn't put up with another year and gave him a letter asking for a leave of absence. My plan was to take a tramp steamer to Australia and farm sheep. Uncle Sid handled my request to leave characteristically: He listened to me, he sympathized with me and he talked with me about my choices. He didn't try to talk me out of it, but he ended our talk by saying he would hold a room open for me in case I changed my mind.

* * *

By the end of my freshman year at Yale, I had dispensed with my plans to farm sheep in Australia. Instead, I did heavy construction work along the Peace River in the outer reaches of Alberta, Canada— sleeping in warehouses where the gasoline fumes were strong enough to drive away the mosquitoes, living with a 350-pound man named "Slim" who did all the cooking, with the main ingredient of each meal seeming to be grease. I had hitchhiked to Alberta with David Salisbury, a school friend who had left Yale at Thanksgiving of our freshman year to study Voodoo in Haiti. He never did return to the school. Seeing him cooled my passion for the drifting life: He didn't seem to have a vision of what he wanted to do next. After taking biology my freshman year the idea of a career in medicine had already started to take hold for me. I decided to go back to the room Uncle Sid was holding open for me, and Australia remains a continent I have not seen.

One thing David did teach me was how to ride the rails. My fascination with railroads had started at an early age, perhaps in part because my great-great-grandfather Melville E. Ingalls had been chairman of the Big Four—the Cincinnati, Chicago, Cleveland and St. Louis railroads. The transcontinental railroad, signed into law by President Abraham Lincoln in 1862 and completed in 1869, served as a great unifier of the country after the divisiveness of the Civil War. To me the network of rails crisscrossing the country spelled adventure. My friend David explained the fine art of hopping trains to me: "First of all, if the train is moving and you grab one of the ladders, you should always grab the front ladder. If you grab the ladder on the rear of the car and the train is moving forward and you can't keep your grip, you will swing between the two cars. There's also a good chance that you would fall between the cars." He added that if you're in an open boxcar you should always jam the runner with a stick. He had almost died once in Nevada when the boxcar door had shut and he broiled in the metal box in the sun for the better part of a day.

After Salisbury and I left Alberta and parted ways at the Montana border, I had my very first experience hopping a train. One morning before dawn, when a fruit express bound for Chicago stopped to pick up ice, I followed Salisbury's advice and grabbed the front ladder of a boxcar. Fruit expresses had no open cars, so I had to ride on top. It was a great way to go: They traveled about 80 to 90 miles per hour, had priority over other trains, and didn't stop unless they had to. This one went all the way to Minneapolis without halting, arriving the next night. There was no way to sleep, because one had to look out for tunnels, and I didn't have any food, but I was so enraptured by the wind, the land and simply being where I was, that I didn't mind.

All I really lacked was the privacy of a bathroom. Instead, at those speeds, I had to climb onto the car's rear ladder, hold on with one hand, drop my pants with the other, and swing out. I was afraid someone would see me and checked the coast for farmhouses and cars. It looked clear. But while I was hanging, a Cadillac pulled up alongside the train. There were two men inside and the passenger spotted me. They slowed down, stayed even with me and drove along laughing and waving.

I hadn't slept or eaten in 36 hours, so when we stopped in Minneapolis, I grabbed a dinner, rounded up some rope and climbed back aboard. I made myself a bed, stuffing my clothes on the catwalk as a mattress and tying my sleeping bag over them. I crawled in as the train slowly began to pull out. The inspectors' lights flashed past me, but the locomotive didn't stop. I figured I had made it.

The train slowed and halted roughly 20 miles later. The caboose man climbed up to the catwalk and shined his light at me. "Okay, kid, get off," was all he said. I asked him to give me a break and let me ride in the caboose. He refused: "They've stopped this whole train because of you, and you have to get off."

After I'd taken my makeshift bed apart and climbed down, the caboose man pointed to the river, where a boat was scanning the shore with its spotlight. "You see that river? Well, that's the Mississippi," he said. "And you see that patrol boat out there? A guy escaped from the penitentiary and they're looking for him. If they see you, they'll arrest you, so watch out." I thanked him for the warning and took off. Each time the search light swung past I hit the ditch. It took me until daylight to reach Minneapolis. I gave up the rails for that trip and hitched the rest of the way. That was my first, but not last, warning about an escaped prisoner in my area.

Hopping trains was not always a lonely existence. I once jumped aboard a northbound freight and swung into an already-full boxcar. A large family of migrants had settled in at one end of the car while a collection of hoboes and winos occupied the other. I didn't want to disrupt the family, but I didn't want to join the hoboes either: They would roll anybody sleeping alone for the price of a bottle of wine. I finally went to the family and asked if I could join them. Without hesitating, they said yes and made a place for me.

The contrast between them and the hoboes struck me powerfully. They represented a fundamental choice between isolation and social commitment: The winos had withdrawn from social bonds, isolating themselves and choosing lives of thievery. But even though the migrants' existence was a daily struggle they hadn't given up. They were a vital unit, each relying on the other, and their commitment to maintaining the common human bond was broad enough to include even me. The migrants had a kind of strength, decency and mutual concern that was remote from my own background's competitiveness and exclusiveness.

*   *   *

I came to an uneasy truce with Yale in my second year there, deciding to use it as my ticket out of the very world it represented. I entered the pre-med program, seeing medicine as an instrument of service. My new plan was to go to Alaska and start a flying medical service for the Native Alaskans.

I majored in American studies, though, aiming to get a broad liberal arts education. One of the last courses that I took was "History of the 20th Century," given by John Blum. It started with the Progressive Era and Teddy Roosevelt and went on into Franklin Roosevelt's New Deal. Blum closely followed Arthur Schlesinger Jr.'s FDR trilogy and brought life to the incredible advances in governance and social welfare during the Depression. Little did I know that I would eventually get to know Arthur quite well and become friends with him.

There was no one in my class at Yale who had ridden freight trains, so I took a mate, Bill Becklean, down to the railyard at night where they "hump" the trains. One night when we were going back and forth, we got on a car that did not stop to be humped, but instead chugged onward out of the yard to New York City. I spoke with Becklean recently, and when I reminded him of our adventure he said, "stupidest thing I ever did." For me it was a great ride. I have told my son Curtis, a musician, that at my funeral I want Willie Nelson's rendition of "Orange Blossom Special" to be played.

I had another unexpectedly long ride with another friend when once again the engineer did not stop to hump in the yard but continued on to Poughkeepsie. Vassar is in Poughkeepsie, so we spent a day with some dates before we returned to New Haven. Another night I was down in the New Haven yard alone, and the train I was planning to hop was going a little bit faster than I had judged. I grabbed the ladder bar, and I was pulled up by the side of the boxcar. I couldn't keep my grip and fell down, doing a somersault and looking up at the wheels of the train grinding past. I can still see the train's undercarriage in my mind's eye, disaster inches away.

I split the summer of 1956, after my sophomore year at Yale, between my two lives. I needed to take a course in qualitative analysis for my pre-med studies. One of my roommates, George Graham, also needed to take the course so we went to Muhlenberg College in Allentown, Pennsylvania, which had the shortest course we could find. So for six weeks we boarded at a funeral parlor, took the course, and passed—despite the overwhelming formaldehyde fumes that engulfed us at night.

I had talked to my other roommate, Norrie Sellar, about going to Mexico on a secondhand Harley 61 that I had recently purchased. Unlike my first motorcycle, the Harley 45 which only had one seat and a rear-end luggage rack with no springs, this Harley had a buddy seat. Norrie and I left from Washington and headed straight down to Mexico City. From Mexico City we made our way through the mountains, staying in a rural areas that were so riddled with bandits we had to stash our motorcycle inside whatever sleeping quarters we found. When we reached Tasco, we stayed with some St. Paul's friends for a night, and then made our way to the great resort on the Pacific, Acapulco. After skin diving for a week, we took the same route back to Washington. I left Norrie there and went up to Canada to our summer spot In La Malbaie.

One night while I was in Canada, I took a girl named Bonnie Cabot out for dinner, picking her up on the Harley. When I returned her to her home in a nearby community, the road was not paved, and I slipped on a turn. Luckily, she was not hurt, but I hit my head on a rock—helmets were not common then—and was knocked out. A car came by in about 15 minutes and it had two Catholic priests who proceeded to give me last rites.

I woke up the next day in the small hospital in La Malbaie. My mother insisted that I get rid of the motorcycle, but I told her that I had to get back on otherwise I might become afraid of it. From our house I drove on a dirt road about 100 miles to our fishing camp, then after a week or so went down to New Haven. I remember going through the Laurentides region in the morning. It was freezing and I had no gloves. But I was back on the bike. By the time I got back to Yale for my sophomore year that fall, I had traveled over 7,500 miles on that bike.

For Thanksgiving break that year, Norrie and I jumped back on the Harley 61 and headed down to Washington. It took us a drizzly six hours to ride from New Haven all the way to DC, and when we arrived we decided to go have a beer. Neither of us looked very presentable: I had a black leather jacket with MOTHER in large letters on the back. After about 20 minutes the hostess came up and said that we would need to leave or pay a fee because entertainment was coming in. We delayed and didn't immediately get up and soon two police officers confronted us. When one grabbed Norrie by the arm he instinctively resisted. The next moment the officer had flipped Norrie onto the floor, and then hit him over the head with his night stick. Blood rushed out (he would require nine stitches at the emergency room). I lost control and went after the policeman. The next thing I knew we were being booked for assaulting police officers, a federal felony in D.C.

I called my mother who said she wasn't going to have anything to do with it and that I should call our friend the Ambassador from Peru, Lucio Berckemeyer. I can only think that Mother was hoping that the intervention of someone with diplomatic immunity would inure to our benefit. Ambassador Berckemeyer got us legal representation and eventually the charges were reduced from a felony to a misdemeanor and then, given the aggressive behavior by the police against two white college boys, they let us off with a fine. I've always wondered what would have happened differently at every step of the process if we had been black. Neither the beat cops nor the prosecutors would have been as lenient with us: At best we would have been tried on the felony charges and probably spent time in jail. Who knows after that? The stream of injustices which sparked the Black Lives Matter movement have been a vivid reminder of our justice system's duplicity. And six decades ago it was even less subtle and more brutal.

In any case, that Thanksgiving break ride from Yale to DC would be the last of my motorcycle days.

*   *   *

While I had always enjoyed sports, playing hockey, baseball, football and squash in high school at St. Paul's, I had really focused on the latter at Yale. Squash is a very competitive solo sport, and it depends totally on that individual and his or her proficiency, which I suppose particularly suited my loner mindset. It's a sport that requires excellent endurance and also enough skill to make the shots. John Skillman was the coach of the Yale squash team and had one adamant admonition: Capture the T and stay on it. The T designates the service boundaries, with one line dividing each side of the court and another running perpendicular, at the center of the court. Why capture the T? You can cut off balls before they get to the rear wall; also, you can keep your opponent moving, eventually tiring him out. The ball was harder than it is today, and as a match progressed it would become more and more difficult to put the now heated ball away—especially for the player behind the T.

I was the top freshman player in my first year. Then in the spring of 1957, when I was a junior, we went undefeated, winning the collegiate championship with Eddie Meyer as captain. He and I ranked first and second respectively. In 1958, my senior year, I was captain of the team, and as we entered the last game of the season— against our archenemy, Harvard—we had another undefeated season going. Our teams were tied 4-4 going into the final match, which pitted the two teams' top players against each other. I would be playing against Gerry Emmet, who was All-American and the favorite to win. At that time matches were played best three out of five. I went down 2 -1 after three games. All Coach Skillman said to me during the break was: "Sloane. Stay on the T." By the fifth game we were 13-all and then went 4-4 in overtime. Heeding my coach, I stayed on the T, in front of Emmett. His return of my backhand allowed me to make a perfect backhand reverse corner shot for the win.

"Yale for the 2nd Year—Unbeaten," Jim Zug wrote in Squash magazine.

*   *   *

I hit the road again in the summer of 1957. Work was hard to come by and I ended up in Rawlins, Wyoming. It was one of those towns that hitchhikers dread: just large enough to get to and just small enough to get stuck in. I'd been standing on the road to Laramie for a while when a little girl walked up. She must have been around eight years old. She asked what I was doing, and when I told her I was after work, she said her dad might be able to get me a job on his road construction crew.

She took me home, and her parents, Dale and Eileen Childers, took me in. They fed me, gave me a bed and made me part of their family. Each morning for almost a week, Dale took me to the construction site where he worked and tried to get me on. Each morning, no luck. I was about ready to give up when the town blacksmith, Jake Thompson, put an ad in the paper for a helper. Summer was his busy season, for it was then that he needed to make the wagons sheep herders lived in during the bitter Wyoming winters.

I took a room at the town's only hotel and spent my summer there. By day and sometimes at nights, I helped Jake with the hammer and anvil work and pumped him for stories. He was about 70 and had lived his life on the frontier. He was big and still strong, a skilled craftsman who took his work seriously. He loved the West and respected the land, and he resented the tourists and developers who were despoiling it. We had that in common.

Two or three nights a week, when we weren't working, I went to the Childers' for supper. The kids treated me like a big brother; Dale and Eileen treated me like a son, and I adopted them as my family. I'd play with the kids and after eating we would all go for walks, Dale and I carrying the little ones on our shoulders. I couldn't imagine finer people. They lived a modest life and the times were hard for them, but they made room for me without hesitation. They later moved to a farm in Arco, Idaho, and we wrote occasionally.

On weekends, I hiked, taking along my sleeping bag and just enough food and water to be safe. The country is open, barren but beautiful, and I would walk for miles and miles, drinking in the vastness. At night, I would build a fire and sleep under the sky, awakening at the first streaks of dawn and watching it grow.

I was not always alone. One morning when I awoke, I thought I felt something next to my leg. The area was full of rattlers and I knew that if I moved, and if it was a rattler, it would strike. I lay there dead still for two hours, fighting against fear and trying to convince myself it was only my imagination. It wasn't. When the sun was high enough to warm the bag, I felt the snake begin to move. He slithered slowly up my leg, up my arm, and out of the bag just in front of my face. I never did know if it was rattler. Those were the worst hours of my life.

*   *   *

In the summer of 1958, after I had graduated from Yale, the song "The Shrimp Boats"—"Shrimp boats is a-comin'/Their sails are in sight…"—was in my head. So I decided to hitch south, toward New Orleans.

I got a ride with a man who was going down to the Gulf of Mexico and when I told him my story, he suggested I come with him to East Bernard, Texas, where Tennessee Gas had a well and a station. It's tough work, he said, but if you like it, I think you could get on. So I went down with him and met the Tennessee gas officials. They said they were laying pipe from a well in the Gulf to the station on land. The work would all be carried out on the ocean and all workers would sleep and eat on a barge. I met the head foreman, who everyone called "Slim," who was about 40 years old and had a big cowboy hat on and was wiry thin. Slim looked me in the eye and asked where I was from. I said I am from Washington, D.C. and he said, "OK Washington, let's see what you can do." He called me Washington the rest of that summer.

I ended up with the job of buffing a 10-inch concrete-covered, metal pipe so that it could be welded. I used to sit on a bucket, waiting for the next pipe to be pushed along. I once got up to use the bathroom and while I was there it started to lightly rain, which caused the pipe to slip and fall—directly on the bucket I had been sitting on. It left a big circular dent. I was glad to miss that one.

The men were hard workers. Many of them were soldiers of fortune who would work for weeks and then go and spend their money in New Orleans. But some had families. The foreman I had first met, Slim, was sympathetic. One day he told me to help him cut the one-inch steel wire we would thread around the pipe. This involved swinging a sledgehammer down onto a cutter which would slice through tough metal wire. One person would hold the cutter while another would swing the hammer. The problem was that the hammer could miss and maim the fellow holding the cutter. Slim told me to swing the hammer. I knew he was testing me: If I said I couldn't do it my fellow workers would think less of me. So I had to take the chance of swinging a sledgehammer and hope I hit the cutter and not Slim. I brought up the sledgehammer and said a silent prayer: "Please, Lord, guide my hand so I don't hit him." The first swing connected solidly with the cutter. "Swing 'er again, Washington," Slim said. I was lucky because I had done a lot of axing and wood-chopping at Eternity. The second swing was also true—but I still never wanted to do that particular act again.

I worked there for two months, getting nine dollars an hour, which was very good money in those days. I gradually gained the respect of the other men and just before I left Slim and his partners asked me to join them for a weekend in Eudora, their Arkansas hometown. It was a wonderful weekend with a lot of dancing and drinking.

I started at Case Western Medical School that fall, hard in body and confident in spirit. The Dean of Admissions, Dr. Jack Caughey, believed in somatotyping all the incoming students—a theory from the 1940s that involved classifying body-types as ectomorphic, endomorphic or mesomorphic. He wanted mesomorphs for the medical school because, the theory went, that body type made the best workers. I guess I passed!

CHAPTER THREE

Seeing the World—
Becoming A Doctor

I had applied to the Case Western School of Medicine in Cleveland, Ohio because its enlightened curriculum, where clinical and preclinical medicine was combined, appealed to me a great deal. My first year there my classmates and I met with a family whose mother was pregnant and followed her and the child through the child's first year of life. Because I had taken only a few pre-med courses whereas most of my fellow students had majored in biology, biochemistry or physics, that first year was difficult for me. It took some time just to get the language of medicine under my belt.

At the end of the first year, I started conducting cancer research with a wonderful professor of neuroanatomy, Dr. Charles Loeser. We focused on the carcinogen 3,4-benzopyrene. This is a cancer-causing agent that was responsible for the chimney sweeps in 18th century England developing cancers in their crotches (because they wrapped their legs around the chimney). The rabbit ear chamber, which we used because it was living tissue which could be studied under the microscope, was created by making a hole in the rabbit's ear and putting a slide over and under the perforation of the ear. When tissue formed between the slides, the benzopyrene was placed in the chamber by lifting one slide. Over time the fluorescence through the spectroscope of the ear would change, signifying an energy change. We could then establish the first chemical change of the compound and so identify the chemical reaction of the carcinogen and the tissue. This would allow us to identify the first stage of carcinogenesis.

Dr. Loeser and his wife, Lucille, both encouraged me to think about taking a year off to complete the work, and I was inclined to do so. But first I did some summer travel.

I started by taking a bus down to visit my friend Reeve Schley, who was living in New Mexico. I had written to him that I would be coming, and he told me to meet him at a movie theatre there. Sure enough, I found him watching "The Nun's Story," with Audrey Hepburn. We rented a bare little schoolhouse where we could sleep in the San Ildefonso Pueblo and every day we climbed one of the mesas around the area. Reeve would paint watercolor landscapes and I wrote short stories.

Reeve's paintings went on to be featured in exhibits, but my stories were not so well-received. I mentioned in a letter to my mother that I was doing some writing and she immediately said that I should send some of my stories to Arthur Krock, the legendary New York Times reporter who also happened to be a family friend. I did and his response was blunt: I was very lucky, he said, that I was able to pursue another line of work!

Next, I flew down to the Caribbean to catch up with my Yale classmate, and fellow Scroll and Key member, Paul Semonin, who was writing for the San Juan Times in Puerto Rico. He was living with another young journalist named Hunter S. Thompson, a gregarious and likeable fellow who would become a friend. Hunter and Paul had gone to Atherton High School together in Louisville. Hunter's future wife, Sandy, was also with them.

Hunter would go on to become famous for pioneering "Gonzo Journalism," with his books *Fear and Loathing in Las Vegas* and *Fear and Loathing on the Campaign Trail '72*. He wrote for Rolling Stone magazine and his articles, particularly about politics, were widely read in the '60s, '70s and '80s. Ironically, in 1974 Rolling Stone assigned Hunter to cover the famous "Rumble in the Jungle" showdown between Muhammad Ali and George Foreman in Zaire. Foreman was the odds-on favorite after winning 40 fights with 38 knockouts, and he was younger and heavier—but Ali scored an upset and prevailed. When Ali came to Louisville at my invitation after that 1974 fight, Hunter called me. He was too bombed to conduct a proper interview with Ali in Zaire, and he wanted some quotes for his article! (Hunter never did file the piece, only adding to his own legend.)

In 1996, historian Douglas Brinkley, who edited Hunter's letters for publication, organized an appreciation night for Hunter in his hometown of Louisville, and he asked me to come and speak at the event. Hunter and I were backstage, watching the evening unfold on a TV monitor, when he reached over to me and asked if I wanted some reefer. I was Commissioner of Health for Washington, D.C. in Mayor Marion Barry's last administration (after he had spent some time up the river on a cocaine charge). I could visualize the Washington Post headline: "Barry's Commissioner of Health Smokes Grass with Hunter Thompson!" I passed.

Hunter, whose mother was a librarian in Louisville, had refined his gift of writing by typing out all of Hemingway's books. Unfortunately, Hunter emulated the great author in a different way as well. In February of 2005, at his home in Woody Creek, Colorado outside of Aspen, he put a gun in his mouth and pulled the trigger. He had been on the phone with his wife at the time. His only child, Juan, was in the next room. "We suspected such an outcome, only not so soon," Juan—who wrote a very good book about growing up with Hunter as his father—later said.

During that summer of 1959, when I was visiting Paul and Hunter in Puerto Rico, Paul and I went to the San Juan Harbor and found a wrinkled old salt who sold us a small 14-foot boat for $250. It had a sturdy hull and a nice gaff rig, but no decking. Basically, it resembled a small lifeboat. We added a canvas on the bow to store our gear and christened her the "Fat City." (The name must have stuck with Hunter: In 1970 he ran for Sheriff of Aspen, Colorado on a platform that included renaming the resort town Fat City so as to keep the "greed heads, land-rapers, and other human jackals from capitalizing on the name 'Aspen.'" He lost by 31 votes out of nearly 400 cast.)

Paul's and my plan was to sail the little craft to Antigua, nearly 300 miles from San Juan, stopping first about a quarter of the way there at St. Thomas in the British Virgin Islands; Hunter thought we were nuts. Neither Paul nor I were experienced sailors—I had done some sailing with my stepfather in the Chesapeake but nothing of this nature. But after a week of preparation we departed, outfitted with some excellent nautical maps and a sailing manual. Heavy seas greeted us. The manual and charts were quickly soaked and torn away by the waves. Paul lost his breakfast about an hour out but recovered, saying "this is a slow dog but unsinkable."

On our third day, we reached Cape San Juan on the northeast tip of Puerto Rico, which had a deadly combination of sharp reefs and strong currents. The outline of the reefs at night was terrifying. At one point we began bouncing and scraping along the reefs, so we got out and tried to walk the boat away from them—but we got stung by sea urchins. We removed the anchor and some weights and managed to float the boat back into open water. Fortunately, two skin divers on the beach were able to show us a channel through the reefs.

Eventually we made it to the island of Culebra, across the largest body of open sea that we had encountered—a bit more than 20 miles. Late in the day we passed a moored U.S. naval ship. We could hear a steel drum band playing on board. The soft music drifting across the water was an almost surreal welcome after the sailing ordeal we had endured.

I was at the tiller late one night on our voyage from Culebra to St. Thomas, with Paul asleep in the bow, when I saw a large ship looming in the darkness. We had a very small light, and I couldn't tell if the ship was coming to our port or to our starboard. But it was soon upon us, and we began waving and yelling and screaming. The skipper of the freighter blew his horn—and narrowly missed us. Throughout the voyage our constant struggle against the water itself and uncertainty about whether we would reach a port kept reminding me of Ernest Hemingway's *The Old Man and The Sea*.

When we finally arrived at Charlotte Amalie, St. Thomas—nine exhausting days after we had started our voyage—several of the locals laughed at the risk we had taken: "Mon, you came all the way from San Juan in that boat?" they asked. Paul and I nodded, and then asked if anybody was interested in buying our craft, since we were abandoning the rest of the trip to Antigua and had no interest in sailing back to Puerto Rico—even though the winds would be in our favor on a return trip. After a day or so we were able to sell the boat for $300—$50 more than we had paid for it. Perhaps our only clever move the entire trip!

From St. Thomas Paul hitched a ride on freighter to Bermuda, and I flew to Haiti to visit the Albert Schweitzer Hospital in Deschapelles, a medical facility which Larry and Gwen Mellon, of the Pittsburgh Mellon family, had opened in 1956. Larry Mellon had become intrigued with Albert Schweitzer in 1947 after Time Magazine called Schweitzer "the Greatest Man in the World." Schweitzer, a medical doctor, had set up a hospital in Gabon in west central Africa and spent fifty years there with his wife, Helene. Inspired by Schweitzer, Larry Mellon went to medical school at the age of 39, and his wife Gwen studied medical techniques and administration. Together they had founded the Albert Schweitzer Hospital, an incredible oasis of healthcare amid the gross poverty and social problems caused in Haiti by the dictator Papa Doc Duvalier. When I was there in 1959, people gathered in the courtyard in the evenings, hoping to be seen the next day, while voodoo drums echoed from the surrounding mountains. Today it serves a population of more than 350,000 people. Larry and Gwen Mellon lived out their lives in Deschapelles and committed themselves to that hospital. Giving up wealth and luxury, they made a great difference to the people of Haiti.

At the end of the summer of 1959, I began psychoanalysis. Both Charles and Lucille Loeser had gone through it, and Case Western was a hotbed of Freudian psychoanalysis. The Dean, Dr. Douglas Bond, had been chairman of the Cleveland Psychoanalytic Society (now called the Cleveland Psychoanalytic Center), an institution which he had been instrumental in setting up. During the Second World War Dr. Bond had been stationed in England with the Army Air Force and had treated many Air Force pilots who were traumatized by their flight missions over Nazi territory. While he was there, he met Anna Freud, who had followed her father in his career as a psychoanalyst. Dr. Bond wrote a marvelous book called *The Love and Fear of Flying* (with a preface by General James Doolittle, who led the daring Doolittle raid over Tokyo) about his work with pilots who served in the war, their inner conflicts and the sexual fantasies they had involving the planes in which they flew missions.

I thought that going through psychoanalysis myself might prepare me for a career in psychiatry, as well as help me come to terms with my background and all the energy I had wasted rebelling, like James Dean in "Rebel Without a Cause." For the next two years my analyst and I met for one hour at 7am, five days a week, at a cost of $25 per session. I was on the couch and he was behind me. Dreams were important and he always asked, "What did that dream mean to you?" or "Why did you feel that way?" or "What was the sexual connotation?" or "What did you feel when your mother insisted on keeping the chaperone-nurse?" or "What did that sexual experience mean to you?" There were times when I didn't have anything to say but would finally think of some event that wasn't necessarily relevant—but which was better than the deafening silence. Today's psychoanalyst would probably be looking at his iPhone! I am not recommending for everyone and I have not done it since, but I believe this psychoanalysis helped me become a more productive and effective person, including and importantly in my relationship with my mother.

At the end of the summer, I also decided to take Charles and Lucille Loeser's suggestion and took the year off from school to devote myself to our cancer research. We published our findings in the journal *Cancer Research* in 1961.

*   *   *

In my junior year as a medical student, in 1962, I joined the Interdepartmental Committee on Nutrition for National Defense on a trip to Malaysia to assess military and civilian nutritional status there. The committee had been established in 1955, after the Korean War, because of malnutrition among our allied troops from the Republic of Korea and Republic of China (Taiwan). There were two dozen of us, including pathologists and general doctors of Chinese, Indian and Malay descent, along with nutritionists and nurses. Families were brought in for nutritional assessments, which required bloodwork, and I was assigned to be the phlebotomist, particularly for infants. Babies' blood had to be drawn from the femoral artery, in the groin, and they often cried. The situation was complicated by the fact that the Chinese mothers often held a traditional belief that an infant's blood would never regenerate, so after the ordeal of taking the blood we gave the mother numerous vitamins and supplements to allay their fears. It was a productive visit because the team included people from the Malay government who could implement corrections for nutritional deficiencies, particularly vitamins A and D, and protein.

The survey team traveled through many rural areas of Malaysia, but not the urban ones. At the end of our visit the American team suggested that both the local and visiting professionals and staff picnic together on the Beach of Passionate Love, on the Pacific Ocean. (The government has since changed the beach's name to Moonlight Beach.) The water was warm, and a lot of people got in. I was a good swimmer but found that I had great difficulty getting back in to shore because of the riptide. And the problem was compounded because about 10 feet off the beach a crosscurrent had eroded the sand and people couldn't stand. The local citizens often couldn't swim very well so hysteria ensued. I saved one doctor who was drowning, and many other people were rescued. However, the Malay head of pathology drowned. This became an international incident because the Malaysian government felt that we had lured their people inappropriately to the beach. After some brouhaha we were finally allowed to leave the country. It was an unfortunate ending, but the trip was still worthwhile, because most of our recommendations to the Malaysian government were implemented over the years. Our hope was that not only soldiers would gain a better nutritional status, but also the country's general population.

At the end of my two-month stay in Malaysia, I got a letter from our family doctor, Dr. Leigh Martin. Mother had cancer.

Returning to see her in Washington, I found that she was determined to beat this disease. This was despite the fact that in those days the survival time for the particular cancer she had—a very aggressive cancer of the pancreas which had not been diagnosed until it had invaded her duodenum, causing her upper abdominal pain— was about six months. I disagreed with Dr. Martin over whether or not she should be told that her cancer was likely terminal. He did not want to tell her, unless she asked directly, but I believed (and believe) that there are a lot of things that people would want to do in the last days if they knew the prognosis. She had to have another laparotomy, which I attended in the Operating Room. The cancer was all over her abdomen. Afterward, the incision area started to grow the cancer and mother finally came to understand that her disease was terminal.

This was a really important time for my relationship with my mother. I was finishing my last year of medical school, and during the six months that she had left I drove the 350 miles from Cleveland to DC every weekend to be with her. We were able to talk about a lot of things that we might not have otherwise discussed. I was able to express some of my anger toward her, and why I had felt I needed to distance myself from her and her society. We played golf and fished together. At one point she said, "Don't you want to see more of your friends?" I told her no, I'd rather be with you.

In the final days that I spent with Mother, we talked about my future, about her joy and sadness. She had married Eddie Graves in 1949, who was a great companion to her in both Canada and Washington and was a good friend to me. She died on April 28, 1963, the day that I took my final medical school exam. I heard about her death just before I went in for the four-hour test, but I felt at peace because of all my time with her in her final months. I took the test— passing it—and then flew to Washington.

The memorial service was led by Rev John Harper of St. John's Church of Lafayette Square and by Sid Lovett, who had become a Congregational minister. Mother was buried in Arlington National Cemetery because Eddie's military service meant he would eventually be buried there. (He died 23 years and a day after Mother did.) Her burial site is about 100 yards from where the eternal flame would soon mark President John F. Kennedy's final resting place, after his death in November of that year.

A year after Mother's death, in 1964, Eddie sold the house he and mother had built on Whitehaven Street. But as my friend Arthur Schlesinger Jr. liked to say, there is a circularity to life. In December 2000, as they prepared to leave the White House, the Clintons were looking for a home. My wife Kathy, by then a real estate broker, had recently helped them find a house in Chappaqua, in Westchester County, New York. We went to the Clintons' last Christmas party at the White House, and as we approached Hillary, she grabbed Kathy and told her she didn't have anywhere to live in Washington—she'd always lived in public housing! (She had just been elected Senator from New York, so she would still be spending most of her time in D.C.)

Kathy agreed to help her and, several days later called me while house-hunting with Hillary. They were looking at a house on Whitehaven Street; why did the address ring a bell, Kathy asked? Because it was the house my mother and stepfather had built, in which I had lived. With Kathy's help, the Clintons bought the house. The owner wanted a guarantee that the Japanese Carp in the pool in the garden would live. President Clinton said he could do many things, but this wasn't one of them!

Years later at a fund-raiser for Hillary at their Washington home, which had once been mine, I went up to my old childhood room and sat with my memories.

*   *   *

For me one of the most important experiences of being in Cleveland was meeting and spending time with the Crile family. Dr. George W. Crile, the first surgeon to successfully perform a direct blood transfusion, had founded the Cleveland Clinic with three other physicians in 1921. His son, Dr. George Crile, Jr.—better known as Barney—was just finishing his career as head of surgery at the clinic in 1958, when I started Case Western. Barney was an incredible person who loved to argue, and to take an unconventional approach. He challenged the medical profession particularly effectively on radical mastectomies, which in the '50s and early '60s were carried out on women who had breast cancer. He argued that it mutilated a woman's arms and chest. He demonstrated through his experiments with animals that if lymph nodes adjacent to the malignancy tested negative and were not removed, the chances of recovery were better. The chest surgeons and the American Surgical Association didn't accept this, so Barney took his case to the lay media and eventually won the day. After his first wife Jane's death from breast cancer, Barney had married Helga Sandburg, the daughter of Carl Sandburg, the Pulitzer Prize-winning poet and writer. In Cleveland I became great friends with Helga's daughter, Paula Steichen. Paula was a terrific writer, and an attractive woman with a wonderful laugh who was game for just about any adventure. She and I would ride horses together, and sometimes Barney's son, George Crile III, would join us. George and I always galloped through the woods at top speed, rides he would later describe as "controlled madness."

George Crile III was a fascinating character in his own right. Unlike his father and grandfather, George III didn't become a doctor.

Instead, he went into journalism and in 2003 wrote the incredible book "Charlie Wilson's War," which was later adapted into a wonderful movie starring Tom Hanks. George's book tells the wild tale of how one Congressman, a Democrat from Texas named Charlie Wilson, was influenced by a very wealthy evangelical woman (played by Julia Roberts in the film) and became obsessed with the need to expunge the Soviets from Afghanistan in the 1980s. Charlie Wilson, a rogue in many ways, was on the House Intelligence Committee and was able to get President Reagan to give more money to the Mujahideen. He promoted a complicated alliance in which five countries, a wealthy evangelical, our CIA and our military all worked with the Afghan leaders to drive the Soviets from Afghanistan. As it happens, Wilson's project was probably the straw that broke the Soviet Union's back. Gorbachev, who was in power at that time, called off the war, which was breaking the Soviet treasury. The Soviet debt in turn led to the breakup of the Soviet Union.

Paula and I wound up being together for several years, and in addition to our escapades in Cleveland, we traveled extensively. We went to Russia, for example, in 1965. She had a lot of contacts with Russian writers and I had contacts with doctors. Our Intourist guides were glued to us in Moscow and Leningrad, but when we departed for the Russian heartland of Kiev, Tbilisi—beautiful old cities—and Yalta (where FDR, Joseph Stalin and Winston Churchill had their first summit during World War Two), we were on our own.

On another trip, Paula and I spent a weekend at Paula's grandparents' home in Flat Rock, North Carolina—called Connemara, it is now a national historic site, administered by the U.S. Park Service. This was a great treat for me, as her grandfather Carl

Sandburg had written one of my favorite poems, "Chicago," which gave the windy city one of its nicknames: City of Big Shoulders. Paula's grandmother, whom Carl had met at a rally for the labor leader and Socialist Eugene Debs, was also named Paula Steichen— my friend had been named for her—and she was the sister of Edward Steichen, the famous photographer and author of the book *The Family of Man*. I was particularly interested in meeting Paula's grandfather—in no small part because he had ridden the rails himself in his youth—and I pumped him on the topic as much as I could. He was working on his memoirs at the time, and didn't appreciate any interruptions, so he was a bit gruff.

In 1968 Paula and I traveled to Kenya, where we visited the great wildlife photographer Peter Beard and his then-wife, Minnie Cushing, in their tent in the Serengeti. A fellow Yale graduate, Peter was a class or so behind me at Yale. (His brother, Anson Beard, who was in my class at Yale, was in my wedding and has remained a lifelong friend.) Peter had done some work with the Kenyan government in northern Kenyan on the border of Ethiopia, studying the lifecycle of crocodiles on Lake Rudolph. When Paula and I visited Lake Rudolph on our 1968 trip, it was the hottest place that I'd ever been—120°F. Evidently a Peace Corps volunteer who was assigned to that area in the early '60s had been told not to get into the water because there were so many crocodiles. But it was so hot that he went in anyway, and a crocodile devoured him. In his photographic study of the Lake Rudolph crocs, Peter had managed to get a picture of the beast that evidently had the unlucky Peace Corps volunteer's leg in his stomach; he kept that photograph in a place of honor his Serengeti tent. Peter's remarkable 1988 book, *The End of the Game*, highlighted the balance between life and death among the great animals in Africa—especially the elephants. Over the years, I have collected a number of wildlife photographs by Peter, and they're absolutely spectacular.

My friend Paula's stepfather Dr. Barney Crile would turn out to be one of the great influences in my life, and the first of a series of important father figures—a role that had been vacant since my youth. In 1963, after I had graduated from Case Western, Barney convinced me to do a Medical Surgical internship under him at the clinic. The first case I scrubbed in on with Barney was an inguinal hernia repair. I marveled at his incredibly quick and graceful hand motions. After a short time, which appeared to me to be only minutes, Barney straightened up, took off his gloves and said to me: "Close him up." And then he headed for the door. I wasn't exactly prepared to do that as I looked into the bloody incision. Then Barney said with a twinkle in his eye as he left: "This man is a preacher and if anything goes wrong, he will say God willed it." Barney was of course a non-believer himself. After about another 25 minutes, the anesthesiologist said, "Doc, how much longer will this go on? I need to get this patient off this anesthesia."

The patient survived intact and was never the wiser.

As it turned out, I would be only the second graduate from Case Western School of Medicine to intern at the Cleveland Clinic. Caldwell "Essy" Esselstyn, who married one of Barney's daughters, had been the first. Essy became a successful surgeon at the Cleveland Clinic but left after he noticed that many cardiac patients were returning to their cardiologist after bypass surgery and were having to undergo more procedures and were taking many medications. He started researching nutrition and eventually published a book on how a plant-based diet can prevent, halt and even reverse heart disease. His rule of thumb: Never eat anything that has a mother or a face. Essy's wife Ann (Dr. Barney Crile's daughter, and George Crile III's sister) and their daughter Jane published a heart-healthy cookbook based on the research. Life sometimes works in strange ways. In 2006 Kathy and I helped Essy get in touch with former President Clinton after his cardiac events. The president followed Essy's diet and has subsequently done quite well. Recently elected Mayor of New York, Eric Adams, claimed Essy has been the only doctor to successfully treat his diabetes by diet.

Although Barney served as my professional mentor and guided me wisely, I would end up pursuing public medicine as opposed to his wish, surgery. Later, when I got involved in health policy, he would argue that physicians should never be remunerated by fee-for-service, which promotes excessive medical procedures, but by a flat salary, and that they should also be rewarded for quality care. This was the practice of the Cleveland Clinic, and is what health reform is striving to do today.

*　　*　　*

For one of my rotations during my 1963-64 internship at the Cleveland Clinic, I was assigned to the emergency room. One day a man with severe chest pain was admitted. He was in his early 30s, nice looking with black hair. He had an irregular heartbeat. The head of the ER was defibrillating him, which brought his heart back into normal rhythm. In about five minutes it happened again. He had a history of very high cholesterol and the head of the ER told me that I would need to be with him all night. I could see from the cardiac monitor if he was going into fibrillation, and after a couple times where I shocked it back into normal rhythm, I said to him that when he started to feel light-headed he should start blinking his eyes and I would shock him. The defibrillator shock is quite uncomfortable but it's better than the alternative. I shocked him back to life 17 times. They were able to get a pacemaker into him the next day and he walked out of the hospital the following week. I don't know what happened to him subsequently but after that night I had a great passion for emergency medicine.

My passion has played out in many ways. In 1967, when I launched the Park DuValle Neighborhood Health Center in a low-income neighborhood in Louisville, one of my primary concerns was the absence of emergency care in the city. Eventually the Health Center had two ambulances as well as arrangements with the Louisville General Hospital for quick response to our runs. After I was elected Mayor of Louisville in 1973, we instituted Kentucky's first professional Emergency Medical Service. When I became Washington, D.C.'s Commissioner of Health in the mid-'90s, under Mayor Marion Barry, I tried—without success—to improve the city's emergency medical services, which were woefully inadequate.

It seems possible I was originally attracted to emergency medicine in part because of my father coming through so many heart attacks. The heart is an amazing organ, beating 100,000 times a day—that's more than 2 billion beats over a typical lifetime. It never rests. Because of greatly improved emergency cardiac care—such as defibrillation, bypass surgery, stent insertions, pacemakers, cholesterol and antihypertensive medications, blood-pressure control and low-fat diets and exercise—death rates from heart disease and stroke have declined significantly, and the use of medication and cardiac surgery have greatly improved cardiac care. When Franklin Roosevelt died, for example, his doctor estimated his blood pressure to have been 300/190. But the doctor just didn't have any medicine with which to bring it under control. The effort over the last 50 years to reduce smoking has also had an important positive effect in reducing cardiovascular disease. Nonetheless, the inequality gap makes itself felt here, as in so many other areas. Unfortunately, lower-income people still die earlier and have much more vascular disease.

*   *   *

The year 1963 was a year of terrible loss not just for me because of my mother's death, but for everyone, because of President Kennedy's assassination. Like so many others of my generation, JFK had inspired me. He had been the first president for whom I volunteered and voted. I had read *Profiles in Courage* and had listened to some of his speeches and had analyzed his background. On Election Day 1960 I looked forward to the New Frontier and, especially, JFK's energy and vision. Any doubts that I might have had about my vote were erased at the inaugural as Kennedy exhorted: "Ask not what your country can do for you—ask what you can do for your country." This was a call to public service, and I embraced it. A new world was being born and I wanted to be part of it.

But by1963 I had started my medical-surgical internship under Barney at the Cleveland Clinic. I was totally engrossed in my work and paid only peripheral attention to the Kennedy administration. I was doing a rotation in the psychiatric service for my Cleveland Clinic internship on November 22, 1963, when suddenly all the patients had their televisions turned on—President Kennedy had been shot in Dallas. It was a totally stunning body blow. I knew immediately I had to go to Washington for his funeral.

I called my old friend and companion, Sid Lovett, who was ministering at a church in Northern Virginia. He and I stood in the crowd, watching the cortege in the funeral procession, with the riderless horse with its stirrups turned to the rear. The previous day the news had come that Lee Harvey Oswald had been shot. Ironically the two men had their funerals on the same day.

It felt like everything was falling apart. We wondered what the hell was happening with the world. It was a highly emotional moment for all who were there. As I watched the procession turn to go over the Arlington Memorial Bridge toward the cemetery, I decided that I wanted to be in elected office. I needed to contribute, to try to pull together the unraveling world around me. Little did I realize that a decade later, almost to the day, I would take the oath of office of Mayor of Louisville, Kentucky.

CHAPTER FOUR

Public Health Physician—
Eastern Kentucky

We have a conversation with the land here.
The land will talk to us.
It will tell us things, like nothing comes easy to the people in the Mountains.
We are a little worn.
We are a little bent.
We are a little broken.
But we are real, we are here.
This is life for us. We ain't got a choice here in the coalfields.
We are fighting back, 'cause it's the only thing we have.

— LARRY GIBSON, "Keeper of the Mountains," from *Mud Creek Medicine: The Life of Eula Hall and the Fight for Appalachia*, by Kiran Bhatraju

I have always viewed medicine as a form of public service. The ability to improve health and relieve pain, to my mind, make it a giving profession. And this is even more true in the realm of public health, where the government should assist those unable to help themselves.

In 1964, after my intern training at the Cleveland Clinic, I decided to apply my medical education to a more direct form of public service. At the time, I needed to make a decision about military service. Vietnam in 1964 really wasn't really an option: The war hadn't ramped up yet, and the idea of spending two years checking guys for VD didn't appeal to me. But in 1954 the Berry Plan offered an alternative to the Armed Forces, as it allowed medical school graduates with at least one year of internship to join the Public Health Service for two years. There was one Public Health Service program which especially interested me—President Kennedy's Appalachian Health Program, predominantly focused on eastern Kentucky. I signed on for it and was assigned to the newly created Appalachian Healthcare Project. I went to Hazard in Perry County, where I joined a team of doctors, nurses and other health professionals who were providing healthcare to families in 16 counties in Eastern Kentucky. We would transport patients from the forks of the creeks and the heads of the hollows to our make-shift clinics (abandoned stores and other spaces) at the county seat. We would give them comprehensive health exams—sometimes the first ones they'd received in their lives. There was massive interest in dental care. Most people never saw a dentist and young women were encouraged to have their teeth taken out and to get dentures so they wouldn't burden future husbands with the cost of dental care.

This work was both gratifying and frustrating. Our intentions were good but much of the local establishment looked upon us as invaders. The members of the Kentucky Medical Association really didn't want "government-paid doctors" coming and taking "their patients"—whom they weren't treating anyway. So, they said we could only refer, we couldn't treat. We could, in other words, offer bad news but do nothing about it but harass the local MDs to treat the referred patients, who had heart disease, diabetes, chronic lung disease and many other ailments. In 1956 the United Mine Workers of America

(UMWA) had established a network of ten hospitals in the Appalachians under the direction of UMWA President John L. Lewis, but unfortunately, they proved to be terribly expensive to run. Eventually, under President Johnson's administration, these hospitals were taken over by the Appalachian Regional Commission. The hospitals were the for the most part responsive up to their credo, and the passage of Medicare and Medicaid in 1965 were of tremendous assistance in providing healthcare in the mountains.

One night a woman suffering from diabetes, Mrs. Denise Crume, called the motel room I shared with another doctor in Inez, Martin County, where I was based at the time. She had gone into a state of acidosis, a potentially fatal condition that disrupts the body's mineral balance. Her fever was already high, and she was scared. The community's only doctor, a man in his 70s, wasn't available, and there was no way until morning to get her to the nearest hospital, which was 40 miles away. We brought Mrs. Crume to our motel room and stayed the night with her. To pull her through, we forced her to drink water and kept feeding her potato chips, hoping they would provide the salt she needed. For all our good intentions, for all our knowledge, that was the best we could offer: comfort, water and potato chips. She survived, and I learned a valuable lesson about the limits of even the best-intentioned programs, especially against entrenched local opposition.

Politics in Eastern Kentucky were intense—and sometimes ugly. My colleagues and I once attended a School Board election in Inez, where the county schools were the main employer in the area. On the evening of the election, we were in an Inez diner when a man came up and told us: "I was bought five times today, Bub, and I didn't vote for any of them."

*   *   *

I love Eastern Kentucky. It is a land of legends, lore and stories. It is insular, but anyone who feels that you're on their side, or that you will help them medically or otherwise, is extremely grateful. Just to drive into the mountains of Eastern Kentucky and feel what has happened over the last century is a unique experience.

Eastern Kentucky is also a land of raconteurs, and Harry Caudill, a country lawyer who lived with his wife, Ann, and raised his children in Whitesburg, Letcher County, was the best raconteur I have ever known. As the esteemed lawyer of the area, he had many tales to tell. Those of us visiting Harry would listen in rapture. One of his best was recorded by his wife Ann in her 2013 book, *The Caudills of the Cumberlands*:

> The situation unfolded in 1962 in the Letcher County Courthouse. My client came into my office with a tale of woe. His wife was a sturdy woman of strong temper, and she had become unusually enraged at him because of an escapade involving one of the young women of the neighborhood. In her wrath, she had armed herself with a bargain-counter .22-caliber pistol with a barrel about one and one-half inches long. She had loaded it with short cartridges because they were cheaper, and awaited his return home,

since she thought he was with another woman. When, humming softly, he entered the front door, she presented him her pistol and vowed to kill him. He took flight through the kitchen and out the back door with his wife in hot pursuit. He fled along a path that led around a hillside to his Buick, while the wife of his bosom fired her shooting iron into his back. Neighbors reported that at each shot he emitted piercing shrieks and wails for mercy. This continued until five cartridges from her Saturday-night special were used up and he reached his car.

He drove at breakneck speed to the hospital where he presented himself at the emergency room with loud assertions that he had been shot square through five times. The doctor removed his blanket-lined leather jacket and his sweater and shirt, and had him lie face down on the examination table. Sure enough, he had been shot five times, but not through. The sturdy leather jacket and woolen garments had acted as a flak jacket, and the feeble cartridges fired from an anemic pistol had merely propelled the bullets partway into his shoulders. They remained half in and half out as the doctor phrased it, and he withdrew them with tweezers. He painted the wounds with mercurochrome, applied bandages, and sent him on his way. My client recovered quickly.

The grand jury was in session at the time and he promptly presented himself at the antechamber.

RIDING THE RAILS

Admitted to tell his tale, he described his ordeal in
florid terms and showed the jurors the five bullet
holes. Before the trial was scheduled, the pain fell and
the turbulent marriage was patched up. At this point
he came in to pay me to defend her for shooting him.
In this new frame of mind he yearned to keep her out
of the penitentiary.

The commonwealth attorney was unsympathetic.
He had read the transcript of the victim's testimony to
the grand jury and deemed her actions a most heinous
crime, a carefully planned attempt to kill her husband.

On the morning of the trial the two sat in court
together, their arms entwined, her head on his
shoulder. I pleaded with the prosecutor, pointing out
that they had children, were reconciled, were deeply
in love, the wounds were minor, and imprisonment
would break the hearts of her son and daughter. The
victim reinforced my pleas with loud and fervent
affirmations. At length, the prosecutor surrendered
to the realities of the case and agreed that the charge
would be reduced: the defendant paying $200 fine for
breach of the peace. Of course, she had no money and
her husband had to pay the fine.

When the judicial proceeding had been
solemnly affirmed by the judge's signature, the clerk
handed my client a receipt for the fine plus court
costs. He stared with a rueful and uncomprehending
gaze at the bits of paper and sighed. 'I just don't

understand this law business. She shot me five times and now I have to pay over \$40 a shot. It ain't fair: I don't care what anybody says.'

The demands of justice had been met. The chastened wife went home and her husband went back to the coal mines. I suspect the lady with the scales managed a little smile.

In 1963 Harry wrote the seminal history of the region, *Night Comes to the Cumberlands: A Biography of a Depressed Area*, a book that raises questions about imbalances of equity and power which left the Appalachian region economically deprived, poverty-stricken and environmentally ravaged. The book so impressed President Kennedy regarding the plight of the region that he invited Harry to come work in Washington (Harry did not go), and he made it a priority to find ways to address the issues. His efforts would be carried onward after his death by the Appalachian Regional Commission set up by the Johnson administration.

The early settlers in Eastern Kentucky were often people who didn't fit into the farming communities of flatland Virginia, or people who were on the run. When the coal and gas barons came to Kentucky in the 19th century and took the mineral rights from the landowners, they did so legally, using the "broad form deed," which separated surface from subsurface mineral rights—largely to landowners' detriment as companies acquired them for a pittance. Sometimes situations got tense. House owners would lay down in front of a backhoe which had started digging for coal right next to their home.

Caudill wrote about how the coal companies continued to illegally risk miner's lives, limbs and lungs.

The situation has improved in years since, but still has major problems: 31 miners were laboring 1,000 feet underground in West Virginia Upper Big Branch Mine in 2010 when an explosion killed 29 of them. Don Blankenship, the CEO of Massey Energy, which owned the mine, was convicted of conspiring to violate federal safety standards. He served one year in prison for the deaths—and then had the gall to seek the GOP nomination for Senate in 2018. (He lost, badly.) New ownership, Alpha Natural Resources, closed the mine in 2012.

Coal companies used the broad-form deed to access the coal under the ground. When these deeds were executed, the rights to the mineral estate transferred from the landowner to the mineral-estate owner. In the mid '80s, 72 percent of the subsurface owners were absentee or from out of state. Horizontal severance allows whoever owns the surface to develop it for agriculture or any other purpose; at the same time someone else can develop the mineral rights under the surface. This was often a bad deal for farmers who didn't realize what they were giving up under the ground. Coal companies would employ agents to approach them to negotiate access to their subsurface resources. They paid a pittance to the poor landowners and made sure the agreements freed them from any liability claims or damages.

In the late 19th and early 20th centuries coal was extracted primarily through underground mining, which caused minimal impact to the surface. But strip-mining eventually became cheaper and more efficient—and more disruptive. Bulldozers, trucks and explosives became commonplace. As technology improved, mountaintop removal became the most invasive type of surface mining, literally involving removing tops of mountains to expose coal seams below.

Removing a mountaintop requires huge earth-moving equipment and displaces a lot of soil. It not only irrevocably fouls streams and drinking water, but also requires coal slurries to contain the liquid mineral contamination. Slurry ponds can break and inundate towns and homes, usually because the coal interests put pressure on the federal and state regulatory agencies to be lenient on penalties. That happened, for example, in Inez, Kentucky, a town where I did a six-month stint as part of the health service. (The catastrophe occurred after I had left.) Perhaps one positive outcome of these mining techniques is that after the coal has been removed, local townships are sometimes able to develop housing or an airfield on the now-flat mountain-top.

It was not until 1988 that the Kentucky legislature amended the state constitution to require that any agreement between the surface owner and the mineral rights owner ensure that both understand the method of extraction. This applied not only to future agreements, but to all those already performed in Kentucky, finally giving the surface owners protection.

Gradually, people realized that coal is a highly-polluting energy source and made changes to its production. Coal prices were taxed in Kentucky through the severance tax, which demanded that a certain amount per ton of coal mined be used to rebuild the state, presumably helping those coal-producing counties. Black lung, caused by long-term exposure to coal dust, predominated in the area and was very difficult to treat effectively. It reduced the lifespans of miners and made them susceptible to other respiratory diseases.

Good health care was a chronic problem in the region. Many babies in Eastern Kentucky were delivered at home. One of the most outstanding examples of innovative missionary help was the Frontier Nursing Service (FNS), set up in 1925 by Mary Breckinridge, a woman who came from a famous Kentucky family. Mary had trained as a nurse in France during the First World War, and the only way the FNS was able to get qualified nurses was to either send them to Great Britain for instruction, or to bring British nurses to the U.S. In the early days, the nurses would go by horseback to families when they were expecting. Later they used jeeps to go up the tortuous roads. The FNS reduced the maternal and child mortality rates significantly, and also set up a training program to ensure there would be enough trained nurse practitioners locally. I had the privilege of working with the FNS for a number of months when I was based in Eastern Kentucky, and I got to know Mary Breckinridge pretty well before she passed away in 1965. This aristocratic woman spent her last 40 years leading the FNS in Hyden, in Eastern Kentucky.

Another impressive woman I got to work with in Eastern Kentucky in the '60s was Eula Hall. Born in 1927 into abject poverty in Pike County, Eula left school after the 8th grade—the local high school was too far away for her to walk, and there were no school buses. When the Second World War broke out, 14-year-old Eula cut her hair, lied about her age and enlisted. She was assigned to a canning and munitions factory outside Rochester, New York to make goods for the war. But when she found the conditions at the factory both unfair and unsafe, the precocious teenage activist organized some of the workers to strike. She was arrested and charged with starting a riot, but when the authorities figured out that she was both underage and a woman, they sent her back to Kentucky. Eula's father, brothers and sons were all coal miners, and by age 17 she was married to a coal miner herself—so she saw firsthand what black lung did to miners, and the poor healthcare they had to deal with it. Described in the Wall Street Journal as "a self-taught social worker who fought for decades to bring medical treatment and clean water to her Appalachian neighbors", Eula participated in miners' strikes throughout the region. When she was elected President of the Kentucky Black Lung Association, this self-described "hillbilly activist" traveled to Washington and testified before Congress about coal miners' needs.

Back when I first got to know Eula in the '60s, she dreamed of setting up a community health center in Floyd County where she grew up—and in 1973 she finally did just that. Eula's Mud Creek Clinic in Grethel, Floyd County (later renamed the Eula Hall Health Center) was one of the first rural community health centers in the country. When the clinic burned down after a few years, Eula went out and raised hundreds of thousands of dollars privately and publicly from the local and federal governments to build a new facility. While the new health center was being built, Eula ran the clinic out of her own home and an empty school lunchroom. She worked at the health center as a patient advocate right up until her death in 2021 at age 93. I went back to Pike County in 2013 because a book about Eula and her Mud Creek Clinic—*Mud Creek Medicine: The Life of Eula Hall and the Fight for Appalachia,* by Kiran Bhatraju—had just been published. Eula was the absolute epitome of the fighting spirit of Eastern Kentucky, and someone who really wanted to make the place better—which she did.

Despite all its good fighting people and innovations in health services, the future of Eastern Kentucky—and of West Virginia and some of the other Appalachian mountain area—is still very grim. Many of the small towns, unfortunately, have almost disappeared. A lot of people in Eastern Kentucky exist in the transfer economy—food stamps, Medicaid and welfare. Nevertheless, there are pockets of hope. Some communities such as Pikeville, Kentucky, are thriving because of educational institutions, especially community colleges, universities and professional schools of osteopathic medicine and dentistry. This has occurred in Pike County largely because of the aforementioned Great Society's Model Cities program, which diverted the Big Sandy River in Pike County so that the community wouldn't be constantly flooded and provided for good transportation via rail and roads.

When I went back to Pike County in 2013 to celebrate Eula, I was impressed, as I've said, by how much better the roads were, thanks in large part to LBJ's Appalachian program. But I was also impressed by how much cleaner the landscape was in general than it had been in the '60s. There were no longer piles of trash and abandoned cars lying around everywhere. In 1981 Paul Patton—County Judge/Executive of Pike County and later Governor of Kentucky—had been the first to institute a sanitation program whereby people paid a certain amount for garbage pick-up, and that has led to real improvements in the water quality. There are all sorts of healthcare options in the area that were not available in the '60s. And four-lane highways! In fact, I think Eastern Kentucky and West Virginia may have more four-lane highways per resident than anywhere.

In 2016 I returned to Eastern Kentucky again, to Martin County, to help longtime "Nightline" anchor Ted Koppel and his wife, Grace Anne, find a community health center where they could establish a chronic pulmonary obstruction disease center through funding from their Dorney-Koppel Family Foundation. Breathing coal dust (as well as smoking) has irrevocably damaged countless coal miners' lungs, and the Koppel's wonderful foundation has helped many COPD clinics get started in West Virginia and other states. The morning I drove from Pikeville and to Martin County I read in the Appalachian Times that the residents of the county did not have potable water and had to buy water in bottles. This was in 2016! Supposedly officials had exhausted the county's bond authority by building a new county courthouse. I went by to see the new building—it had Gothic columns! Perhaps not the wisest use of County funds..

In 2017 federal health reports documented that 10 counties in the U.S. actually had adults who were dying at a younger average age than their parents. Seven of those 10 counties were in Eastern Kentucky, and Martin County was one of them. It is past time to promote more comprehensive healthcare and stress smoking cessation, healthy lifestyle and nutrition and to stop drug abuse and promote rehabilitation.

One of the fascinating things about Eastern Kentucky, though, is that while many of the young people moved out to get jobs in cities such as Cincinnati, Detroit, Cleveland or Pittsburgh, on weekends you see lines of cars going back to Eastern Kentucky as these young people head home for a few days to be with their families. Eastern Kentucky runs deep in the people who grew up there. They never forgot it and it is always a part of them.

*   *   *

In addition to immersing me in the nuts and bolts of public health, my stint in Kentucky brought about several relationships that would have a profound influence on my life. Early in the fall of 1964, during my 6-month stint in Inez, I sent a note to Barry Bingham Sr., the publisher of the Louisville Courier-Journal. This was at the suggestion of my friend Kay Halle, the sister-in-law of Barney Crile and an heiress to the Halle Brothers department store in Cleveland. Kay was generous in hosting me when I was in Washington, D.C., and she became an important figure in my life. She had worked in the Office of Strategic Services in the Second World War (where her boss, William "Wild Bill" Donovan gave her the nickname Mata Halle) and then as a newspaper reporter. Kay was at attractive and engaging woman who never married, despite proposals from such luminaries as Randolph Churchill and Averell Harriman.

As it happened, Kay's insistence that I contact Barry Bingham Sr. would have a huge impact on my life for years to come. Mr. Bingham immediately wrote back and invited me to lunch at his home in Louisville the following Sunday. After lunch he and his wife Mary and I walked around their estate. The Binghams were just absolutely out of breath with all sorts of things to talk about. When he heard that I had no way of getting news on a daily basis in Inez, he had The Courier-Journal delivery truck drive the 30 miles from Prestonsburg to deliver the paper to our team every day in order to keep us connected to the wider world.

In the '60s and '70s The Courier-Journal was among the top ten papers in the nation. In his famous 1962 "last press conference," for example, Richard Nixon listed The Courier-Journal as being one of "the great papers in this country" before warning the assembled press corps that "you won't have Nixon to kick around anymore." Barry Bingham Sr. had placed talented people in top positions and had progressive principles. Like his father—Judge Worth Bingham Sr., the former publisher of The Courier-Journal—Barry Sr. believed deeply in President Franklin Roosevelt and had served in the war, returning to Europe to help implement the Marshall Plan. His wife, Mary Bingham, ran the editorial page during his absence.

Barry Sr.'s father, Judge Robert Worth Bingham, had served briefly as Mayor of Louisville in 1907. He was appointed Jefferson Police Judge in 1911. Judge Bingham had been a great supporter of FDR, who appointed him to the Court of St. James as U.S. Ambassador to England from 1933 through late 1937. Unlike his successor, Joe Kennedy, Judge Bingham was a great force for intervention in the approaching world conflict, and The Courier-Journal (which Judge Bingham had bought in 1918) supported that position vigorously, especially FDR's lend-lease program, which lent military supplies and clothing to England and Russia before the US had entered the war. The paper's support of lend-lease had generated some distaste in the local community at the time. But when I met Barry Sr. and Mary Bingham in the mid-60s, they fully supported Lyndon Johnson's war on poverty—so we immediately connected.

Barry Bingham Sr. really became a mentor for me, and he and his family's counsel and support would prove very important to me in my Kentucky years. In 1975, during my first term as Mayor of Louisville, the paper's support for the implementation of court-ordered busing would prove critical. Barry Jr. was at the helm of the paper by that time (he took over for his father as publisher and editor in 1971), and he was a tremendous help in ensuring that accurate information and not rumors were published by the Louisville media. My family and Barry Bingham Sr.'s family grew close over the years, and it always was a joy to be with them. Kathy and I cherish their friendship. Our daughter, Abigail, was Barry Bingham Sr.'s goddaughter. I should add that Barry Sr. and I always kept our personal and professional relationships separate. I never asked a political favor of him and he never did of me.

During our Kentucky years Kathy and I got to know many other members of the Bingham family—including Barry Sr.'s daughters Sallie and Eleanor, and his sons Worth and Barry Jr.—and they became an important part of our life as well. Worth and I first got to know each other in the mid-60's, and we became close. I remember flying with him to Washington, D.C. one weekend on a private plane (because there was an airline strike). We played cards the whole way with the stakes being the cost of chartering the plane. I lost! I never saw him again because shortly after he went to Nantucket, where he died in a tragic freak accident: a surfboard in the back of the car he was driving hit a parked car, swung around and hit him in the back of his head. His family was in the car with him at the time. Sadly, Worth's fatal accident occurred only two years after the tragic death of his brother Jonathan (whom I never met), who was electrocuted while stringing lights up for a party at their home, Melcombe. Worth and his wife Joan's son Rob, who would serve as press secretary in my run for the

Senate against Mitch McConnell 1990, would also die at a tragically young age. Their daughter Clara became a friend of Kathy and me.

Unfortunately, it was not just personal tragedy that darkened the Bingham's lives. Barry Bingham Jr. had taken over the editorship of the paper from his father in 1971, but his tenure ended unhappily, consumed by intrafamily squabbles that saw him force his mother and his two sisters, Sallie and Eleanor, off of the paper's board. The differences that festered between the siblings led to Barry Bingham Sr.'s decision in 1986 to sell the paper to Gannett for $300 million. This marked the end of an era. The Courier-Journal had been a locally owned Kentucky newspaper since 1868, and the 1986 sale of the paper to Gannett was a great blow to the Bingham family, to Kentucky journalism—and to me and my family. Over the years the paper had supported me in all but one of the ten races that I ran, the general election for Mayor 1981 being the exception. It also supported the three referenda I was out front on: the Transit Authority of River City, or TARC, and two city-county mergers. In addition to being considered one of the ten best papers in the nation in the 1960s and in the '70s, The Courier-Journal had won many Pulitzer Prizes over the years. As one distinguished journalist, John Ed Pearce, said, "There was always a Courier-Journal reporter around to challenge the timber cutters, the strip miners, the polluters, the corrupt." But a tragic disagreement in the Bingham family brought all that to an end.

At the news conference announcing the sale, Al Neuharth, Gannett's chief, claimed he had achieved the Triple Crown in buying the Des Moines Register, the Detroit News and The Courier-Journal. Unfortunately, The Courier-Journal diminished under Gannett's stewardship, suffering declining circulation and eventually eliminating its editorial page. In 2021, the Gannett company announced that it was shuttering the paper's local printing press and would produce the paper copy in Tennessee and Indiana. In April of 2021, Gannett put The Courier-Journal's building up for sale, yet another sign of the decline of a once-great institution.

Not long after the sale of the paper, in 1988, Barry Bingham Sr. died from a brain tumor. He had endured two surgeries to try to treat it. His devoted wife Mary had permitted the second operation, at Mass General, after the first didn't deal with the problem. That second operation greatly compromised his speech and she deeply regretted allowing it. She later recounted to Kathy and me how he was so angry at her for allowing the operation that he wouldn't speak to her. Nevertheless, they were the most loving couple I've ever witnessed. Mary vowed to Kathy and me that she would never let that happen to her, and she joined the Hemlock Society, which advocated for terminal patients' right to die.

Mary lived for nearly seven years after her husband's death and distributed most of her proceeds from the sale of The Courier-Journal and other media properties to various charities in Kentucky. In 1995, during her opening remarks at a Louisville gala where she was being recognized, she joked that the event was so flattering that "the best thing would be for a big pink cloud to come down and take me away." Partway through her remarks, as she was criticizing the destructive nature of the Newt Gingrich revolution, she had a massive and fatal heart attack and collapsed on stage. She died, as they say, with her boots on.

*　　*　　*

Some months before my tenure in the Public Health Service ended, I was called to Washington for training to ensure the Medicare and Medicaid compliance with Title 7 of the Civil Rights Act of 1964. This meant that no health provider receiving reimbursement from Medicare or Medicaid could discriminate—hospitals had to have biracial room assignments and an integrated staff to be eligible for funding.

The trainer started with the appropriate language to be used. "Negro," (the official term at that time) "is pronounced 'Neegro,'" he said as he slapped his knee, "and not 'Negra.'" He told us to meet with local civil rights organizations to get the lay of the land.

My first assignment after my training was a hospital in Western Kentucky that was owned by a surgeon. When I arrived there a tall man in a white coat greeted me. He said, "Well, son, it is nice to meet you." I am sure I looked like a med student to him. After I explained why I was visiting, he took me around the hospital. No surprise: The white patients were on the top two floors and the Black ones were in the basement.

After the tour I asked if we could meet privately. The first question I asked was why he separated the races. He drew himself up to his full height, about six inches taller than me, and said, "We have studied this situation fully, son. If you put a white man after surgery in the same room as a Negro man, the white man's surgical wounds won't heal."

I said, "Oh, I never heard that in medical school, but I will report this to my superiors in Washington."

I called the civil rights officials and then I returned the next day, and after greeting the surgeon-proprietor, told him, "Unfortunately the wound resolution problem of your white patients does not afford an exemption for the biracial room assignment requirement, and if that continues you and the hospital will not be eligible for reimbursement of services from either Medicare or Medicaid."

Weeks later I learned that his hospital had complied. Hospitals and physicians across the country came into compliance because the issue was not a black or white problem anymore, but a green one. Unlike the implementation of fair housing or desegregation of schools and colleges, there were no demonstrations or white-sheet rallies. No hospitals suddenly privatized. It was a very quiet revolution.

*　　*　　*

If one looks upon life as a series of adventures from childhood to death, in my opinion the chance to both work and "do good" is the most fulfilling combination. My earlier summers of being on the road, hitchhiking, riding the rails and working from Alberta, Canada to the Gulf of Mexico were unforgettable adventures, but I don't think they benefited anyone else but me. In Eastern Kentucky, though, I both had an incredible experience and also made a difference. Again, I turn to the Oliver Wendell Holmes' quote: "As life is action and passion, it is required of a man that he should share the passion and action of his time at peril of being judged not to have lived." For me, Appalachia and Eastern Kentucky in the mid- and late-'60s was a center of action, thanks in large part to both President Kennedy's and the Great Society's focus on fighting poverty there. A few years later my work establishing the Park DuValle Community Health Center in Louisville—which has been in operation for 54 years now—would be an even more intense experience of the joys and satisfaction that can come with public service.

Once again, in this period of my life as in so many others, some of the most profound developments seemed to occur almost accidentally, as a kind of cosmic domino effect. John F. Kennedy did not have much experience with rural poverty before his presidential bid. But in 1960, after beating his fellow Senator Hubert Humphrey for the Democratic presidential nomination in the Wisconsin primary, John F. Kennedy went to the West Virginia primary. He went there hoping to overcome the perception that a Catholic could not win in a mostly Protestant electorate, but what struck him most on his visit was the vast rural poverty in the mountains, the hills, the hollows and the flood-prone plains of the Mountain State. He won the primary in part because he was well-funded, but also because he demonstrated to the coal mining country people that he understood their dilemma and really cared, even though he himself had never known mountain poverty.

Kennedy's interest in helping the Appalachian people was then carried onward after his death by the Appalachian Health Project, for which I worked. President Johnson's administration focused its anti-poverty efforts through its Office of Economic Opportunity (OEO), its Model Cities program and its Appalachian Regional Program on rural mountain poverty. Johnson got Sen. Robert Kennedy on board by extending the geographic area to include mountains in New York. Media from all over the world came to depict the lives and poverty of the people, and not without some danger: One Canadian film producer was shot to death by a landlord when he didn't get permission to film the tenants and their houses—the juries in two neighboring counties could not come to a verdict for the murder because the film director was allegedly "trespassing without permission." The landlord received a greatly reduced sentence and he got time off to rotate his crops.

I could not have known in 1960 that JFK's primary campaign visit to West Virginia would have an indirect but lasting effect on my own life. The ostensibly two-year stint in Kentucky that I started in 1964 would wind up stretching into the next quarter century of my life as I became captivated by Kentucky and its people.

On January 2, 2022 The New York Times had a front-page article entitled "Coming Soon to This Coal County: Solar, in a Big Way." The article explained that renewable energy would be generated from a shuttered coal mine site in the heart of Appalachia, where poverty grinds on in the aftermath of the coal industry demise. This project will be carried out by Edelen Renewables. The President, Adam Edelen, a former Kentucky state auditor, will lead a 231-million-dollar project to place solar panels on 72 acres of land where a mountain top was removed for a former mining project in Martin County, in eastern Kentucky—the same county where I spent six months in 1965. At that time the county had a population of around 12,000 and was rated the poorest white county in the world. The main employment back then was the school system. In 2000, Martin County suffered a massive oil spill of 250,000,000 gallons of coal mine refuge sludge from a breached coal pond—a spill that was 26 times greater than the Exxon Valdez oil disaster—that spoiled drinking water in the county for over a decade. The Edelen Renewables project is the first effort to use eastern Kentucky land on an abandoned coal site to produce clean energy. The solar panels will provide renewable energy and new jobs, making the abandoned eastern Kentucky and West Virginia mines economically productive—and bringing a welcome ray of light to a long-suffering community.

CHAPTER FIVE

Phan Rang, Vietnam

After my stint with the Public Health Service in Kentucky, I signed up with the American Medical Association (AMA) exchange program and headed out to Vietnam.

There's some interesting history here: According to LBJ aide Joe Califano, when President Johnson was meeting with the AMA leadership in 1965 to talk about passing Medicare and Medicaid he asked, "Are you people going to help our boys out in Vietnam?" He was assured that the AMA would, through was called the AMA's Voluntary Exchange Program of Doctors. I don't know where the word "exchange" came from—certainly there were no doctors coming from Vietnam to the United States.

I chose to go to Vietnam because that was where the action was in 1967. In 1964, when I joined the Public Health Service in Kentucky, Vietnam was not yet a major issue, but by 1967 it was on everyone's minds. I was opposed to the war by then, but I still felt an obligation to serve in some capacity—and I also wanted to get a first-hand look at the situation—so I joined the AMA volunteer program. By the time I left the embattled country two months later, I was firmly opposed to our involvement.

Phan Rang, Vietnam

The French colonization of Vietnam had contributed almost nothing to the development of a medical system or to the training of indigenous physicians, so those of us in the "exchange" program were sorely needed. When I arrived in Vietnam in 1967, there were relatively few doctors caring for the millions of Vietnamese civilians. As part of the war effort, the United States military forces were developing the most sophisticated emergency medical system ever, saving many lives in the field through medevac helicopter squads that picked up the wounded—both US soldiers and those fighting with them—and ferried them to army hospitals. The medics in this program were saving men in battle and exposing themselves to great danger by doing so. Unfortunately, when they came back to the United States, these heroes were not integrated into the medical system here, and they were unable to leverage their experience into medical jobs. What a waste of valuable experience and training! The citizens of Vietnam, needless to say, did not have medical care comparable to the men in battle.

I was assigned to a provincial hospital in Phan Rang, a medium-sized city on the Pacific Coast, about 200 miles northeast of Saigon. I flew to Saigon in late September of 1967, and although I had only a few days of orientation there, I was glad to get out of that city. Everyone was on edge—the Viet Cong Tet Offensive months later, in 1968, would prove these fears justified.

At the provincial hospital where I served, there were only a few Vietnamese physicians and certainly not enough to meet the needs of the civilians. We were overwhelmed with patients. In the clinic room where I worked there were numbers of people desperate to get in, to get some kind of medical care. Some tried to crawl through the windows. The Viet Cong and the South Vietnamese dressed similarly and had similar medical needs. Security wasn't an issue because everyone desperately needed medical attention, so I never had an ugly incident. Fortunately, I had an interpreter when I saw patients. Thankfully, I had brought my Merck Manual, given to us at medical school, so I could look up drugs to be used for the many tropical diseases I encountered that I had only studied in my medical training.

But it was a lonely existence since I didn't speak any Vietnamese. My lodging was in a small cabin near the hospital. The sounds of the nearby jungle were haunting at night, and I was always glad when the sun rose. I welcomed the occasional letter from the U.S.—always from a friend, because I had no family at that point. It was one of the few times in my life I felt really lonesome.

One of the problems we faced at the hospital was a cholera epidemic. Cholera causes diarrhea and eventually dehydration and death if the patients are not rehydrated. We had 100 cots, each with a hole in the middle for the patient to defecate into a bucket. I made rounds every morning and would dip a stick into the bucket to determine how much saline and glucose we needed to put into the IV to replace the one or two liters the patient had lost. We saved most of the adults, but the infants were so dehydrated when they arrived that their veins collapsed, and we couldn't start IVs. Unfortunately, there was not a vaccine available for the Vietnamese civilians, unlike Americans, who received one.

During my stay there I went up to the mountains by medevac helicopter and spent two weeks helping the Montagnards, who were native to that area. Working with army medics, I pulled teeth, cleaned abscesses, gave antibiotics and did anything else I could to aid them.

Unlike the civilian Vietnamese, the Montagnards were more respectful and appreciative of any attention. Both the Viet Cong and the Vietnamese suspected the Montagnards of being traitors and so, tragically, one side or the other killed most of them.

*   *   *

One of the most disturbing developments during my stay in Vietnam was Secretary of Defense Robert McNamara's decision to defoliate Vietnam's jungle. He believed doing so would make it easier to see the Viet Cong from the air and then kill them. I was situated on the edge of the jungle, but I walked into it to get a sense of what defoliation would mean. I could tell that the United States was going to have to destroy *all* the vegetation to accomplish its mission. They did so by using herbicides with names like Agent Orange and Agent White. But this tactic didn't slow down the Viet Cong, because they infiltrated most areas through tunnels, largely moving by night.

Tragically, Agent Orange proved toxic not just for the jungle foliage and vegetation, but also for crops the South Vietnamese farmers were harvesting to stay alive. Inevitably, humans were affected as well. It is estimated that we dropped 20 million gallons of toxic herbicide onto South Vietnam, affecting about 4.8 million people. The dioxins in these herbicides, made by Monsanto and Dow Chemical—who falsely stated that they were safe—were responsible for many immediate deaths as well as long-term cancers and genetic defects. A disturbing incidence of cancer began to appear in American veterans. In 1990, Adm. Elmo Zumwalt Jr., who had been the commander of the U.S. Naval Forces in Vietnam, issued a report which excoriated the chemical companies' official corporate mendacity.

The Department of Veterans Affairs eventually drew up a list of 14 diseases, including several kinds of cancer, related to Agent Orange. Anyone who suffered from them could claim disability compensation. There was a separate list of birth defects added for the children of male veterans, and 18 other conditions for the offspring of Vietnamese women who survived in Vietnam. Even when our government acknowledged the problems Agent Orange caused, veterans had to navigate a bureaucratic maze to get relief—the burden was often on them to prove that they were ill because of Agent Orange.

Vietnam had a long history of war and occupation. Like many other countries in Southeast Asia, it had been repeatedly attacked and invaded by China for more than 1,000 years. France occupied the country for three-quarters of a century. As many as 2 million people had died from famine in the brutal Japanese occupation during World War II. But the war we were involved in was a civil war, between the North and South of Vietnam.

I recently watched the 2003 movie "The Fog of War," which is largely narrated by McNamara. He said that in 1967 he didn't understand that the Vietnam war was a civil war, and that he believed in the domino theory of the Southeast Asian countries—that one toppling would cause the rest to fall, one by one, allowing Russia and/or China to take over all of Southeast Asia. JFK also believed this, but I doubt he would have committed a half-million troops to a war which eventually killed 58,000 Americans.

In the 1968 presidential primary, Minnesota Democratic Sen. Eugene McCarthy aggressively mobilized opposition to the war and, after Johnson dropped out, Vice President Hubert Humphrey eventually emerged as the party nominee. After he was nominated, Nixon claimed that he had a "secret plan" to end the war, but it continued until 1974, by which time Nixon had resigned and Gerald Ford was president. Ford had to order the withdrawal of troops because Congress had cut off money for the war. The exodus was chaotic and had to be done rapidly as Ho Chi Minh's army was coming into Saigon and killing many South Vietnamese. Unfortunately, we left behind many friendly South Vietnamese who had helped with translation and intelligence. Rory Kennedy, Robert F. Kennedy's youngest child, made a wonderful documentary in 2014, "Last Days in Vietnam," which recounted these dark days.

We were applauded internationally for pulling out and, strangely enough, the Vietnamese regrouped and developed friendly relations with the United States. Many South Vietnamese were able to immigrate stateside and become citizens and I have never found much hostility to what we did to the country through eight years of war.

Unfortunately, we learned little from Vietnam and the disastrous effects of invading other countries. We invaded Iraq during the Bush administration because of faulty intelligence concerning weapons of mass destruction. As then-Secretary of State Colin Powell said, "You break it, you own it." And for a decade, we owned not only Iraq but were stuck in the Middle East and its tribal sectionalism and religious conflict between the Shiites and Sunnis.

CHAPTER SIX

Park Duvalle Community Health Center

I moved back to Kentucky in 1968 and settled in Louisville, in a very attractive rental house on Belgravia Court, a beautiful street in Historic Old Louisville. It was a year of uncertainty and tumult for me and for the nation.

I had reached a crossroads. After years of charting my course within the guardrails of education and obligation—Yale, Case Western, the Cleveland Clinic, the U.S. Public Health Service and the American Medical Association—an open horizon spread before me. With my mother's death five years earlier, I was also now functionally bereft of family ties drawing me anywhere (excepting my summer excursions to La Malbaie).

My experiences in the U.S. Public Health Service had taught me the importance of local action to generate positive change, and I had moved to Louisville with the idea of starting a community health clinic there. After much consideration and with the input of a number of friends and community activists, I decided to focus on the Park DuValle neighborhood.

Park DuValle was a poor, predominantly Black community in Louisville's West End. Its origin dated back to the years after the Civil

War, when thousands of former slaves settled it, calling the area "Needmore." That moniker was eventually replaced with "Little Africa," before urban renewal programs leveled the area and built the Cotter Homes subsidized housing with no services such as grocery stores or barber shops. Most Park DuValle residents had to go to the other side of town, to General Hospital, for medical care—which was no easy feat given that public transportation stopped running at 5pm. The number of black physicians in Louisville's low income communities had plummeted over the years—many gifted young black people found the time and cost of getting a medical degree daunting—and young white doctors weren't filling the gap.

Once again I met a range of resistance, from open criticism to a snide belief that, left alone, the center would collapse under its own weight. The Jefferson County Medical Society voted to send a board member to participate in the clinic but did not endorse it. There were the familiar warnings of "socialized medicine" and complaints from white doctors (who weren't treating people in the West End anyway) that we were taking their patients. Even the Falls City Medical Society, a professional association of black doctors, looked askance: They were worried that we were going to poach from the new group of patients which Medicaid had created.

There were, however, several key supporters of my efforts. At the time four granddames of Louisville society—Sally Lyons Brown, Mary Bingham, Mary Helen Byck and Jane Norton, who owned WAVE-TV, Kentucky's first television station—dominated philanthropy and civic action in the city, and these women were all tremendously helpful. (Today their children and grandchildren have taken up that philanthropic mantle.) Mary Bingham's husband Barry Bingham Sr.

was another early supporter, as was his son, Worth. But what really saved our proposal was the committed support we got from the Park DuValle community itself. Through Worth Bingham, I had been working with the dedicated people of the American Friends Service Committee, a local Quaker group which had helped introduce me to the Park DuValle neighborhood. The head of the Committee, a wonderful woman named Dora Rice who had escaped Nazi Germany, was a dynamic champion of our project. The Office of Economic Opportunity (OEO), part of President Johnson's Great Society series of ambitious initiatives, had a "maximum feasible participation" mandate that required that at least 51 percent of each community health center's board be made up of patients, and this also tied us into the community in an important way.

Another critical supporter I met through the American Friends Service Committee was a local activist named Vernice Hunter. Mrs. Hunter had grown up in Park DuValle, and though she had little education she had become a community leader through instinct and sheer force of will. When the community thought that a specific intersection—Wilson Avenue and DuValle Drive—needed a traffic light because too many pedestrians had been killed there, Mrs. Hunter took charge. City Hall was unresponsive so Mrs. Hunter, who had been crippled by a stroke and used a crutch to walk around, went into the middle of the street at rush-hour and directed traffic with her crutch while 50 supporters marched on the sidewalk with placards. Of course, everything was messed up and the police came and arrested her. She was eventually fined a single dollar for obstructing traffic— and thanks to her efforts the city put up the light.

Mrs. Hunter immediately understood the idea of the community health center and its importance, and she provided the community leadership to make it happen. When we finally got the health center started, she chaired the board, presiding over the often-contentious meetings about hiring staff and setting the course for the health center's future. She understood how to lead, and she had universal respect from the community. Without her we would have had a much more difficult time establishing Park DuValle Community Health Center. Thanks in large part to her vision and leadership, the center will celebrate its 55th anniversary in 2023.

To get funding, I went to Washington to visit with OEO officials about establishing a community health center in Louisville. My first appointment was with Sargent Shriver, who was head of both the Peace Corps and the OEO at the time. He said he had heard about me, and he immediately referred me to Dr. Joe English, the OEO's Director for Health Affairs. Joe had been the head psychiatrist for the Peace Corps for five years and was close to all of the Kennedys. When President Johnson asked Shriver to take over the OEO as well as the Peace Corps, Shriver had asked Joe to come over and head up the office for Health Affairs. Joe is an immediately likable and engaging person, and when I went in to see him, we really hit it off. When I told him about what I wanted to do in Louisville and explained that the Bingham family and The Courier-Journal were fully behind the health center, Joe said he would like to come down and talk to members of the Bingham family and other key Louisville players, and explain the opportunities and difficulties he was encountering as head of Health Affairs.

Not long after, Barry Sr. and Mary Bingham had a grand luncheon for Joe at their Glenview home, and invited an assortment of Louisville luminaries, including many people from The Courier-Journal. Barry Sr.'s son, Worth Bingham Jr., was being groomed to take over the paper and was interested in the neighborhood health center because he, too, was on the American Friends Service Committee. He wrote an editorial in support of the health center, to help with the Kentucky delegation in the U.S. House, and when Joe got back to Washington armed with this editorial, he distributed it to the members of the Education and Labor Committee. Carl Perkins, the Kentucky Democrat who chaired the committee, invited me to testify. After l gave him an elaborate picture of what the health centers could do, he said, "Now, Doctor, will the centers take care of all the people of Appalachia?" I said: "Not all, but it's a good start."

In fact, it was a good start. The community health center was immediately approved, and the OEO gave us a $1.4 million grant. It was exciting to hire a new staff, coordinate with a Model City program in the same neighborhood (another OEO initiative) and utilize job training programs, Head Start, and other Great Society initiatives. For me this was the culmination of a dream that I had worked for since my days with the public health service in Eastern Kentucky. As the seventh community health center anywhere in the country, and the first in Kentucky, it demonstrated that such concepts could be successfully executed. In 2018 my family, Joe and I were invited to the 50th anniversary gala of the Park DuValle Community Health Center. As one of more than 1,400 organizations running more than 11,000 facilities serving 27 million people nationwide, it is still going strong. Joe has continued to be a friend over the years, and I later asked him to be godfather to our youngest son, Curtis.

*   *   *

Nationally, 1968 was a very fraught year. Vietnam continued to dominate U.S. politics, and other areas as well. In early January, Dr. Benjamin Spock was indicted for counseling young men to avoid the draft. Dr. Spock had taught me at Case Western and I greatly admired this tall, gentle man who talked in such a loving way about babies and childcare, and how mothers should trust their own instincts. It was from him that I had begun to see the importance of the very early years in child development. Dr. Spock wrote *The Common Sense Book of Baby & Child Care* in 1946 and eventually 50 million copies were printed and distributed in many languages. By 1968, Spock had married his concern for youth to the crisis of the moment, protesting in the streets against the war he saw was unjust.

In Southeast Asia itself, the palpable anxiety over security which I had felt the previous fall in Vietnam, especially in Saigon, had been borne out by the January 1968 Tet Offensive. North Vietnamese forces struck simultaneously across the south, hitting five major cities as well as towns, villages and military bases. It shocked the U.S. public because it demonstrated that the Viet Cong could devastatingly attack anywhere in South Vietnam. It prompted CBS News's Walter Cronkite to travel to Vietnam and film a one-hour special report, concluding that the war was not winnable: "To say that we are mired in stalemate seems the only realistic, yet unsatisfactory, conclusion," he told a stunned nation at the end of February.

After Lyndon Johnson almost lost the 1968 New Hampshire Democratic primary to Sen. Eugene McCarthy, Robert Kennedy decided to enter the Presidential race. (I supported Bobby.) I will not forget the evening of March 31, when President Johnson told the nation: "I shall not seek, and I will not accept, the nomination of my party for another term as your President." This immediately changed the Democratic landscape and the future of the country.

Four days later, on April 4, Dr. Martin Luther King Jr was assassinated in Memphis. Riots erupted throughout the country, particularly in Washington D.C. One notable exception was in Indianapolis, where Robert Kennedy's inspiring expression of grief to African American residents managed to quell their anger.

That summer I went to Kenya with Paula Steichen. We met Mr. & Mrs. Barry Bingham Sr. in Nairobi, where an international newspaper conference was being held. That's where we were on June 6, when Bobby Kennedy was assassinated in Los Angeles just after his victory in the Californian primary. This was a totally devastating blow to me - after John Kennedy, Malcolm X, and Martin Luther King, Jr. yet another inspirational leader taken from our nation as it spiraled out of control. "We have lost John, Malcolm, Martin and Bobby in less than five years," I told Paula. "I just can't go back to another funeral and wrenching emotions. Let's climb Kilimanjaro and get away from it."

So we set off to climb Kilimanjaro—without preparation or training. It nearly did us in. Kilimanjaro, at nearly 20,000 feet, rises majestically above the African plains. It is the tallest mountain in Africa, and I had been fascinated with it since reading Ernest Hemingway's story, "The Snows of Kilimanjaro." Neither Paula nor I had trained to ascend the great volcano, which left us vulnerable to altitude sickness. But we pushed through, ascending with guides we hired—three days up and two days down.

Paula, the gamest woman I knew, didn't climb the final ascent. I started out at 1 am with a guide cutting steps in the ice. The thin air was debilitating: Every five steps I would have to stop to catch my breath. Finally, around midday, I made the ascent and saw the most wonderful panoramic view of the African plains. With an excruciating headache, I peered over the volcanic top and threw up. The descent was much easier.

Despite the troubles and tragedies of that year, my interest in politics was undiminished. I wanted to go to the 1968 Democratic Convention in Chicago, which held the potential for being both of great consequence for the nation, as well as a likely scene of real violence. I went there as an alternative delegate for Joan Bingham, the widow of Worth Bingham Jr.—my friend who had done so much to help me get the Park DuValle Health Center started, but then had died suddenly and tragically in 1966.

It was a fascinating week in Chicago. I got to see the ebb and flow of what was happening internally in the convention. The assembled masses went wild for a documentary about young Sen. Ted Kennedy of Massachusetts, the youngest and only surviving Kennedy brother. The enthusiasm for that film would prove to be one of the few moments of unity that week. Several Southern states had competing slates of delegates (some all-white, some mixed), which prompted floor fights. Anti-war demonstrators were in the streets, and the events out there soon made their way into the convention hall. I will never forget Abraham Ribicoff, the liberal senator from Connecticut, standing at the podium and decrying "Gestapo in the streets of Chicago" as kids outside were beaten up pretty badly by the police. He directed his wrath at Chicago Mayor Richard Daley, who was on the convention floor. Incensed, Daley rose and started gesticulating and used an antisemitic epithet when yelling at the senator "you have never been a mayor!" Daley's idea of being a mayor was issuing the insane orders that police should "shoot to kill" arsonists and "shoot to maim" looters.

The next day, after the encounter with Ribicoff, Daley had almost all the city employees—thousands of them—descend on the convention with big banners saying phrases like: "We Love Daley." You knew who was mayor, and whose town you were in.

After the convention week I was totally exhausted but felt as though nothing had been accomplished. Vice President Hubert Humphrey had emerged as the Democratic nominee, but his ascendance seemed anticlimactic. Johnson wouldn't give his number two any leeway to create daylight between him regarding Vietnam, which let down Humphrey's young supporters. Former Vice President Richard Nixon had seized the opportunity to build a lead. But when Johnson stopped bombing North Vietnam and talked about peace negotiations, the race narrowed. In the end, Nixon would beat Humphrey narrowly—by less than 500,000 of the popular vote—in a three-way race with Alabama Gov. George Wallace, a Democrat, winning five states in the deep South on the segregationist American Independent ticket. The loss permanently disrupted the Democrats' New Deal coalition, which had dominated American politics since 1932. Twenty years of basically Republican national political victories ensued. We learned many years later that Nixon had actually interfered in the negotiations between Johnson and the South Vietnamese government by telling the foreign leaders that he could get them a better deal. This was a treasonous intervention in U.S. foreign policy—a foretaste of impeachable offenses to come.

Despite all the political turmoil, the three years following JFK's assassination had been exciting in terms of developing ideas about fighting poverty and its effects on communities. Johnson's Great Society brought forward a plethora of great ideas as well as enthusiasm and volunteerism. The initiatives were broad: From ground-breaking civil rights laws to Medicaid and Medicare to National Public Radio to the National Endowment for the Arts to school lunches and new education initiatives, Johnson was able to get landmark legislation passed. The capstones were the Civil Rights Act and Voting Rights Act. LBJ told Everett Dirksen, the Republican Senate leader, that if he joined him in passing the civil rights law, future schoolchildren would know the names of two Illinoisans: Abraham Lincoln and Dirksen. And of course, there was the Community Health Center movement, which really had begun around 1964. In many ways we are now living more in the Great Society than in the New Deal. Johnson's programs have largely continued in one way or another, although unfortunately the Vietnam War interrupted the full development of some of his initiatives. Joe Califano, Johnson's close aide and a fellow board member on The Century Foundation, later described LBJ's accomplishment this way:

> He put the federal government forcefully on the scale
> for the vulnerable among us. He hauled and dragooned
> talented people into public service which he felt was the
> highest calling a person could have. At the risk of
> nagging, he said that God and history would judge us

not on how Gross National Product grew, but on how we spent it. Not simply on how many millionaires a booming economy produced, but how many millions of people it lifted out of poverty.

Of course, many Democrats as well as Republicans criticized Johnson. Califano blamed this on the fear of being labeled a "liberal", which by those days was an increasingly unpopular term. Johnson was more caustic: "The difference between liberals and cannibals," he once said, "is that cannibals eat only their enemies."

CHAPTER SEVEN

"That Barefoot Doctor From Kentucky"

As it happens, 1968 was also a milestone year in my personal life. That fall, as I sat I down at the rehearsal dinner the night before George Crile III's wedding in Washington, D.C., I introduced myself to my partners on my left and right. I had just said "I'm Harvey Sloane," when a voice behind me spoke up: "Oh, Harvey Sloane, I have heard of you! You are that barefoot doctor from Kentucky." I looked around and was immediately captivated by the brunette woman speaking to me. It turned out that her name was Kathleen McNally. It took only five seconds for me to say to myself: "I am going to marry that woman." Nine months later, I did.

We wed at the Heinz Chapel in Pittsburgh, where Kathy was born and raised, on June 7 of 1969. Sid Lovett officiated alongside a Catholic priest. I had made many friends in the Park DuValle community that we invited to our wedding. They were enthusiastic about coming and traveled together on a chartered bus. The Medical Director of the center, Dr. William Moses, was an usher. Dr. Milton Young, another Park DuValle ally, came and photographed the entire event. Kathy's mother, Nancy McNally, arranged for us to have our reception at her country club, which there may have been African American servers, but no Black members. Kathy asked her mother if the club would object to us having African American guests. Her mother, who was wonderful, assertive, and direct, responded: "If they do, I will resign."

Kathy and I spent our wedding night at the Plaza Hotel in New York, which Donald Trump would buy in 1988. (I am very glad he hadn't bought it yet in 1969) We had debated our honeymoon destination. I wanted to go to Alaska, because what I eventually wanted to do was to set up flying medical service there. Kathy was not enthusiastic. We ended up going to Dubrovnik in old Yugoslavia and to the Greek islands.

At the end of June of 1969, we headed back home to Louisville. I had made a new life for myself there, members of the Park DuValle community, including Vernice Hunter and her colleagues Rosemary Cook and John Thompson, as well as new friends, including John and Nancy Bell, Mr. and Mrs. Barry Bingham Sr., Jane Norton, Ian and Roberta Henderson, Joe Ardery, Cy and Wig McKinnon, Allen Bryan. Now I was bringing my bride home to this life, and I was totally excited about it.

I convinced Kathy that we should stay in the house on Belgravia Street—her caveat was that we buy it—and live in downtown Louisville, cutting against the tide of prosperous families moving to the suburbs. My view was that you couldn't work on inner city problems while enjoying the shade of suburbia. Besides, we loved the historic architecture of Belgravia Court and Old Louisville.

Louisville was a laid-back city in those days, but one still open to new ideas. It was a mix of old Southern- and whiskey-gentry and blue-collar workers. My Kentucky experience up to that point had been in the hardscrabble hills in the eastern part of the state, so Louisville had been an adjustment when I moved back there fulltime in 1968. Around the Kentucky Derby it could seem positively cosmopolitan. Situated on the Ohio River, it had always been a crossroads of sorts, a city in a Civil War border state, a key launching point as the West was opened and won.

Kathy threw herself into the life of the city. Right after she moved into the Belgravia Court house, a neighbor, Winnie Chamberland, knocked on our door and explained that urban renewal was planning a 9th Street thoroughfare project that would severely affect one side of Belgravia Court. Kathy immediately joined the cause to fight the project, attending and speaking at many town meetings. The Urban Renewal and Community Development Agency eventually dropped the project. Kathy also co-founded and was president of Louisville's first Preservation Alliance, and she took a deep interest in the arts. She chaired the Kentucky Dance Council, and she pushed to bring the famous African American ballet dancer Arthur Mitchell to Louisville. A couple of other women on the committee approached her after one meeting, concerned: "We don't want to embarrass you," they said, "but you know these people (Blacks) can't get *en pointe*, don't you?" (Getting *en pointe* is a very basic ballet technique.) This only presaged other problems: The stagehands didn't want to work with African American performers. But the show itself was a big success, and it broke the color barrier for the performing arts in Louisville.

Marrying Kathy ushered in a new epoch for me. To be married at age 33, and then after a couple of years to have our first child, Abigail—and always your first child is your most wondrous—was marvelous. Kathy wanted to have a natural childbirth. We both went to Lamaze classes, which wasn't exactly a common practice in the early '70s in Louisville. Kathy went into labor and we went to the old Norton Hospital just five blocks from where we lived. Kathy was in labor for over 20 hours and wanted me to stay with her so that we could breathe together. She was scared that if I left the room the nurse would insist on putting morphine into her IV.

Abigail was finally born at 2:15am on May 30, 1972. The next day, when all was well, I left for a meeting in the District of Columbia—an act Kathy has never let me forget. Her mother Nancy and our friend, the reporter Jimmy Walker (a cousin of the Bush family), brought her and Abigail home from the hospital.

Kathy subsequently had two miscarriages, and then in 1976 she had our son Patrick on May 30—within 15 minutes of Abigail's birthtime. Kathy became pregnant with Curtis the next year, so she went to the hospital on May 30. When the OB resident said that she had not dilated and so was not in labor, Kathy responded: "Well, I have all my babies on May 30th." But Curtis waited until June 16th!

I never had brothers and sisters and had only one parent after I was 10. Having an intact family has meant so much to us, and to me. All three of our children have been blessedly healthy and each is their own, distinct person and personality, although they all get along fabulously. If Kathy and I criticize one, the other two immediately take their sibling's position. Our kids are the greatest.

They have all pursued different paths in their lives. Abigail started with the pollster Peter Hart—the greatest pollster of his era—out of college and now she is a partner at Hart Research. (Peter did all of my ten campaigns for office. We won seven and lost three—all three losses were outside of Louisville. I always won my home base). Abigail is happily married to a wonderful guy named Todd Davenport who is a communications executive, and they have two terrific kids—a daughter, Sloane, and a son, Charlie. One of my favorite memories is Todd coming out of the delivery room and saying: "You have a granddaughter, and her name is Sloane." Charlie and I have been golfing partners since he was six.

Patrick is a Managing Director at JP Morgan Chase. He is married to the former Erin Gentry Holt, a partner and prominent attorney at Wilmer, Cutler, Pickering, Hale, and Dorr. Erin was the first person to suggest that I write a memoir. They have two vibrant boys, Fox and Winslow, who are younger than Abigail's children and are doing quite well. Both are good athletes and students and live in New York.

Curtis spent a lot of his life on the West Coast, graduating from the University of San Francisco and then playing guitar in a band. Then he decided to come back East, ostensibly to be with his family, and also to have the opportunity to work with his mother in real estate at Brown Harris Stevens in New York. At first, we all questioned whether that was really going to work out, but after six years, it certainly has. Curtis is a star in the company.

It has been a delight to have the association and enthusiasm and, really, friendship of all these children and grandchildren. All of these grandchildren are way ahead of where we were at their age, and they are much smarter. It is a great pleasure to be their grandfather.

Our whole family goes up to La Malbaie for a week or two every year and it is a spectacular time. I marvel at how lucky I am to have this intact family, to have a partner who is so vibrant, and so busy in her own sphere of work and influence but always still an incredible family person. She allows me distance. She lives in New York and I live in Washington, D.C. and we go back and forth on weekends. We have children and grandchildren in both cities. In a modern era of easy travel options, it works out well. The children are a great comfort to me, and I look forward to being with them as often as I can.

CHAPTER EIGHT

"He'll Be Lucky To Carry One Ward."

I started thinking of running for mayor of Louisville in 1972. Despite my deep interest in public service, deciding to run for mayor was no foregone conclusion. In medical school in Cleveland, I had thought that there could be few worse jobs than being mayor of a city—a humdrum business of tending to local nuts and bolts while the truly significant action of the times went on elsewhere. Indeed, while I had a longstanding desire to go into government, I had always thought of politics as Washington, D.C. and the federal government, never something like city hall. (That view has seemingly been flipped today, where qualified candidates are skipping races for federal office because success would bring gridlock, acrimony and little prospect of accomplishing anything.)

The first thing I did was get Kathy's buy-in. She had already made a tremendous change, moving from New York City and a job at Harper's Bazaar to Louisville. Now I proposed to take us into a life of politics. As a woman of Irish heritage, she extracted only one promise from me: That if I won, I would reinstate Louisville's St. Patrick's Day parade, which had last occurred in 1916 and then closed down because of the war. I did restart it and it is still robust today. (Also, it made for good politics in a Democratic primary.)

In 2023, the hosts of Louisville's St. Patrick's Day parade, the Ancient Order of the Hibernians, invited me to join in celebration of the 50th year since it had been restarted. Kathy, our three children, and our three grandsons joined me in the festivities. (Sloane could not join us because she was studying in Dublin.) I was humbled and honored by the warm reception we received 50 years after I was first mayor. It reminds me of President Kennedy saying that visiting Ireland was "as good as it gets."

One of the reasons I had started thinking about running for mayor was my dissatisfaction with city services, especially in relation to the Community Health Center. Air pollution was a real problem, particularly in the West End. There were many chemical plants located in that area, undoubtedly because it was not affluent—they would have never been placed in the East End. Companies like Louisville Gas & Electric, our major utility, American Standard, which made toilets (and was one block from where we lived) and the aptly named Air Reduction spewed all manner of particulates and noise into the air. A stench permeated the city from local industry, and on especially bad days white material caked onto cars in the West End—a visual reminder of what we were breathing. So in 1969 I had followed my activist instincts, starting an air pollution group, called Action for Clean Air.

We demonstrated in downtown Louisville wearing gas masks. One time, after a heavy rain which caused the city waste disposal landfill to flood, another Action for Clean Air activist, Tina Heavrin joined me rowing a boat to the old city dump. A photo of our protest ran in the paper during the election for County Judge/Executive, between incumbent Judge Tom Sawyer and Todd Hollenbach. Judge Sawyer's daughter, Diane (who would go on to have a prominent career as a national television reporter), had encouraged her father to appoint me to the Louisville-Jefferson County Air Pollution Control Board. The Courier-Journal also favored my appointment, and Judge Sawyer appointed me. Some local manufacturing groups immediately struck back by criticizing Standard Gravure—The Courier-Journal's printer—for emitting pollutants. This was embarrassing but it forced the Bingham empire to comply with local and federal air pollution control standards.

Unfortunately, Judge Sawyer died in an early morning accident on the way to work in September of 1969. Democrat Todd Hollenbach won the November election for County Judge/Executive that year. In city politics, Frank Burke, a Democrat who had served in Congress from 1959 to 1963, was elected the Mayor. Mayors of Louisville back then served one four-year term and were not allowed to serve consecutive terms, so as I saw it a run for mayor after Burke's term ended was my logical next step. Not everyone agreed: Many people suggested I aim for a more achievable office, like Alderman, first. Others just told me I was crazy.

In 1972, the most knowledgeable person around about politics in general and Kentucky politics in particular was a man named Ed Prichard. So it only made sense for me to turn to him when I started thinking about a mayoral run. I had first met Prich, as everyone called him, when I had moved to Louisville in 1964. (Again, my introduction was thanks to Kay Halle, who had insisted that I contact two people in Kentucky: the aforementioned Barry Bingham Sr. was the first, and

Ed Prichard was the second.) Prich and his wife Lucy had graciously welcomed me to their house in Versailles, and I enjoyed any opportunity to see them thereafter.

The back story on Prich is an interesting one. He was a prominent New Dealer and FDR Brain-Truster who had returned to Kentucky after FDR's death and attempted to engage in local politics. Politicians of the day were sure he would either be governor or president, given his brilliance and political connections. But in 1948 he stuffed ballot boxes in eleven precincts. "I thought of it as something you did for fun," he said years later. "It was sort of a moral blind spot."

Prich later confessed about stuffing the ballot boxes to someone—it's never been clear who—who then alerted the FBI. The Judge of the Federal District Court in Lexington sentenced Prichard to two years in the Federal Correctional Institution in Ashland, Kentucky about 100 miles east of Lexington. He served time there until President Truman commuted his sentence to time served. The incident cost Prich his law practice, and when he got out of jail, he was so furious at the government that he refused to pay taxes. Bill Wester, a close friend and the Administrator of the Kentucky Department of Health, saw that Prich was unemployed, helped him get contracts with the department and made sure he resumed paying his federal taxes.

Prich slowly managed to restore his reputation, and by the time I arrived in Kentucky in the mid-'60s, he was again a visible, if still controversial, figure in state politics. He gave a legendary stemwinder in the 1963 Democratic primary between Edward T. "Ned" Breathitt, Jr. and former Gov. A.B. "Happy" Chandler. Campaigning for Breathitt from the back of a flatbed truck in Hindman, in Knott

County, he accused Chandler of directing contracts to his son-in-law, Jimmy Jack Lewis, during his second term as governor in the 1950s. "Fill up the sack for Jimmy Jack," Prich would tell audiences. Ed Easterly, Breathitt's press secretary, recorded it and distributed it widely, a joy for those of us who cherish skillful use of language and metaphor in politics as well as deep ridicule of opponents. He told another classic joke about a farmer and his son watching a hungry calf chasing after a bull in hope of getting some milk. When the alarmed son points this out to his father, the man replies: "He'll know the difference when supper-time comes." Voters will know the difference at supper time, he would conclude, if Chandler were to win.

The final decision to run for Mayor really crystallized for Kathy and me when we held an event at our house for Democratic presidential nominee George McGovern in the fall of 1972. McGovern didn't stand a chance of winning Kentucky, but we wanted to do the best we could. We asked Prich to be the headliner at the event, to come stir up the McGovern supporters. He did a great job. After the McGovern event Kathy and I drove Prich home. I told him about my aspirations. We parked near our home and talked for two hours about the 1973 Democratic mayoral primary. He advised us on who the legislative district chairmen were, who was the most important and how to go about starting the campaign. "Go to the North End Democratic Club and help them fix their roof," he said, telling me to get to know George Lucas, the chairman there—and I did.

Prich proved to be a keen adviser to me on many fronts, and really helped me expand my Kentucky network. He introduced me, for example, to former Governor Bert Combs, from Eastern Kentucky, a not very tall man who was often known as the "Little

Judge". Prich had helped Combs during his 1955 gubernatorial bid against Chandler. Perhaps still stinging from Prichard's acid wit from four years earlier, Chandler accused Combs of harboring a "jailbird" in his campaign. Combs lost in 1955, but went on to win the Governorship in 1959, and Prich became an unofficial adviser to the new Governor.

Combs was a great Governor for Kentucky. In addition to serving as a judge in Eastern Kentucky, he was a distinguished World War II veteran. He established a community college system in Kentucky, had a strong civil rights record and above all supported education, especially in low-income counties. He built the Mountain Parkway, which went from Lexington to his former residence of Prestonsburg. Combs and I got to be good friends, and he would wind up advising me in important ways during my first run for mayor.

*   *   *

Once Kathy and I decided to go for it, I started assembling a campaign team. It included Allen Bryan, whom I had met through my close friends John and Nancy Bell and who had done significant radio work, and Joe Ardery, a bright Harvard graduate who went on to be in my administration. Everybody recognized that my race was a long shot. I had been in Louisville for only four years and I had only been cursorily involved in politics. The Democratic establishment opposed me. "Sloane is a loopy liberal," one alderman told The Courier-Journal early on. "He'll be lucky to carry one ward in the primary."

Dr. Carroll Witten, President of the Board of Alderman, was Burke's heir apparent. He was a general practitioner of some renown and was the president of the American Academy of General Practice. The Democratic nominee was usually chosen by the crowd on 4th Street—the Louisville political machine at party headquarters—and the incumbent Democratic officeholders. A vibrant primary was an exotic exception.

On the other hand, even though I had only been in Louisville a relatively short time, I had a good record. The Park DuValle Neighborhood Health Center generally got good publicity and I was known as an activist; and I had resources to help fund my campaign. Louisville might just be ready to have fresh leadership; the Burke administration had concentrated on downtown development, as opposed to helping residential neighborhoods. There was also a political scandal in the police department which was getting steady attention from WHAS-TV's Jimmy Walker.

Over the course of that 1973 Democratic primary, Kathy and I went to 250 coffees. We met many wonderful people all over the city who were interested in volunteering. But most important, we heard about their hopes, dreams and concerns. The volunteers we met proved to be tremendously important. We developed one of the first "instant-organizations" in the country for Election Day: Volunteers were assigned specific blocks (usually close to where they lived) to ensure my supporters got to the polls. By early January we were intensively preparing a series of policy papers on every major issue, from police protection to neighborhood development.

Luckily some people experienced with Louisville politics joined our campaign, including state senator Lacey Smith, who chaired the campaign; legislative district chairman Creighton Mershon; and Danny Briscoe, an excellent operative. Without their expertise and enthusiasm, we would not have won the campaign. They helped me organize campaign staff and volunteers and get professional media advice. We hired Jack Bowen and Doug Bailey from the Washington-based political consulting firm Bailey Deardourff. I was the first Democrat that their firm had ever worked for! Bailey would later work for both of my campaigns for governor, and Bowen for the first. (In 1987 Bailey would go on to found the daily political tip sheet "The Hotline.") During the early phases of our campaign our original TV spots, produced by my longtime friends Reverend Al Shands and Joe Ardery, were absolutely crucial.

Even though the primary was in late May, we didn't hire a pollster until April. Through Briscoe's mother, who had worked as a telephone interviewer at Hart Reserach, we retained the aforementioned Peter Hart, a pollster who was just then starting a very promising career. Peter called to say that he would come to Louisville to brief me on the poll results. He said, however, that as a practice he did not involve spouses in such debriefings. I suggested this might be a problem in our household because Kathy was very involved in the campaign. He relented and gave us the most marvelous briefing. He outlined our strengths and weaknesses, and our opponent's strengths and weaknesses and what we could do to correct them. Peter would go on to handle all ten of my races for office, as well as the three referenda I introduced as Mayor with the County Judge.

Unfortunately, we were behind by 27 points and the primary was just six weeks away. My campaign's big issue was neighborhood development. The downtown was getting attention and the Fourth Street Mall was being built, but residential neighborhoods had been neglected. I pledged to set up a specific office for neighborhood development with staff to directly work with neighborhood organizations and individuals who had local concerns.

This promise, to help people where they *lived* rather than worrying solely about businesses, struck a chord. In part, it tapped into a backlash against urban renewal and a fear that unresponsive, aloof bureaucrats would tear up neighborhoods without regard to local wishes. There was a more local angle to the anger too. As Sharon Wilbert, who was one of my most trusted aides in my Kentucky political career, later described it, I was the first Louisville politician in a long time who actually seemed interested in voters themselves. "Those who had direct impact and power over our neighborhoods were not evident in our communities," she told me. "The Courier-Journal and Louisville Times told us they were at business meetings and Chamber of Commerce gatherings, but they were unknown to us, unless there was a ribbon-cutting or they were passing through."

One issue Peter Hart identified as a vulnerability for my opponent, Dr. Caroll Witten, was a property tax increase the Board of Alderman had enacted under his leadership—despite President Richard Nixon instituting federal-local revenue sharing. Every professional instinct I had was to provide more support for public spending, so when I had a press conference to criticize Witten for the tax increase, my knees literally shook. Luckily, I did not get any searching questions on the topic from the media or my opponent.

Financial disclosure was another big campaign issue for me. I had disclosed my finances, showing about $2 million worth of assets, but Dr. Witten refused to do so. Our campaign started asking why: Why did Dr. Witten not want to disclose his assets and income tax returns?

I don't think he had anything to hide. He likely didn't do it because it wasn't a regular part of the political culture and he didn't take me seriously enough to do anything different. But the question had legs.

*   *   *

My biggest personal priority as a potential Mayor was establishing Louisville's first professional emergency medical service. This not only stemmed from my medical background and longtime public health concerns, but also from a personal experience during the campaign. All the mayoral candidates were scheduled to speak at a Veterans of Foreign Wars Post one night in April. Irving Hibbs, who represented the Seventh Ward on the Board of Aldermen and supported Witten, got up to speak and immediately collapsed. I pushed my way through the crowd, up to the stage and found him lying unconscious on the floor. I could not find a heartbeat. The police had been called—they provided emergency medical services at that point—but no one was giving him CPR, so I started.

It took 20 minutes for the police to arrive. He was wearing Witten's bright yellow campaign pin and as the minutes passed and I started to become short of breath, it would go in and out of focus each time I tried to blow life into Hibbs.

The police finally arrived with the vehicle they used for emergency medical services: a station wagon. I got in the back with Hibbs and continued to perform CPR. There were no straps for the stretcher so each time the car stopped we would get thrown toward the front seat and then when the car took off we nearly went out the back.

From the time the police were called it took 45 minutes to get Hibbs to Louisville General Hospital. When we got there he had no pulse and I knew he was gone. I vowed then and there that if I won, I would establish a professional Emergency Medical Service.

Late in the campaign, Witten sensed that I was generating excitement and interest, so he started accusing me of trying to buy the race. "Louisville is not for sale," became his slogan. He also started attacking me as a carpetbagger, noting that I had been born in New York City. I had only spent my first week in that metropolis, but in 1973 it was a national symbol of urban incompetence and decay. When reporters asked me about it I was able to defuse the attack with humor: "I just wanted to be near my mother when I was born," I said.

Kathy thought that we had little chance of winning the primary, but that May I carried all twelve wards. Hart has credited that race as a springboard for his career. It was also the beginning of our enduring friendship with Peter and his wife, Florence.

*   *   *

The fall campaign would be an arduous one. We needed momentum and credibility. Louisville is a Democratic town, but the Republican nominee was a former Police Chief, Colonel Columbus J. "C.J." Hyde. He was a decent and likeable person, but he was really not cut out for politics and had a limited appeal. His big issue was how many police we would have and how they would be deployed.

Our team, again led by Lacey Smith, felt the best way for me to really become acquainted with Louisville (and it with me) was for me to walk around the city—all around the city. I walked some 275 miles.

Each day a volunteer went ahead of me so that neighbors would know that I was coming in case they wanted to have a meeting or talk to me individually. We had a whole team that went out and of course distributed campaign literature. My walkabouts exposed me to Louisville's neighborhoods, roads, ambiance and the Ohio River; but they also were a great way to see and to get to know Louisville's alleys, blighted areas and the run-down housing that would need attention.

As we campaigned intensely through that lead up to the election I learned a lot about the city, but I also learned a lot about myself. I was reminded of a moment in 1961 when the newly elected Vice President Lyndon Johnson was asked how he felt about President Kennedy's appointments for the various Cabinet positions, all of which were high-powered private citizens who have been presidents of foundations or heads of prominent companies. Johnson's retort was: "I would feel a lot better if one of them had run for sheriff". Running for office and asking for people's votes is a humbling and character-building experience.

On November 4, 1973, the hard work paid off. We won with over 70 percent of the vote. Todd Hollenbach handily won his reelection as County Judge/Executive, so the city and the county would be run by two elected officials in their 30s.

CHAPTER NINE

"We Didn't Know What We Couldn't Do."

I took the oath of office at just after midnight on December 1, 1973, standing in our living room. I hadn't waited for the normal midday ceremony because I wanted to demonstrate that this administration would be moving from the get-go.

There is no job in the world like being mayor, especially of a city like Louisville in the early 1970s. It was large enough to face the full array of modern urban problems but small enough that both individuals and government could have a positive, tangible effect on how life is lived. As one staffer, Lou Byron, later recalled: "We didn't know what we couldn't do."

My approach, as I said in my inaugural address that afternoon, would be "people, not buildings; people, not highways; people, not sprawling and unmanageable growth."

I had campaigned on a responsive administration, promising that I would list my home phone number so that I could be reached when needed, day or night. We got all sorts of calls, though *mostly* at decent hours. One night shortly after I was inaugurated, I got a call from a good citizen who said that there was a pothole in the street outside his door and every time a car went over it, it would wake his wife. I received this call at 2 o'clock in the morning. The next day I made sure that the public works director personally oversaw the pothole's repair. I then called the good man back—at 2:30 the next morning—and asked him how he felt now that the pothole was repaired. He said that he hadn't noticed the repair, so I said, "Sir, I would really appreciate it if you would go out and personally look at it." It was a cold December morning and he never called back again.

Among the small group standing in my living room that night was Jay Rockefeller, whom I had met in the '60s when I was a public health officer assigned to Kentucky and he was a VISTA volunteer in West Virginia. After he finished his VISTA stint, he had stayed in the Mountain State and was elected first to the state legislature as a Democrat, and then as West Virginia's Secretary of State in 1968. As Jay said, "Harvey and I have the absolute pleasure of being kindred spirits. We are entirely alike in every way that matters and I take joy in our friendship."

The previous year, Jay had been defeated in his first run for governor of West Virginia against the incumbent Arch Moore. Jay had courageously come out against strip mining—not a popular position in West Virginia in the early '70s. Jay would recall that Moore's campaign had a bumper sticker that said, "Make him spend it all, Arch!", referring to the fabled Rockefeller riches. Governor Moore eventually went to jail on corruption charges, and in 1976 Jay would win the governorship on his second try and serve two terms as Governor, followed by four terms in the U.S. Senate. (When Jay retired in 2014, Arch Moore's daughter, Shelly Moore Capito, won his senate seat.) He, his wife Sharon (who would become President of the flagship public television and radio station WETA for over 20 years),

Kathy and I would wind up spending many very wonderful times together over the years, especially at the Kentucky Derby.

After that swearing in ceremony in my living room, I hit the ground running. My first order of business as Mayor was to make good on my pledge to focus on neighborhoods, punching through a cosseted status quo to try to make city politics less insulated. My neighborhood focus would entail creating a linkage between the new administration and neighborhood organizations throughout the city. Not surprisingly, perhaps, my agenda quickly ran into typical political turf wars. The Board of Aldermen hated this idea, fearing that these new neighborhood representatives would be politicking to replace them. This is the nature of dealing with an entrenched political system; it becomes a battle of attrition, to see which side can outlast the other. It would take another election, in 1975, to break the logjam and finally move forward on my neighborhood agenda.

*   *   *

The first major crisis of my administration tore through the city, literally, on April 3, 1974.

I was out of the country when the tornado hit. I had been working nonstop for two years, first getting the campaign started and then setting up the administration, and I needed a break. I had gone up to Eternity for a week, to spend some time in the wilderness with my old friend and guide Jean-Marie Menier. We both had Ski-Doos and snowshoes, and we walked and Ski-Dooed around the lakes. It was a whole different experience to be up there in the winter. Jean-Marie and I would make lunch, melt some snow for water and eat peanut butter sandwiches. He carried twigs in his backpack so we could start a fire and make tea. I loved looking out over the vista of those familiar rolling mountains, which were now white. We slept in the main room at Eternity, warmed by the fire there. Every two hours we took turns putting more logs on the fire, to keep it going. It was really cold. We had to haul up water from the lake, because the stream from which we got water in the summertime was frozen.

On the last morning a man came Ski-Dooing down from the top of the lake, about seven-and-a-half miles away. He was yelling and screaming: "Louisville, Louisville gros orage! Gros orage!" In English that meant that there had been a great storm in Louisville. In fact, it had been a tornado, and a massive one.

Jean-Marie and I de-camped, getting out of there as fast as we could. I was able to catch a passenger flight out of Canada from an airstrip at a Canadian Air Force base about 40 miles away—but no planes could land in Louisville itself, because of the damage from the tornado. When I finally managed to get there, I took a helicopter ride over the city. I had never seen anything like it. The tornado had felled 10,000 trees in 90 seconds in Cherokee Park in central Louisville—it looked like a meat cutter had sliced into the park. Many buildings and homes throughout the city had also been destroyed.

The private and public sectors immediately pulled together into action. For security reasons, streets were blocked off—downed power lines had to be removed. Amazingly, there was no vandalism, and no arrests were made. Representatives from my new Neighborhood Development Office went door to door in stricken areas, to survey residents' needs and to connect them with available resources.

The most encouraging sign came in the period just after the immediate crisis: Residents needed to make decisions about whether to rebuild or move away. Most people in both the city and the county decided to stay and rebuild. It was a unifying moment for the community. The first task was to remove the incredible amount of debris and fallen trees, and not damage the terrain further. Importantly, residents insisted that the original Frederick Law Olmsted design for Cherokee Park be honored in its reconstruction. Olmsted is acknowledged as the father of American landscape architecture, and Louisville is blessed with three separate Olmsted parks. Everyone in the community agreed it was essential to retain his classic design. We had our Parks Department go to the Olmsted Firm in Brookline, Massachusetts and get the original plans for the park. We hired a landscape company out of Michigan and insisted that they work closely with the various neighborhoods in the rehabilitation. The private sector started an organization called Trees, Inc., and thousands of trees were planted over the next decade. All these combined efforts worked. Today the park looks virtually the same as it did before the tornado.

Ironically, the tornado disaster helped my administration to follow through on my campaign promise, because it forced us to focus on neighborhoods. We insisted that the planning commission, led at the time by Don Ridings, develop neighborhood plans presenting various options—whether to close an alley or build a park or alter traffic—to which the residents could react. Zoning was not changed to allow higher development, and residential areas were honored.

The city and the county, under Judge/Executive Todd Hollenbach, were not always great at working together—turf rivalries would sometimes get in the way, not to mention self-reinforcing habits of each doing its own thing. But in this instance, crisis was the mother of cooperation and we worked hand in hand to deal with the aftermath of the storm. Rick Northern, a county employee, served as the bridge between the city and county governments. Even within the governments, employees did their part and did not try to grandstand or do anything that would make their department look better. It really was a team effort.

Looking back, I am convinced that the way the natural disaster pulled the community together helped prepare the city and county to work together on the issue of court-ordered busing that would be coming in the next year.

*   *   *

A month after the tornado hit, I had a far more pleasurable duty: my first Kentucky Derby as Mayor of Louisville.

Wendell Ford, the former Governor and US Senator of Kentucky, used to tell this story about the Kentucky Derby, which was recounted in his New York Times obituary: One Kentucky Derby day, a man walking in the Churchill Downs grandstand spied a box with a prominent empty seat. Next to it sat an older woman. "This is the first empty seat I've seen today," he told her. She explained, "Well, it belonged to my husband, but he died." The stranger then asked, "Why didn't you give it to one of your relatives?" The woman replied, "I would have, but they're all at the funeral."

Coming from Eastern Kentucky to Louisville in the mid-'60s had been not only a rural-to-urban transition for me, but also a cultural transformation. Eastern Kentucky, with its scarred mountains and rural poverty, was elemental with few frills. Louisville, by contrast, had asphalt, old buildings, universities, air pollution, the Ohio River—and, perhaps most dramatic of all, the Derby.

Why has this horse race continued without interruption for more than 140 years? I went to my first Derby in 1966, and I still remember being in the infield where: 1) I couldn't see the race; 2) good times and drink and merriment were had in abundance; 3) it took about three and a half hours to get out of Churchill Downs. My friend Hunter Thompson may have had it right in his 1970 gonzo journalism article for Scanlan's magazine, entitled "The Kentucky Derby Is Decadent and Depraved." Maybe he was in the infield and couldn't see the race.

But the longer I lived in Louisville, the more I appreciated how deeply the event is embedded in Kentucky culture. As James C. Nicholson describes in his book *The Kentucky Derby: How the Run for the Roses Became America's Premier Sporting Event*, the Derby has run continuously since 1875. This so-called "Greatest Two Minutes of Sport" was originally modeled on the Derby at Epsom Downs, one of England's oldest and most famous racecourses, but over time it has been embellished by conspicuous American displays of wealth and luxury. Over the years the Kentucky Derby developed its own pageantry and became an integral part of Kentucky's identity, along with Daniel Boone—the classic rugged woodsman who died more than a half-century before the first Derby and who actually had no connection with horse-racing.

Nowadays the Derby—with its iconic mint julep, roses, hats and Stephen Foster's "My Old Kentucky Home"—has become a celebration of place, as well as a milestone in the annual calendar. The lyrics, however, have been deleted at the opening of the Run for the Roses because of the racial implications. In Louisville, one got into the habit of saying, "I will do such-and-such right after the Derby." And the Derby is not just about the race itself. It is also a full-blown civic celebration, spanning the two-week Kentucky Derby Festival and going right through the presentation of the trophy. Louisville comes alive, with spring flowers abounding, the streets meticulously cleaned, and residents dressed in their Derby finest. During Derby season there are now a number of other races that feature just about anything you can think of: Colorful hot air balloons drift across the Louisville sky; rodents run on a miniature track; waiters and waitresses maneuver through an obstacle course with trays of wine glasses in the "Run for the Rosé". One of the best-known events is the Great Steamboat Race, featuring the historic Belle of Louisville versus the Cincinnati Delta Queen in a skullduggery-filled race on the Ohio River for the grand trophy of Golden Antlers.

My personal favorite Derby-inspired event is the Kentucky Derby Festival Mini-Marathon, which I helped start in 1974. Originally called the Mayor's Mini-Marathon, it drew 301 runners its first year—including, of course, me. Now the Mini routinely draws 12,000 runners, and the companion full marathon draws another 3,000. In 2016 the Festival issued 301 commemorative Mini T-shirts, and I was honored to be presented with one, along with other memorabilia; and I was invited to return for the 50th annual Derby Festival mini and Marathon in 2023. I ran in these Derby 13-mile marathons every year I was in office—12 years.

My first Derby as Mayor, in 1974, set an attendance record of 163,628; this was the year after Secretariat had won the Triple Crown with an unbelievable 31-length victory at the Belmont Stakes. "There is absolutely no doubt in my mind that he is the finest athlete of any race, color, family, genus or species ever to have lived," one turf writer commented. That year not only marked the 100th running of the race, but also coincided with the 200th anniversary of the first permanent Kentucky settlement, Harrodsburg. Wendell Ford, Kentucky's governor at the time, boldly predicted, "The 100th Kentucky Derby will be the greatest thing that ever happened on the face of the United States." No editorial or writer dared make fun of the remark.

In 1975 Kathy and I and our children moved to Magnolia and South Fourth St., literally ten minutes from Churchill Downs. The buses carrying Derby-goers from downtown would come by our house and the drivers would yell out: "There is the Mayor's house, with the flag." It was an occasion for us to invite prominent guests, such as Jay Rockefeller and his wife Sharon, the Tom and Meredith Brokaw, revered statesman Averell Harriman and his wife Pamela (the famous Washington, D.C. hostess), CBS News anchor Dan Rather and his wife Jean, Pam and Tom Wicker, Jimmy and Rosalynn Carter (it was the year he ran for President) and many others. I had always downplayed fancy cars, but the Mayor's motorcycle escort was a thrill for all of our guests—and it got us into and out of Churchill Downs in record time.

One of the most challenging parts of Derby season as Mayor was trying to attend all the numerous Festival events, and especially Derby parties. Kathy and I were typically invited to a dozen parties on the Friday evening before the Derby and the Saturday night of the Derby. Working with the driver and the police in advance, we would come in the front door, where we were greeted by the hosts. Most would line up a picture with us, and then we would gradually work our way to the rear of the house and leave through the back door into the waiting car to go to the next party. Sadly, we rarely had time to linger.

Few of the out-of-town Derby attendees were thoroughbred-racing aficionados, and many didn't even know what a pari-mutuel bet was (it involves the payout from a bet coming from a pool of all bets placed). But on that first Saturday in May, most Americans wanted to at least watch the "The Run for the Roses."

I have attended 22 Derbies in my life—and I believe I will watch the rest on TV!

*   *   *

June of 1974 brought a crashing return to the reality of urban politics. The city's sanitation workers went on a wildcat strike. The nature of their grievances was not entirely clear, especially because the Teamsters, who represented them, did not sanction the walkout. State law prohibits public employees from striking, so I was facing a decision to fire the 500 employees—which I did. Working with Charlie Roberts, an imposing man and born leader who was our Director of Sanitation, we immediately set up a process for rehiring the fired workers—but only those who were not actively involved in the strike and who had a good employment record. We were conscious of the Memphis sanitation strike in 1968, and wanted to avoid a similarly prolonged situation in Louisville. (Martin Luther King, Jr. was assassinated in Memphis in 1968 after he had addressed a group of sanitation workers to encourage their continued commitment to the strike.)

As a practical matter, the garbage still had to be collected, so all of us who were in administrative roles played our part. I worked as a tipper on the garbage truck—the person who picks up the cans and dumps the garbage into the truck—and went to some of the neighborhoods in the West End, which were predominantly African American, to pick up the trash and empty their garbage cans. Many of the sanitation workers came from there and they obviously were not happy with me. Anticipating the route that the garbage truck I was working on would take, they put heavy rocks into the garbage cans. We had garbage thrown into our front yard at home. Fortunately, that was as bad as it got.

Around this time, I decided I wanted to do something for the city's kids during the free days they had in the summer. I had heard that Boston had a "Summerthing" program which exposed kids to the arts. I asked one of my staffers, a bright and effective woman named Mary Moss, to look into creating something similar for Louisville. I had first met Mary when she was a reporter at WAVE covering consumer and environmental issues (she was one of the first journalists in the country on these beats). Mary investigated the matter and said she thought we could do it better than Boston.

The idea was to have activities in the neighborhoods, particularly low-income areas, which involved the arts—dance, storytelling, puppetry, singing—to allow Louisville kids to really experience what many more-affluent children were able to enjoy. Mary began contacting the private and corporate sectors about funding. Coca-Cola, Philip Morris, Standard Oil and Brown-Forman, as well as a number of banks, all agreed to chip in and she set up a foundation to fund the events. We rented trucks from which the programs would run around town and got Barry Bingham Jr. to ensure that The Courier-Journal would publicize their locations on a daily basis. Muhammad Ali also got involved with our version of Summerthing—which we called Summerscene, and was a big help. He attracted a lot of kids and did all sorts of things to entertain and encourage them: storytelling, singing—he just had so many talents.

Holding these summer festivities in low-income inner-city neighborhoods was particularly important, especially after federal court ordered cross-community busing in 1975, during the second year of my administration. Often the inner-city students wound up being bused in greater numbers and farther distances than suburban students, so it was nice for them to have enriching cultural opportunities in their home neighborhoods.

That first summer 150 children came to Summerscene events, and it proved to be a tremendous success. It was a big triumph not only because of Mary's initiative, drive and imagination, but more importantly because the private sector, which loaned 15 trucks for the effort, was a real partner. It turned out to be one of the great public-private enterprises developed by my administration. Unfortunately, the mayor who succeeded me—William Stansbury—was not very interested, and eventually he let it die.

Another big challenge we faced that year was saving the Louisville and Jefferson County bus service. The Louisville Transit Company was privately owned and could not make ends meet, which forced them to raise fares, which in turn caused them to lose riders. An established and resourceful attorney, John Tarrant, represented the Louisville Transit Company, and was very firm about what they would agree to do in terms of allowing the city to buy them out and operate the service. The bottom line was that the company wanted a lot of money—and Tarrant was the man to squeeze every last dime out of us. I asked around for who was the toughest and most effective attorney in the city. The name of Rucker Todd, a partner in another major Louisville firm, came up again and again. I knew Rucker slightly, and I told him we had to get this done or the whole busing service would collapse. I needed someone tough to work on behalf of the city and the county. Thankfully he agreed, and he did a great job.

Getting funds to operate the system would be even more difficult, as it would require voters to authorize a dedicated tax by ballot referendum. We decided to increase the occupational tax which both the city and the county employees and employers already paid. It was tricky because both the city and the county were in somewhat of a recession and the last thing that the labor folks that supported me wanted was a tax increase. We retained Peter Hart to gather information as to what the community would support and why. Again, Peter did a marvelous job picking through the conflicting attitudes of the electorate who wanted bus service but did not want to pay for it. Citizens were mainly concerned about continuing public transportation to get to work. We devised a plan and an agenda.

The first order of business was getting the county's Fiscal Court and the city's Board of Aldermen to approve putting the referendum on the November ballot. This was complicated by the fact that many of these individuals would be up for re-election the following year. Todd Hollenbach, the County Judge/Executive, planned to challenge incumbent Gov. Julian Carroll—who had succeeded Wendell Ford when he left to become US Senator—in the Democratic primary. The Board of Aldermen was stuck in a tie vote to authorize the referendum, until Danny Meyer, a United Auto Workers employee, switched his vote in spite of his labor background. Meyer's vote put the referendum on the ballot. The fiscal court also approved, giving the community a chance to vote to finance the bus service.

My campaign for the referendum was touch and go. I used my annual October walk through neighborhoods to highlight the need for bus service. (The walk was organized by Cass Harris, a trusted aide who put all of my walks together.) These treks would become a symbol of government meeting people and were quite positively received. We had advance work done by the neighborhood staff, and we left literature regarding the upcoming November referendum. I brought the various department heads to walk with me, so that as we received complaints we would be able to respond as quickly as possible. Most people were inclined to go with the referendum, which would increase the occupational tax by one-fifth of 1 percent. Labor didn't take a position on it, which was very important because we certainly would have lost if they had opposed it. There was good support from the media, both electronic and print, and the fact that there might not be a bus service without it was a strong motive to vote for the tax.

I campaigned harder for that referendum than I had for my own election. I would get on buses during the morning and evening rush-hours, meet everybody and give them a little literature about the referendum. Then I would get off that bus and get on the next one. This was obviously a sympathetic audience, but they needed to understand that they had to vote.

Toward the end of October, the employees in the transit union became concerned about their future, and their remuneration. It looked like *they* might strike. I went to the meeting of all the workers in the union to plead for them not to do so. First of all, it was illegal, and they would have to be terminated; but as importantly, if they struck and the community reacted badly, their future, as well as the community's, would be jeopardized. It was a raucous meeting but after I left, they voted not to strike.

Surprisingly, the referendum passed going away, and the Transit Authority of River City, or TARC, was established. As I described in the introduction, less than a week before the vote on this referendum and half a world away, Louisville's most famous son—Muhammad Ali—had squared off against reigning boxing champion George Foreman in the famous "Rumble in the Jungle" in Zaire. After winning in eight rounds, Ali had delivered the shout out—"Louisville is the greatest!"—that prompted me to send him a telegram inviting him home. I was delighted when he took me up on my invitation and arrived a mere five days later. Between saving the city's bus service and escorting the heavyweight world boxing champion around his hometown, it was a hectic but thrilling week for me as Louisville's new Mayor.

$*$ $*$ $*$

At the end of my first year in office a controversy erupted involving alleged inappropriate behavior by some of my staff. In December of 1973, just after I had won the election for Mayor, an insurance advisor for the previous administration offered me a $5,000 contribution. I consulted with my friend and advisor, former Governor Bert Combs, as to whether I should accept such a contribution. After thinking for a moment, Combs said, "I don't think I would." He was right. A year later, State Sen. Lacey Smith, who had managed my campaign and then served as my special counsel, was indicted by the Republican Commonwealth Attorney for having allegedly accepted $5,000 from the same insurance advisor. I had not accepted money from him, and was not implicated in the political scandal, and Smith was eventually acquitted. But I was asked to go before a grand jury to answer questions.

Over the 16 years that I have been involved in management of various organizations—two years at the Park DuValle Neighborhood Health Center, eight years as Mayor, four as County Judge/Executive and two as Washington, D.C. Director of Health—I have been criticized for not always being organized and attentive to detail. I plead guilty to that criticism. Neither my formal education—college and the medical school process—nor being a public health officer ever prepared me to manage a large organization.

Whether it was establishing the community health center, dealing with the busing crisis, spearheading the referendum to pass the tax for TARC, moving the city's natural history museum to its current Main Street location, dealing with a contract system for HIV aids procurement in Washington or working to improve TB control in a Russian prison. I was always much better at analyzing the situation and identifying the big picture solution than figuring out the details of execution. My forte was always people: choosing the best people I could find to run departments, managing the budget and resolving personal issues. My philosophy was to hire the most qualified person possible and give them latitude in fulfilling their responsibilities. After setting the course, I would only intervene when there was an intractable situation.

After testifying for the grand jury, I vowed never to leave myself open to criticism of inappropriate ethical behavior by myself or by those working with me. I appointed an ethics committee to receive and judge any potential improprieties that I witnessed or that were brought to my attention, with the proviso that their findings would be made public. To avoid any conflict-of-interest issues, I made sure this strict ethical review would include any transactions involving the city, including my wife's real estate practice. The process served the city well, and I never had to go through a grand jury investigation again.

CHAPTER TEN

"Mayor Sloane Did Everything Possible To Give Us Security."

In my second full year in office, in 1975, I faced, with Hollenbach, the biggest challenge I would confront during my political career: At the end of July, a federal judge ordered that the schools in the city and surrounding Jefferson County be desegregated in what would be the first instance of cross urban-suburban busing anywhere in the country: Louisville children would go to schools out in the suburbs and suburban children would come into the city.

We had suspected something like this might be coming and had started to prepare. In early July, Kathy and I had attended the U.S. Conference of Mayors' meeting in Boston, a city which had had a disastrous busing situation in 1974. Violent protests had broken out and many students of both races simply didn't go to their assigned schools. We met with Boston Mayor Kevin White and his staff to learn of his experience handling the issue; I also consulted with Tom Winship, the editor of The Boston Globe, and his staff. We got three take-aways: First, train up the police—Boston hadn't readied its police force enough and it showed; second, encourage the judge to be as stern as possible because in Boston's case the judge had been too lenient, allowing small demonstrations which would then flare up into big problems; and finally, create a rumor-control center with the cooperation of the local media in Louisville—rumors had run rampant in Boston, feeding the fear and anger that was engulfing the city. That last effort would not be possible in today's media environment, but with the help and influence of Barry Bingham, Jr., who suggested it to all local print publications and broadcast media, we were able to create and implement a rumor-control center for the desegregation process.

When U.S. District Court Judge James Gordon, from Owensboro, Kentucky, issued his order we only had six weeks before the start of the new school year to merge two entirely different—and, frankly, plainly unequal—school systems. The racial and resource differences between the city and county schools were so stark that it wasn't possible to desegregate solely within the city or solely outside of the city: 90 percent of the Louisville students were Black while 90 percent of the suburban Jefferson County students were white. Gordon had ordered that all schools—city and County—have between 15 and 50 percent Black students. Dr. John Bell, on the Louisville School Board, and Newman Walker, the School Superintendent, emphasized the city school system's financial distress—thereby encouraging the liquidation of both the city system and the city school board—and both city and suburban schools were managed by the County.

The fact that Gordon ordered the merging and integration of the two school systems was critical politically. In 1974 Detroit had initially moved to merge its city schools with the surrounding county system, but later buckled to citizen disapproval. Detroit and its suburbs never have been able to desegregate. Gordon mandated that a total of 11,300 Black students and 11,300 white students would, in effect, switch places, transported on 250 buses to 165 different schools. The idea was that white students would bus for two years while black students could do so for up to ten years. Some black teachers were also bused.

Ninety percent of citizens were opposed.

When Gordon issued his order, Cy MacKinnon, a friend and an executive with The Courier-Journal, suggested that I seek the assistance of Frank Rose of the LQC Lamar Society, a pragmatic Southern political group. Rose had been president of the University of Alabama when Gov. George Wallace vowed to stop the integration of blacks into it. It had been a tense situation and Rose worked as an intermediary between Wallace and the Justice Department to resolve it.

Frank and I had long talks about the implementation of Gordon's order. One of the big problems was opposition in the African American community, where many resisted the idea of sending their children into a potentially traumatic situation. Frank suggested that he and I meet with Black ministers to enlist their support for the integration effort, which we did. If the African American community had resisted the order, we would certainly have had turmoil.

The first day of school, Thursday, September 4, was tense. There was confusion about school assignments for both teachers and pupils. There was confusion about which city and which county buses would be used (made worse by the fact that the city buses were publicly owned while Jefferson County's were private). I rode on one bus with the African American kids heading out to their new suburban schools.

Dozens of angry local parents awaited them and lit into me: "Where is our freedom?" they demanded. "My family and I moved from the [predominantly Black] West End to [predominantly white Southwest] Jefferson County so that our children would have a better education. We are mortgaged heavily, both of us working and now you are busing our kids back to the schools we took them out of. This isn't freedom—it's tyranny." This wasn't the time for a discourse on desegregation. I confined myself to observing that we had a federal court order and that we were going to peacefully enforce it.

Black Louisville families were not entirely pleased either: They didn't like having their children travel so far and were scared for their safety. African American ministers had to persuade parents to keep their children in school.

By Friday evening, the end of the second day of school, violence erupted around the county but not in the city itself. Thousands of students rioted at one suburban school, setting fire to buses, throwing rocks and wounding nearly 30 police officers. "We had bricks, rocks, bats, sticks, fists, spit and profanity hurled at us and our bus drivers as we transitioned from the school to the bus," one student told The Courier-Journal years later. "We were powerless. We struggled to understand the madness, but we knew that busing us across the county was [a] means to [an] end. We were on the heels of the civil rights movement."

The city police had been well-trained for crowd control and were in two buses waiting to be asked to come into the county to help the police there. But Hollenbach never asked for the help. We got word that the city police sitting in the buses had not eaten. Good Catholic that she was, Kathy said, "I will help," and called the nuns at St.

Vincent de Paul Convent. They came over and served meals to the dozens of police officers.

The night was punctuated with riots in the suburbs around Louisville, but there was peace in the city. That was going to end, though, as a protest rally was planned for Saturday in downtown Louisville. The Ku Klux Klan planned to be there. I decided to call Gov. Julian Carroll to ask him to mobilize the National Guard. Carroll was in the midst of his own reelection campaign so the last thing he wanted in a very conservative state was to be identified with the Louisville busing controversy.

We called and he hesitated.

"Governor, let me put Charlie Roberts, a prominent black Louisville leader and also the head of the Department of Sanitation, on the phone with you," I said. Carroll asked Charlie what would happen if he didn't send in the National Guard. Charlie responded: "Well, if the police are going to protect the whites on Saturday in Louisville and you don't call out the Guard to protect the Black people, the next night you're going to have a racial riot." So, the governor called up the National Guard, though we insisted that they not be armed with bullets. The Governor continued to be a positive force throughout this chaotic period.

The anti-busers were organizing with CB radios, so Don Cox, a brilliant city lawyer, insisted that I declare a state of emergency and ban both any assembly downtown, and also the use of CBs, which were being used to organize the demonstration. So, with a massive congregation of the National Guard and state and local police we were able to keep the demonstrators out of the downtown. These actions were questionable legally, but they had to be done. And I never got sued for them. Fortunately Judge Gordon was very strict about his federal court order. Unlike Judge Garrity in Boston, he disallowed even small demonstrations.

Another factor that made the situation more complicated was that many members of the Louisville police force lived in the suburbs. The head of the Fraternal Order of Police came knocking on our door at 2 o'clock in the morning on the first Monday after busing had started to tell me that his members were not going to ride the buses to provide security because they disagreed with the order. I had to wake the federal marshal in charge of implementing the desegregation order, and then relay his response: If the cops didn't get on the buses, they would no longer be cops. Some of the police officers had buttons that read "Stop the Busing!" I told our Police Chief, John "Jack" Nevin, to get the buttons off of their uniforms. That resolved the situation.

I felt it was important for me as mayor to be visible and present throughout this controversy, so I made a point of continuing my annual neighborhood walks. Many of those I met were hostile, particularly in white neighborhoods. Many white parents said they were not opposed to the desegregation order but how it was to be carried out—they were uneasy about their children's security going to school. The families of the black kids were even more afraid because of the violence which they had seen in Boston the year before during that city's busing crisis. Luckily, I had earned a great deal of credit in the black community for spending six years establishing the Park DuValle Community Health Center and getting it off the ground. And then for hiring a new police chief, Jack Nevin. Decades later some of those black students formed Pioneers of Desegregation and Forced Busing to commemorate the experience. I was touched by the invitation Kathy and I received to come down to one of their events, which we accepted. Their leader, Edith Nelson Yarbrough, honored us by saying, "Mayor Sloane did everything possible to give us security."

The situation drew national attention. President Gerald Ford canceled an October trip to the city, over my objections, out of concern for his safety. I had better luck the following month with a Democratic Issues Convention, arguing to party Chairman Bob Strauss that we couldn't run from the issue, literally or figuratively. As the Democratic leaders debated inside the Louisville Convention Center, protesters outside rocked cars. I stood behind the center with the Chief of Police, both of us holding a firehose which we would have to deploy if the situation worsened. Fortunately, it did not: The conference leadership, especially Stan Salette, defused things by inviting some of the protestors in to express their strong concerns.

Sen. George McGovern of South Dakota, who had been the Democratic presidential nominee three years earlier, was scheduled to give the closing address, and when I learned that it was going to be on busing, I asked him to switch topics. The community is barely holding together, I explained. Nevertheless, McGovern gave a stemwinder about the great civil rights issue of the 1970s: busing. "The issue is all of us Americans, and the evil we have done to each other, and how it must be undone," he told the crowd. (I saw him a year later at another party event and he apologized: "I know I didn't do you any favors, Mr. Mayor," he said, "but that was the only speech I had!")

These were tough times for our family. I received a lot of blow back about busing on my neighborhood walks and received threatening phone calls. In 1976, after we had moved to 4th Street, our car on the street was set on fire once and windows were broken multiple times—we did not know if this was by people unhappy about busing or if they were attempts to intimidate me during our administration's contract negotiations with the Fraternal Order of Police. A bullet was also shot through our front window around this time. Then in 1977, while appearing on Meet the Press, I was asked how busing was going in Louisville, and I responded that it had been implemented successfully. Shortly thereafter, the FBI notified me that a contract had been taken out on my life for $35,000. My first reaction was, "is that all I am worth?" For weeks after that, police officers were stationed at our home, and I had to wear a bullet-proof vest at all times—even when jogging.

It was touch-and-go for several months, and the scars from the conflict took years to fully heal. But busing worked: Private financial support was provided for computers and other student needs. Leadership from the schools and Jefferson County Board of Education as well as parent organizations worked together to improve the schools, and over all we managed the tensions in Louisville well. Our city became a model of how to handle the busing issue. Years later, on March of 2015, "The Atlantic Monthly" published an article entitled: "The City That Believed in Desegregation: Integration isn't easy but Louisville, Kentucky, has decided that it's worth it." Louisville still buses, the article noted. "Indeed, it could be argued that Louisville, an economically vibrant city in a highly conservative and segregated state, is a success today in large part because of its integrated schools and the collaborations among racial and economic groups that have come as a result," it reported. The following year The Century Foundation issued a report on integration in Louisville, noting that more than 40 years after instituting busing, the city was "unique, in that it is one of the only districts that has maintained a staunch commitment to integration."

*   *   *

The U.S. Supreme Court ruled in 2007 that it was unconstitutional to use race to determine student school assignments, effectively making busing illegal. "The way to stop discrimination on the basis of race is stop discriminating on the basis of race," Chief Justice John Roberts wrote at the time. It was almost as if all the work Louisville had done to integrate was suddenly meaningless. I said publicly: "I couldn't believe you can't bus students for racial purposes. What was this all about in 1975? Now how will the Supreme Court Brown v. Board of Education decision in 1954 be implemented?"

But an amazing thing happened, which was a credit to the city and county (which had officially merged the school systems by then): They decided to keep busing—but to bus on the basis of economic background instead of race. Assigning students based only on race had concentrated more lower-income students together anyway. To this day Louisville still buses.

Despite this seeming success, I was distressed to read a 2021 series in The Courier-Journal about how the unintended consequences of busing had hurt the areas it was meant to help, including the West End, where many schools have closed and those which remain are designated as in decline. This was in part a result of the 2007 decision to bus students based on income rather than race, which meant that while a large number of African American kids from the city were being bussed to schools in the suburbs, not many white kids were being bussed into the city schools. Louisville's West End schools were essentially drained. It was heart-breaking to read this—but I still feel the effort was worth it. I take pride in the fact that so much of Louisville remains committed to dispelling inequalities in education. The whole experience is a reminder that any attempt to fix such sensitive problems requires ongoing attention and resources.

Sadly, race remains a divisive issue across the country and was only exacerbated by Donald Trump's four years in the White House. The deaths of Breonna Taylor and George Floyd, among many others, at the hands of police, are just the latest reminder of the kind of injustices still visited upon a portion of our citizenry because of the color of their skin.

In 2020, Louisville had an intense moment of racial conflict when police broke into Breonna Taylor's apartment, a botched raid which tragically ended with her shooting death. The incident caused massive protests in Louisville and around the country for months. Louisville, like many communities throughout the country, needs to work on police reform to ensure that such tragedies do not keep occurring. This incident, as well as the murder of George Floyd in Minneapolis, forced the country to consider with renewed urgency its legacy of racial injustice and institutional racism. It also led the governments of Louisville, and then Kentucky, to institute police reforms. Perhaps it will lead to a major revitalization of the West End of Louisville, as Mayor Greg Fisher proposed in 2021.

*　　*　　*

Despite their overall terrific performance during the busing crisis in 1975, during my first term as Mayor the Louisville police proved to be an ongoing thorn in my side. Their contract expired at the end of June 1976 triggering a protracted and unpleasant negotiating process over a new one. The city had collective-bargaining agreements with six other unions, and those negotiations were all conducted professionally and smoothly. The city administrator, Joe Elam, knew the budget and conducted the negotiations at a time when the city was facing budget problems. He was a real pro and had the respect of the union leaders. He was responsible for maintaining the city's programs and performance during a time when we were suffering a recession.

But dealing with the FOP was a different experience. The leadership wanted to bargain not just on pay but also on departmental policies and procedures. Worse, they didn't know their stuff when it came to the budget, and they tried to set up special privileges for their membership. They were consistently obnoxious and uncooperative and deeply resistant to even the most reasonable reforms. Allen Bryan, who by then was my Safety Director and thus the civilian boss of the police force, was a focal point for the FOP's rage. He came from a media background rather than from law enforcement and had helped me in the election and in early days of my administration, including with the successful referendum on the bus service. He was very strict about not permitting special privileges for the FOP. He was strongly supported by Joe Elam, who had labor's respect and knew the budget inside-out.

In retrospect, I probably should have gotten more deeply involved in the negotiations early on, but I didn't want to set a precedent since our negotiating team was very effective. I wanted to let them do their jobs and only come into it when they needed me.

The police eventually turned on me—literally. When we broke ground on the new Hyatt Regency hotel in August of that year, A.N. Pritzker, who was vice president of the Hyatt board, came to Louisville for the ceremony. When it was my turn to speak, all the police who were guarding the outdoor event turned their backs on me. After I had finished and sat down again, Pritzker leaned over to me and said, "Well Mayor, you must be doing something right in this town!"

The confounding thing was that the police had done such a terrific, professional job for the city during the busing crisis.

These tensions went on for months and, unfortunately, they would have an effect on the next mayor's race in 1977. I supported Creighton Mershon in that race, who had been an effective president of the Board of Aldermen and had run on my Democrats for Progress slate, having come in with me in 1973. He caught the brunt of the police hostility and William Stansbury, another Alderman who constantly courted the police, won the election.

Throughout my first term we periodically got complaints about racist behavior on the part of the police. John Nevin, my police chief, had earned the respect of the community. Through him we were able to resolve many of these complaints internally and not on the street. Nevin was very good about following up on every complaint and doing what he could to fix any problems.

I tried hard to maintain good relations with the Black community, including by bringing more African Americans into the police force. I think that my periodic neighborhood walks also helped a lot: Residents of all races knew that I was interested in and responsive to their needs. "That is why I believe you did not have the kinds of problems [Louisville has been] experiencing," Ernie Allen, who would be my Public Safety Director in my second term as Mayor, recently told me. "You built trust. People knew you cared about them and their problems. They knew you would respond. They believed you had their best interests at heart. When public officials lose that trust, you can't repair it."

* * *

Throughout these years we were pushing ahead on my neighborhood development agenda. One small example was the first Portland Festival, in June 1975, which was designed to show off the French, Irish and German heritage in the city's Portland neighborhood. Louisville's neighborhoods often hold summer festivals to celebrate their past as well as their hopes for the future. Portland is a neighborhood in west Louisville which was once a riverfront town in its own right. The festival had everything from hot air balloons to historic house tours, bands—and lots of food. The event was run by Sharon Wilbert, a Portland native whom I had gotten to know during the 1973 campaign. I had appointed her to the Louisville-Jefferson County Planning and Zoning Commission in October 1974. A single mother who raised two daughters, Sharon was fearless and unflappable.

The festival drew an estimated 100,000 attendees, and it might have proven disastrous but for Sharon's leadership and quick thinking. As the crowd was starting to gather mid-morning on the day of the event, the ground started to shake and a bone-shaking roar arose—the Outlaws, a notorious Louisville motorcycle gang, was arriving at the festival in force. The gang had set up a headquarters in the neighborhood and everyone lived in fear of them. The approaching rumble of the bikes immediately triggered a sense of fear and dread in the assembling crowd.

Sharon decided that there was only one thing she could do: She ran straight down Northwestern Parkway, toward the oncoming biker horde. Their leader, Sharon recalls, "looked like a hairy bear in dirty jeans." Her mad dash left them with two choices: run her over or stop. They stopped.

"Welcome!" she shouted. "We're so glad you came! We want you to come and have fun, but I am very sorry you cannot ride your cycles into the festival. We have arranged for your bikes to be parked just the other side. Is that OK?" The hairy bear laughed, and the gang parked where they were told to. He and Sharon shook hands and then she co-opted them: We couldn't afford security today, she said, would you please help us keep the peace and make sure everyone has fun? The bear agreed. There wasn't a single fight. And nearly a half-century later, the festival still occurs every year.

Sharon would go on to be elected to the Board of Aldermen in 1977, and we stayed close. When I served a second term as Mayor, I appointed her to be director of Housing and Community development. And then when I later served as County Judge/Executive, she enlarged her development responsibilities to include the whole county. In my 12 years of service to the city and county I was truly blessed to have a number of dedicated city employees like Ernie Allen and Sharon who helped secure so many achievements for the people of Louisville, across so many fronts.

In 1976 Maury D. S. Johnson, the chairman of Louisville's Citizens Fidelity Bank, approached me about getting a developer for the Galleria, a commercial office/retail development on 4th Street. Maury was one of the most dedicated and public-spirited businessmen I ever met. We went to Minneapolis, and then to Calgary and Edmonton, Alberta in Canada to see their downtown developments. The downtown leadership, headed by Maury and President of the First National Bank A. Stevens Miles, chose the Edmonton-based Oxford Properties, led by Don Love, as the developer for Galleria. At the same time, plans for the state of Kentucky to work with Louisville to develop a center for performing arts in the city were percolating. The historic Seelbach Hotel, which bordered the downtown area, needed new development, and the actor-entrepreneur Roger Davis, with the help of the city, took the lead in that restoration.

The Galleria and surrounding office buildings were successfully built, but unfortunately, like most small malls these days, it could not retain retail stores. These days the Galleria has been redeveloped as Fourth Street Live, a tourist destination filled with restaurants and bars.

*   *   *

Although I had won the election for Mayor handily and remained popular, throughout my first term I still faced hidebound resistance from the Louisville political machine. The Board of Aldermen in particular fought me on practically everything. As The Courier-Journal editorialized in the spring of 1975: "With a few notable exceptions, the incumbent aldermen have, in fact, been plainly obstructionist."

I was somewhat at a loss about how best to deal with this recalcitrance. I considered supporting individual primary challenges to uncooperative Democrats or even putting forward a whole slate. We especially wanted to replace Joe Kotheimer, the finance chairman of the Aldermen, who had held up my budget. Peter Hart was doing some polling and so inserted the name of Mark Shields (a then little-known journalist who would go on to great prominence politically and also become a close friend), someone with no name recognition at all in the city. When the results came back, voters supported Shields by a wide margin. That told us that Kotheimer was eminently beatable. We eventually enlisted a local Episcopal minister and teacher named F. David Banks, who beat Kotheimer in the primary.

I decided to support a complete slate in that spring's primaries, calling them Democrats for Progress. They included Banks, Creighton Mershon, Mary Margaret Mulvihill, Danny Meyer, E. Porter Hatcher, Rev. W.J. Hodge and Jerry Abramson. Although all of the establishment candidates were favored in the polls, our slate won a sweeping victory, knocking out four Democratic incumbents in the primary. One of our winners, Abramson would go on to become the longest-serving mayor of Louisville.

Thus, even with the recession, we were able to keep our program intact.

* * *

In 1976 a crisis arose that called for an overlap of my political and medical experience. The country appeared to be facing a swine flu outbreak. Soldiers at Fort Dix in New Jersey got the flu and spread it to some other soldiers and there was great concern that this would evolve into an epidemic similar to the Influenza pandemic of 1918. President Ford convened a meeting at the White House with representatives from the governors, the mayors and officials in the U.S. government as well as distinguished scientists. I was chairman of the U.S. Conference of Mayors' Committee on Health, so I was included.

At the meeting I sat between Albert Bruce Sabin and Jonas Salk, the developers of the polio vaccine. After a lot of discussion, President Ford asked, "Is there any reason that we shouldn't start a country-wide vaccination program against the swine flu?" There were no dissenters.

I went back to Louisville and started a vaccination program and personally vaccinated Louisville citizens. Then after a month or so, side effects started appearing from the vaccine—Guillain-Barré neurological disease in children, for example. During this period the swine flu did not spread beyond Fort Dix, so President Ford, with some embarrassment, called off the countrywide vaccination initiative. He was unfairly blamed for starting it—the scientists should have given him better advice in the first place—but at least his instinct was to act. Unlike Trump and COVID.

*   *   *

Great Mayors of Louisvillle

Louisville, Kentucky in the late 19th, 20th and 21st centuries has generally had very good government with minor corruption. There have been at least four outstanding mayors in my estimation and I have known three of them.

The first mayor that really broke the mold and gave Louisville lasting benefits was Charles Donnell Jacob. He lived from 1838 to 1898 and he had four terms. The two overwhelming contributions were: number one he open the southern Exposition in 1889 and secondly and more importantly he established the first Frederick Law Olmsted landscape park.

Mayor Jacob brought the great landscape architect Frederick law Olmsted to Louisville to design the Iroquois Park. This led to the parks around the city that connected the outskirts of the city including Iroquois, Cherokee, and Shawnee Parks; they were spokes that serve the south, east and west of the city. The citizens of Louisville insisted that the parks be well preserved and maintained for posterity. I saw this after the 1974 tornado that really broke up Cherokee Park in the East. In spite of the fact that many homes and neighborhoods were destroyed the one unifying demand was to reestablish Cherokee Park as it was before the hurricane which tore down 10,000 trees a minute. For the rehabilitation at the park I was strongly encouraged to go back to the original Olmsted design which was at their office in Brookline Massachusetts. We retained that firm and got a Michigan company to carefully remove the wounded and dead trees and to make certain that the park was reestablished as before. Private groups such as Trees, Inc. donated thousands of trees to help Cherokee return to its natural state.

Wilson Wyatt who was the mayor from 1941 to 1945 came in just before Pearl Harbor and established the civil defense system and the planning and zoning for the city. He served in the Truman administration as headed up the Office of War Mobilization. He has been council to the Courier Journal and other media properties of the Binghams. In 1956 Wilson ran for the US Senate against in Republican Thruston Morton but was barely defeated. He served as Lieutenant Governor with Governor Bert Combs in 1959-63. Wilson was a sage for many young politicians as myself and he was always someone to get advice from.

Charles Roland Farnsley—Charlie Farnsley was a colorful character and extremely popular. He instituted the occupational tax which was a very imaginative approach to taxation particularly from the standpoint of bringing the city and the county together. If an employee worked in the county but lived in the city, the occupational tax would be paid to the county and likewise if he/she lived in the county and worked in the city that money will go to city. This really helped with economic development of the whole community. Charlie also did imaginative things with little money like having streets "half soled." He was very popular with the people and always answered complaints. In 1964 he was elected to Congress. This was the first Congress after Lyndon Johnson became president. This Congress passed landmark Civil and Voting Rights legislation as well as Medicaid and Medicare. The Poverty Program was also enacted which provided funds for the community health center I started in Park DuValle in 1968. It was a wonderful time for those of us dedicated to social progress. Mayor Farnsley was part of my Brain

Trust a la FDR in my first administration and gave me great advice on the controversial issues I faced in my first term.

Jerry Edwin Abramson served as Mayor 21 years and was the first Metro Mayor. He was a popular leader who helped consolidate the city and county government through Kentucky state legislation as Indianapolis and Lexington had. Jerry was a builder and expanded the Louisville International Airport and the Waterfront Park that we both started when I was Mayor and County Judge Executive. Jerry was a pleasure to work with in our joint terms of Mayor and County Judge Executive.

Jerry was the Chairman of the US Conference of Mayors and Co-chair of Mayors Against Illegal Guns after Louisville's first mass shooting in 1989. He served as Lt. Governor with Steve Beshear, and he went on to work in the Obama White House. Jerry was a member of Democrats For Progress for the Board of Alderman that I supported as Mayor in 1975.

My parents, George "Tod" and Kay Sloane

My father, George "Tod," holding me

Mother and me at our home on Whitehaven Street, NW in Washington, DC – which was purchased by Hillary and Bill Clinton in 2000.

Patrick, Abigail, Curtis, Kathy, Bathsheba, and Harvey shoving off to paddle down the river.

Sailing Fat City on the Caribbean with Paul Semonin

Harvey at the tiller

Harvey and Norrie return from Mexico

Helga Sandberg and Dr. George "Barney" Carile Jr.

BARRY BINGHAM SR.   MARY BINGHAM

Mr. and Mrs. Barry Bingham

Abigail (age 2) takes mic to annouce 1973 Primary election.
Harvey's wife Kathy was absent due to fear of a loss. Kathy's mother, Nancy, was in attendance
(far left).

From left: Kathy, Ned Chilton, Harvey,
Jay and Sharon Rockefeller, and Betty Chilton at the Derby

Pegasus Parade at the Kentucky Derby (1982)

The First Kentucky Derby Mini Marathon (1974)

Start of the Neighborhood Walk

The Neighborhood Walk in Portland (1974)

Charlie Roberts, Sanitation Director, points out trash to be picked up.

A vigorous neighborly discussion

The necessary visit to the pool hall

The anti-busing rally (1975)

Democratic Presidential nominee Jimmy Carter meets Patrick (1976)

Harvey was the first mayor to endorse Jimmy Carter

Harvey and Governor Burt Combs

Abigail and Harvey

Curtis, Harvey, and Patrick

Curtis, Patrick, and Harvey at the Grand Canyon

A good laugh

Ali regains the heavyweight championship with win over
Foreman in Zaire (Rumble in the Jungle, 1974).
It was after this fight that Ali said: "Louisville is the greatest."

A wonderful moment

Abigail and Harvey with The Greatest

Ali trys out the Mayor's chair

Lonnie and Ali's wedding at Harvey and Kathy's home which was officiated by Harvey (1986)

Re-election in 1981

Mayor Jerry Abramson and County Judge Executive Harvey Sloane form a partnership (1985)

Louisville Congressman Romano "Ron" Mazzoli – a helper in Congress

Committee of 100 for National Health Insurance – Senator Ted Kennedy and Harvey

The Clintons and the Sloanes

Conservationist, Larry Rockefeller, and his wife Wendy, who have helped preserve and restore the Beaverkill Valley in the Catskills

With Russian TB doctors at the Nizhny Tagil Prison Hospital

The next generation – Winslow, Fox, Sloane, and Charlie

Harvey, Kathy, and grandsons Fox and Winslow Sloane at
50th anniversary of Louisville St. Patrick's Day parade.

CHAPTER ELEVEN

One Thousand Miles For Governor

Until the state legislature changed the law in 2005, you could not serve consecutive terms as Mayor of Louisville. Unable to succeed myself, I left office in December 1977. Kathy and I went down to the Bahamian island of Exuma to visit Al and Mary Shands, who had become close Louisville friends of ours. Al was an Episcopal minister. Mary was the daugther of Jane Norton, the owner of the WAVE television station in Louisville; and her uncle was former U.S. Senator Thruston Morton. We enjoyed the beautiful water and relaxed. I had already set my sights on the 1979 Kentucky governor's race, which promised to be an uphill battle: Even though I was quite popular and had had a great term as Mayor, the state had a bias against the city—most Kentuckians were rural-dwellers and viewed it with suspicion—and had never elected a Louisville Mayor to be Governor.

I had gotten good marks for the term, even though we were disorganized when we started. We had to face a number of issues, starting with the tornado, the sanitation strike, the transit referendum and Muhammad Ali's visit, and of course busing. I was convinced that walking around Kentucky as I had Louisville would be a great way to introduce myself to the rest of the state. Once again I hired Doug

Bailey, not simply because of my past experience with him, but because he had just finished working on Lamar Alexander's successful 1978 bid to be Governor of Tennessee—a campaign which had started with a 1,000-mile walk across that state to introduce Alexander to voters. Of course, our pollster and strategist was once again Peter Hart. Peter had done the primary and general election polling for my mayor's race and then for the 1974 referendum on raising the occupational tax to help fund the bus service.

My trek across Kentucky was a marvelous experience. Cass Harris, who had masterminded each of my annual mayor's walks, carefully planned and executed this 1,031-mile hike. We had fun with it: Bailey penned a song, "Walking and Talking with Harvey Sloane." But it also served an important political and personal purpose: I stayed with a different family every night. I listened to their hopes and dreams and made many friends along the way. It was an unforgettable experience. Kathy would join me about three days a week and then go back to Louisville to be with the kids. Sometimes, if I was going to be passing through a town with a festival, she would bring the children out to join us.

The plan was for me to walk from the western Tennessee border to the Illinois border, to the West Virginia border to the Ohio border, and back home (the Indiana border). River-wise, I would start near the Mississippi and hike up to the Ohio River, all the way across to the Big Sandy River, and back up to the Ohio River (twice). The logistics would be much easier today, with GPS and computerized maps and social media to spread the word. Instead we had to rely on a 1977 Kentucky Department of Transportation Highway and Parkway Map, a basic list of contacts and a ton of planning.

It didn't begin auspiciously: Kathy and I started the walk from the International Banana Festival in Fulton, Kentucky, in August. Fulton is on Kentucky's far western tip, on the Mississippi River. Now, Kentucky produces a wide variety of crops, but bananas are obviously not among them. In the late 1880s, however, bananas were shipped up from South America to New Orleans and then loaded onto refrigerated rail cars. By the time the cargo reached Fulton, the fruit needed to be re-iced, and Fulton happened to have the only icehouse between New Orleans and Chicago. The small town came to be referred to as the Banana Capital of the World, as over 70% percent of the bananas consumed in the U.S. passed through Fulton.

To celebrate this unique historical feature, Fulton and its twin city of South Fulton, Tennessee, stage an annual festival. The highlight is always the Banana Parade, which features a one-ton banana pudding. I made the mistake of devouring a large plate of it before starting out on what proved to be pavement that was 98 degrees hot. We covered just over 12 miles on what would be the first of many hot, sweaty days.

Over three months I worked my way through Central Kentucky then on to Eastern Kentucky in the Appalachian Mountains. I would traverse the state, south to north, west to east, on country roads, on downtown streets and on busy highways, through small villages and large cities. From the Jackson Purchase in the west up through coal fields to Henderson and Owensboro, back down to Bowling Green. Through central Kentucky and east into the mountains and coal mine country. North to Newport and Covington, then back to Lexington and the Bluegrass, before returning to Louisville. We mapped out supporters' homes in towns across the state.

I had a red shirt with a sign on the back which said, "Sloane for Governor," and people would honk. Sometimes when there were long stretches between towns, I would jog. My friends John and Nancy Bell's son, Victor Bell, who went on to become a family physician and now practices in Virginia, was our driver, trailing me most of the way. David Rose, another energetic young Kentuckian, shared driving and advance duties.

The advance team would make preparations in whichever town was next. Townspeople were alerted before I came in, and volunteers would go around and distribute campaign literature and paraphernalia. I made a point of talking with everybody I could. Kentucky is hot during August and September! And at the end of the day, I would use chalk to mark the spot where I had finished walking so I would know where to start the following day. Reporters would sometimes check to make sure I wasn't trying to trim a few steps off of my journey. Then when I came to where I was going to stay for the night, I would drink multiple cans of cold Sprite.

One day, in Lyon County in Western Kentucky, I had my second escaped prisoner experience. A state trooper stopped and told me to get off the road because a convict had escaped from the nearby Eddyville penitentiary. I did get in the car for a few minutes, but I made sure to go back later and cover that short distance.

I walked, talked and listened, visiting country stores, government buildings, college campuses, plants and every public health clinic or facility we could fit in. There were appearances on local radio and television shows and speeches to community groups. I rode in Battlefield Commemoration and Tobacco Festival parades. We took every opportunity to meet Kentuckians and hear their concerns, and to explain my positions and proposals.

I encountered hostility only once. I was jogging down a road coming out of Madisonville in Western Kentucky, moving against traffic as was my practice. A car came toward me at a good speed and a guy opened the window and threw something at me, hitting me in the chest. It was a full can of beer. I flagged down Victor in the campaign car and told him to let me take over. I turned the car around and we went after the car, finally getting them to pull over. I got out and said, "You know, you could've killed me by hitting my head while going that fast." They apologized. It turned out that the car was filled with Army soldiers coming back from leave. They didn't have a problem with me as such but were just swept up in ignorant exuberance.

In Eastern Kentucky, going past a house that was off the highway, I saw an older man rocking in a chair. I went up to him and said, "I'm Harvey Sloane. I'm running for Governor and would appreciate your vote." He looked up and said, "Well, I'm for Jesus." I thought a moment and said, "I'm for Jesus too, but He's not running in this election. I need your support." I don't know if I ever got his support, but we parted company on a friendly basis.

On another occasion, I met an older woman, again on her porch, and asked for her support. She asked, "Have you been born again?" I paused for a moment and said, "I am working on it."

Eastern Kentucky is mountainous and in the 1970s the roads were not good. The main roads were relatively narrow, and when the big coal trucks rumbled by they took up half of the road—going fast. You had to look out for them: Sometimes they would whip around the curves and a few errant pieces of coal would fly off of the back. I was lucky I was never hit by one. But the people in Eastern Kentucky were friendly. In Knott County, for example, there were a lot of Slones. Gene Autry Slone assured me that way back we were connected genetically, and he adopted me as one of his blood family.

From Eastern Kentucky, I went north along the Ohio River and visited some of the farms in the communities going up to Covington and Newport, and then came down to Lexington with its beautiful Bluegrass.

*   *   *

I took one break from the road, in September. Carson Porter, a Louisville attorney who was my finance chairman, suggested that Muhammad Ali's endorsement would be important both for raising money and in the Democratic primary. Ali was getting ready to face Leon Spinks for what would turn out to be his third undisputed world heavyweight championship. Spinks had beaten Ali in a dramatic upset seven months earlier, and the two were set for a rematch in the Superdome in New Orleans. Porter and I went down to see the boxer and were joined by a key figure, a former Louisville cop named Joe Martin. Martin had been running a Louisville recreation center in his spare time when, in 1954, a skinny 12-year-old came into the gym looking for help. Someone had stolen his new red Schwinn bicycle (which his father had given him for Christmas) and he had heard that as a cop Martin could help him file a report. The young man was threatening to beat up whoever had taken the bike. "You better learn to fight before you start fightin'," Martin told the young man, whose name was Cassius Clay. Martin ended up training the boy who would later become Muhammad Ali, the greatest boxer of all time, and Ali revered him.

Carson and Joe Martin and I flew down to New Orleans in the middle of my walk around Kentucky because we had heard one had to meet with Ali in person to get a commitment. It was September 15th, the day Ali was going to face Spinks. Joe helped me get into the locker room before the fight. He said I was going to be governor, and so Ali would want to see me. Ali was sitting down on a stool and I said, "I've got to have your help in this race for governor. Will you give it to me?" Ali looked at me and said yes. Then he went out and beat Spinks in 15 rounds, reclaiming the heavyweight championship.

On a cold Sunday night nearly three months later, December 10th, my long walk finally led me back to Louisville, and Ali joined me for the last mile. We walked and jogged together along Hurstbourne Lane, past fast-food restaurants and gas stations all the way to the Bluegrass Convention Center where 1,000 of my supporters awaited at a rally. News cameras were just ahead of us as we jogged, and the champ voiced his support the way only he could: "If you don't vote for this man, I will…" he said, finishing his thought with a pretend punch into the lens. Although "the Greatest" may have had some detractors because he avoided military service and was a Muslim, it was, it was both a great honor and a comfort to have his support.

Ali spoke at the rally that night, as did Prich and Col. Harland Sanders, the founder of Kentucky Fried Chicken, who was, as always, dressed all in white. I had the backing of "the greatest fighter of all time and the greatest businessman of all time," Ali told the crowd.

Colonel Sanders was another wonderful campaign companion. Although he was born in Indiana, Harland Sanders was a real Kentuckian. His father had died when he was six, and because his mother worked, Harland quickly became responsible for feeding his brother and sister—which led to his love of cooking. Years later he was running a service station in Corbin, Kentucky while also serving food there, most notably his fried chicken. He had devised a special kind of pressure cooker for the chicken, and the results were so good that he moved his business to a restaurant across the street. In 1935 Gov. Ruby Laffoon named the self-taught chef a "Kentucky Colonel"—the highest title the governor can bestow. When his restaurant closed in 1956, Sanders started franchising his fried chicken, traveling from eating establishment to eating establishment, getting five cents for each chicken they purveyed. He eventually sold his interest in the business to a businessman named John Y. Brown (who, it happened, I would face in that 1979 primary for governor) and became a salaried brand-ambassador for Kentucky Fried Chicken. But he became highly critical of many of the franchisees for the quality of their food: He felt that Brown hadn't respected his recipe and was making a lot of money off of franchises with substandard food. It was rumored that he didn't want his name associated with it.

I enjoyed getting to know Colonel Sanders during that Governor's race. He was particularly interested in education for children, having received little himself. He claimed algebra had chased him off. We would drive around to different counties, and he would always be warmly received. His support was important, and I was honored by it. My campaign appearances with Muhammad Ali and Colonel Sanders, two of the most recognized figures in the

Western world, one white and dressed up as a Kentucky Colonel and the other a Black Muslim, showed that our campaign had broad representation.

The "official" walk route map, recorded on a 1977 Kentucky Department of Transportation Highway and Parkway Map, is yellowed and worn through on the creases, and the route line has faded. The accompanying daily route and schedule pages in the official red Walk Binder, with their hand drawn maps and last-minute notations, are browning and brittle. I wish I had the space to name all of the hundreds of volunteers and dedicated supporters who made this walk possible. All of their names—among them David & Jeannie Yewell of Owensboro, Gene Tichenor of McLean County, Rapier and Violet Smith of Bardstown, Bess Douhitt of Louisville, Gene Autry Slone of Hindman, Tom Rouse and his parents Clyde and Margery Rouse, Steve Miller of Owenton, Jerry Anglin of Franklin County— are recorded on those daily walk pages. So many wonderful folks walked with us and pounded on doors, roped in all their friends, hosted campaign rallies, and put us up; some of them are no longer with us, and all have grown older. But every one of them played a role in making this a unique experience and an enduring memory; they all have my endless gratitude for helping me through those 1,031 miles.

*   *   *

My next big campaign trip was only around 700 miles, taking me to New York City in February (not walking, happily). Kathy worked with Arthur and Alexandra Schlesinger to plan an event to raise money and publicity for our Kentucky race at their Manhattan home. Ali and Colonel Sanders and Prich—also an old friend of Arthur's—all attended.

I first got to know Arthur in 1974, when I joined The Century Foundation (then called the 20th Century Fund), a nonpartisan, progressive think tank. It had been founded in 1919 as the Co-operative League by Edward Filene, who also co-founded the department store chain of the same name with his father and brother. Filene was an ardent New Dealer who corresponded extensively with FDR and helped pioneer credit unions (and also helped create the U.S. Chamber of Commerce). Asked about the onset of federal income taxes, Filene responded: "Why shouldn't the American people take half my money from me? I took *all* of it from them!"

The Century Foundation has been a leading voice for school integration, which research has found is one of the best ways to promote social mobility and social cohesion. Although it is politically difficult to integrate schools, as I had discovered in Louisville, Century Foundation researchers, led by the invaluable Richard Kahlenberg, demonstrated that there are politically viable ways to achieve integration by providing incentives in the form of attractive magnet programs. When the Supreme Court struck down Louisville's efforts to integrate by race in a wrong-headed 2007 decision, the Foundation showed how using socioeconomic factors could produce racial and economic diversity in a way that is legally bulletproof. Between 1996 and 2020, the number of school districts or charter schools using socioeconomic factors to integrate student bodies increased from 2 to 171. And the results for students have been very encouraging: higher test scores, higher graduation rates and reduced bias. Recently, the Foundation launched the Bridges Collaborative to bring 57 school districts, charter schools and housing organizations together to learn from one another about the best ways to produce integrated schools. I've been proud to have been associated with its efforts to make the promise of Brown v. Board of Education a reality for more students.

Filene wanted scholars to promote progressive policies and many of the original New Dealers sat on the League's board. When I joined the group in 1974 my fellow members included former LBJ aide Joe Califano, David Lilienthal (the architect of the Tennessee Valley Authority), Jim Rowe from Roosevelt's White House, Ben Cohen, who was in FDR's brain trust, and of course Arthur, who had written extensively about FDR. Ted Sorensen, JFK's top domestic policy aide and speechwriter, joined later with his wife Gillian and they both became great friends with Kathy and me. One of my closest friendships in the group was with Peter Berle, whose father, Adolf Berle, was a New Dealer who had been chairman of the 20th Century Fund. Peter had a distinguished career in conservation, including as Commissioner of the Department of Environmental Conservation under New York Governor Hugh Carey. Another friend I made through the Fund was Richard Ravitch, who became the Lieutenant Governor of New York after Governor Spitzer resigned.

My relationship with Arthur and his family was an example of what Arthur liked to call the "circularity of life": Kathy had dated Arthur's son Stephen, and I had dated Arthur's daughter Kathy, who had worked in the hills of Eastern Kentucky as a VISTA volunteer. His youngest son, Robert, assisted me with this memoir. On that long ago night of my fundraiser chez Schlesinger in 1979, a seven-year-old

Robert delighted in shadowboxing with Ali, who was the first person to arrive at the event.

When Kathy and I got to the Schlesingers' East 64th Street brownstone, the line to get in stretched down the block. Kathy had contacted Bobby Zarem, a Yale classmate of mine who was the prominent New York City publicist who designed and implemented the "Big Apple" campaign which refurbished New York's tarnished image in the early '70s. Bobby enlisted The New York Post's Page Six column, the epicenter of city gossip, to run an item about the event and it was suddenly a hot ticket. Ethel Kennedy had to wait an hour just to get in.

It was an unforgettable evening. At one point, Eunice Kennedy Shriver was sitting on Muhammed Ali's lap, and vowing to remain there until he agreed to be a major supporter of her Special Olympics program, now a huge success and well-known worldwide. As always, Ali was in terrific form. When Sanders jokingly wondered to the crowd why I had "called on you New Yorkers," Ali interjected with a stage whisper: "Money, money, money." It was a $50-per-person fundraiser and the champ chided the crowd for contributing so little when he had given me $1,000. "All these rich, white folks here and nobody is going to match me?" he quipped. "I'll be standing by the door."

The event didn't make very much money in the end, but it did put our campaign on the liberal map. Unfortunately, I'm not sure how many voters were persuaded in Kentucky.

*   *   *

One prominent Democrat whose support I did not have during my gubernatorial campaign was President Jimmy Carter. He had come to the 1975 Democratic issues conference in Louisville (where George McGovern had delivered his busing stemwinder) and really stood out among the 1976 hopefuls. I had been the first mayor in the country to endorse him for president. Kathy and I held a fundraiser for him and Rossalyn and we hosted them both at the Kentucky Derby that year. During the presidential primary I went down to Atlanta and attended a workshop to help develop policy for Carter, and also worked with Dr. Peter Bourne to develop the candidate's national health insurance plan. One of his administration's great tragedies was that he never introduced that national health insurance bill. I think that was the main reason that Ted Kennedy got into the 1980 primary against him, which did so much to damage Carter for the general election against Ronald Reagan.

When I was running for governor in 1979, Carter threw his support behind Terry McBrayer, a former state legislator, incumbent Gov. Julian Carroll's preferred candidate. (Carroll had also supported Carter three years earlier.) Nevertheless, Carter called me, once more seeking my help in his own primary the following year, against Kennedy. Many people close to the Kennedys had supported me financially and publicly, so I sided with the Massachusetts Senator. When I politely explained that I was disinclined to help him out this time, he asked what about Kathy? I responded that he would have to talk to her. So, the next day Rosalynn Carter phoned my wife; their talk turned to the ongoing hostage crisis in Iran. "Why don't you have Muhammad Ali go over there?" Kathy said. "He's the most recognized, respected Muslim in the world." Two nights later we saw on the news that Ali was in Iran trying to help find a diplomatic solution to the crisis. I turned to Kathy: "If we're making foreign policy in this house in Louisville, this administration is in big trouble!"

President Carter is a totally decent man who has promoted human rights throughout the planet and has unquestionably been our most extraordinary former president. His efforts at the Carter Center, with Habitat for Humanity and working in Africa to abolish the disabling Guinea worm (a tropical parasitic infection)—as well as many other activities in the field of human rights—certainly give him a position of excellence as an American public figure.

*   *   *

Kentucky's Democratic gubernatorial primary in 1979 ended up having five candidates. I came in a close second behind the wealthy investor (and son of a former congressman) John Y. Brown, who I mentioned earlier bought Kentucky Fried Chicken from Colonel Sanders and transformed it from a chain of restaurants into a global fast-food megabrand. Brown's promise to run Kentucky more like a business apparently appealed to Kentuckians amid the financial uncertainty of the late 1970s. He jumped into the race impulsively, interrupting his honeymoon (with new wife Phyllis George, an ABC Sports announcer and former Miss America) to announce his candidacy in March for a late-May primary. Brown beat me by 4 percentage points. Nonetheless, it was a great race, and really the most fun of any campaign I ever had. I loved the long walks, and the opportunity to meet new people and to see the state. Brown would go on to win the governorship, serving a single term.

After the primary, I went to the small town of Hazard in Eastern Kentucky for an event to thank my supporters. As I went through the diner where it was being held, I overheard two older gents talking. "I wonder what happened to that fella Sloane. I had my eye on him," one of them said. The other fella replied: "Well, you know, I think if he just had had a car, he would have won her." I told this to Bailey, who had written the song "Walking and Talking with Harvey Sloane," and he responded: "Maybe you should have a bicycle next time!"

CHAPTER TWELVE

Second Runs,
One Loss One Win

In 1981 Kentucky's state Democrats tried to recruit me to run for County Judge/Executive a position akin to being mayor of Jefferson County. They thought that the incumbent, an ambitious young Republican named Mitch McConnell, was vulnerable. But I had loved being Mayor—it's the best job in politics—and sensed that the job of Judge/Executive just would not be as stimulating. State law prevented me from serving consecutive terms, but not from running again after four years out of office, so I decided to seek a second term as Mayor of Louisville. I passed on the race against McConnell.

In retrospect, my decision to give a run against Mitch a pass may have been a mistake. He squeaked by in his race with a few thousand vote-margin, while I scored a lop-sided victory in my mayoral race. Politics, like life, is full of what-ifs, but I wonder how our nation would be different if I had nipped McConnell's political career in the bud. Perhaps any highly-conservative Republican Senate leader was bound to be as destructive as Mitch has proven to be with his filibuster abuse, conservative court-packing (not to mention dreadful treatment of Merrick Garland and President Barack Obama), determined inaction in the face of Russian interference in our 2016 election, shameless collusion with the Trump defense team in the former President's first impeachment trial and refusal to vote to convict during the second trial, even as he excoriated Trump for fomenting a violent riot. Sometimes one person really does make a difference—a bad difference in this case.

The Courier-Journal and the Louisville Times, the city's major afternoon newspaper until it closed in 1987, had been generally supportive of my work at the health center and of my first term as mayor. The newspapers and the Binghams (who owned both publications) had gotten behind most of my efforts in public office, such as neighborhood development, the TARC referendum, the restoration of Louisville after the tornado, managing court-ordered school busing, historic preservation and downtown development.

But when I ran for mayor again in 1981, Barry Bingham, Jr., then the publisher, supported George Clark, who founded Louisville-based fast food franchise Burger Queen, against me in the general election. Bingham felt that, ethically, newspaper owners needed to be independent of candidates and office holders. And I think he also felt I had been too close to his father. Nevertheless—in spite of Clark, his money and the Courier-Journal's endorsement—we won the general election with 70 percent of the vote. (The paper also supported McConnell's 1981 re-election to be County Judge/Executive. Shortly before his 2006 death, Barry Jr. told the editorial page editor, Keith Runyon, "the worst mistake we ever made was endorsing Mitch McConnell.")

After my resounding victory, The Louisville Times' editorial page embraced me as the "antithesis of the current mayor, William Stansbury, whose lackluster administration has been such a disappointment. In contrast, Dr. Sloane, 45, seems to have an almost magical appeal to the people of Louisville, who recall his term as a time when neighborhood pride, concern for the needy and interest in downtown redevelopment were kindled." The editorial concluded: "It's now up to the mayor elect to prove that their trust was deserved. That's not by any means an easy task, but it is an exciting challenge because Louisville's future depends so much upon whether he succeeds."

Mitch called me the day after the election and came over to my home for breakfast. "We both want to run for state-wide office," he said, bluntly. "If we fight it will hurt us both." Instead, he said, we should make a point of working. This was the epitome of McConnell: pragmatic, power-hungry and a planner. He wanted to run for Senate in 1984 and he knew I was eyeing another run at the governorship in 1983.

His idea made sense and we did work well together for the next couple years, twice collaborating on unsuccessful referenda to merge the city and county governments. He was easy to work with because at that time he was still a reasonable politician, and because good relations made both our jobs easier. I had worked effectively with his predecessor, Todd Hollenbach, and later during my tenure as Judge/Executive (from 1985 to 1989 I developed a strong relationship with Louisville Mayor Jerry Abramson).

In the years since, Mitch has become much more of a hard-edged conservative—a reflection, I suppose, of the changing politics of Kentucky. The population has remained largely static over the last 40 years, but attitudes have shifted tremendously. Kentucky and West Virginia alike used to be quite Democratic: Democrat Bill Clinton won both states in his 1992 and 1996 Presidential elections, for example. But in the last couple of decades environmental (coal regulations) and cultural issues (gay marriage, abortion and guns) have taken on new salience and the state has drifted further and further to the right. The state has a relatively small Black population— only around 8.5 percent—and nearly half are situated in Jefferson County. Kentucky is now reliably Republican: Donald Trump won more than 62 percent of the 2020 vote there (though I'm proud to note that Joe Biden carried Jefferson County).

*   *   *

The start of my second administration was much different than the first. In 1973 I didn't know much about the operations of city government; I considered a small range of candidates for nomination to the various departments and had limited knowledge of how we could best improve quality of life. We had goals such as neighborhood development, revival of the bus service and the establishment of emergency medical service, but we were unprepared for emergencies such as the tornado, the sanitation strike and the busing order. I made a point of starting my second term, in December 1982, much more deliberately. Planning for the administration was well under way before I took the oath of office. Attorney Wallace "Skip" Grafton, my campaign manager, gathered the best and brightest of the previous administration, plus downtown movers and shakers and neighborhood leaders to help chart my next term.

The first order of business was to recruit a police chief. Always an important appointment for a new Mayor, selecting a new police chief was especially important because the department had been racked by scandals and turmoil in the term between my two administrations. Also, I had had difficult relations with the police in my first term. I appointed a 12-person search committee to find the right person for the job and asked Ernie Allen, director of the Louisville-Jefferson County Crime Commission, to head it up. They made relations between the police department and the Black community a top priority in their search. They eventually sent me two names and I settled on Richard Dotson, who had been a Captain in the narcotics squad and had, as The Courier-Journal put it, an "arrow-straight" reputation: Police scandals had accumulated during Stansbury's term and we needed someone whose reputation was beyond reproach on the issue.

Dotson was the man for the job. He made community policing a focus of his tenure: We wanted the police to be a visible part of the community, interacting with people and building connections with residents. They went to community meetings and engaged with community leaders. The idea was to rebuild trust and respect, especially in the Black community.

For Safety Director, to whom not only the Police Chief but also the Fire and EMS Chiefs reported, I reached out to Burt Deutsch, who had served as City Law Director in my first administration. The next order of business was setting up a managerial task force made of business executives who could look into all the various departments and evaluate their effectiveness and recommend alterations. The economy was soft, so the budget was not flush, and we needed to streamline departments and create a much more effective cabinet system.

I was encouraged to get a top administrator, preferably one with state government experience. James O. King, who had just finished serving as Gov. John Y. Brown's cabinet secretary, was the logical choice. Jim was a former administrator at the University of Kentucky and had the backing of my good friend Bill Wester (whom I had gotten to know when I served in Eastern Kentucky, and who was the administrator of the Department for Public Health under Dr. Russel Teague and a close friend of Ed Prichard).

When Jim King returned to state government after my state campaign, Burt Deutsch stepped up to become Secretary of the Cabinet. Burt was a skilled strategist who always had a handle on everything that was happening in City government, down to the most minute program. To fill the resulting Safety Director vacancy, I was glad to promote Ernie Allen, who had led the search for a police chief. He had given me excellent advice about the police even before I ran the first time and he was well respected by both the police and the public, as well as by people in my administration. When I later became County Judge/Executive I would ask Ernie to be my chief administrative officer, a position he filled with great distinction. Ernie was later recruited to be the President and CEO of the National Center for Missing & Exploited Children, where he earned enormous admiration from both Congress and the public for his work. In the 2000s Ernie informally consulted with the Vatican about how to handle the child abuse scandal.

After filling the cabinet, the next order of business was renewing the downtown. This involved appointing directors for both the Broadway redevelopment project and the Galleria (now called Fourth Street Live!) and setting up an Office for Economic Development and appointing Charles Buddeke, a widely respected Louisville businessman who served for a dollar per year, as its director. Another area of development we focused on was the Louisville waterfront along the Ohio river. The I-64 expressway separated the downtown from the waterfront, but it was elevated and by clearing the industrial land under it and next to the waterfront we could reestablish one of Louisville's greatest assets. In November of 1985 the new County/Judge Bremer Ehler and I jointly appointed the Louisville Waterfront Commission, which was headed by respected former state senator David Karem. Over the next four years, Jerry Abramson, my successor as Mayor, and I, as Jefferson County Judge/Executive, worked to begin the process of revitalizing the waterfront, which had been neglected for many years. Under Karem's gifted guidance, and with the leadership and support of succeeding officials, particularly Jerry, the waterfront was gradually transformed into a beautiful community asset—a welcoming spot for residents and visitors alike.

Another major objective during my second term as Mayor was to revitalize and renovate such central neighborhoods as the areas around the medical center in Phoenix Place and the Chestnut Street project. One of the most successful partnerships involved rebuilding the old General Hospital, which had fallen into disrepair. When I started my second term, there was no coordinated movement to build a new hospital. But Humana, the health insurance company, was one of our great Louisville companies, having started out in nursing homes before moving into hospitals. I approached Humana's CEO, David Jones, about working with the state, the city and the county to build a new hospital which would eventually be run by the University of Louisville. David was the essential figure in the remarkable coordination of effort and finance. The new hospital, the Humana Hospital University, was spectacular and served the needs of indigent citizens.

Years later, when I became the Commissioner for Public Health in Washington D.C., that city faced a similar problem: The old General Hospital was inadequate and in decline; it was eventually used as a homeless shelter before being torn down in 2020. It took over 25 years for D.C. to initiate and finance a new hospital, in no small part because it didn't have the kind of private sector partnership that we had with Humana. D.C. General still has not been replaced. What we did in Louisville with the Humana Hospital University is an example of what a well-run city-state-private partnership could do and stands in contrast to what a dysfunctional city like Washington could not do.

*   *   *

Quality of life remained a focal point for my administration in my second term. This involved initiatives like celebrating neighborhoods with festivals, staging citywide events such as "Light Up Louisville" (the annual holiday light display), and the highly successful "Look what we can do, Louisville!" campaign, which highlighted all the new opportunities and accomplishments in the area.

We worked hard at improving residential areas, by creating an adopt-a-neighborhood program, by rehabilitating many housing units and by stricter enforcement of housing laws. This included removing roughly 1,400 illegal space heaters, which were a huge fire hazard. Once again, we placed a lot of emphasis on resolving neighborhood complaints, including establishing a citizens' guide for direct access to diversified city services. We also worked with the University of Louisville to put on a series of leadership seminars in order to encourage future city leaders. Each year the summer youth and beautification program employed 2,000 to 2,500 young people between 14 and 21 years old to help clean up neighborhoods. They filled over 300,000 trash bags and received the Golden Broom Award for their efforts.

Homelessness remained a challenge. I set up a Christmas turkey fund as well as a task force on homelessness to provide 3,500 people with shelter and good meals during the severe 1984 winter. We distributed critical items such as heaters during subzero temperatures around Christmas. The remarkable and most generous Blanche Cooper, the city's Human Needs Director, led these efforts.

Like many cities across the country in the 1980s, we had to deal with safety and crime. The first step had been appointing Dotson as the new police chief. Another important move was the creation of a 911 system, which Louisville previously did not have. We were able to reduce crime in the city every year from 1980 to 1985, with a total reduction of about 60 percent.

In 1985 a Rand McNally study of most livable metropolitan areas—which looked at qualities like healthcare, the environment and transportation—ranked Louisville eighth in the nation, a considerable improvement from 1981, when we were 19th. The 1985 ranking placed us behind only Pittsburgh, Boston, Raleigh-Durham, N.C., San Francisco, Philadelphia, Nassau-Suffolk counties in New York, and St. Louis.

*　　*　　*

In January of 1983, in the middle of my second term as Mayor, I decided to run for Governor again in that year's election. I had placed a close second to John Y. Brown in 1979, and the main candidates for the '83 race were Lieutenant Governor Martha Layne Collins and Grady Stumbo, a physician from Eastern Kentucky who had been Governor Brown's Human Services secretary.

We were already off and running that January, and I was driving in a Jeep from one stop to the next while campaigning in Eastern Kentucky, when I suddenly got severe back pain. I could neither sit up or stand up. When I returned to Louisville, I had to conduct a campaign meeting lying on the floor.

I went to Jewish Hospital the next day and an MRI showed I had a slipped disc. Dr. John Guarnaschelli said I would need laminectomy, a procedure which involves removing part or all of the vertebral bone, to be able to continue the campaign. So, I had the operation and a week later formally announced my bid for governor—from my hospital bed. It was two months before I fully recovered, however, which proved a major campaign impediment. I couldn't work the state, which I had come within a hair of winning four years early.

The biggest mistake I made in that race, however, was also one of the single stupidest decisions of my entire life. There was a statewide push for a "right to work" law, which would have permitted people to take jobs on union sites without joining the union. I had been strongly pro-labor my entire career and had enjoyed their support. But I allowed myself to be convinced by some Louisville business leaders not to promise to veto the legislation if elected Governor. Instead, I stayed carefully neutral on it.

One day Owen Hammond, a UAW labor leader I knew well and had worked with closely for years, came into my City Hall office and asked me point-blank: What are you going to do on this right to work bill? I temporized: "I've got to see the legislation before making a commitment." He knew an inartful dodge when he heard one, so Owen and his associates just got up and walked out. (The legislation failed in any case, though Kentucky would pass a "right to work" law more than three decades later, in 2017.)

My attempt to straddle the issue reminded me of an Eastern Kentucky saying: "The only two things in the middle of the road are yellow lines and dead skunks." My mistake was doubly stupid because I so strongly believe in the labor movement, which was one of great positive forces in the U.S. in the 20th century. Labor unions supported some of our most important social causes: workers' rights, child labor laws, worksite safety and broadened access to healthcare. The fact that labor has been so hollowed out over the last 40 years is one of our real national political tragedies.

So, I lost the union endorsement and lost the race by 4,000 votes out of more than 650,000 cast. Collins won and would go on to beat Republican Jim Bunning in the general election that fall. She ended up being a pretty good governor. She brought me with her on her first trade mission to Japan, during which she was able to make a groundbreaking deal for Toyota to have a plant in central Kentucky.

*   *   *

After my second unsuccessful run for Governor, I re-embraced my agenda as Mayor with great energy. McConnell and I worked together on city-county issues as we had agreed. The most important one was trying to merge city-county government. Having two distinct governments operating side-by-side, and at times overlapping each other, was a duplicative waste: We didn't need two sets of police and other services. Experience told us there could be upsides to merging. Other metropolitan areas, such as Lexington, Kentucky and Indianapolis, Indiana, had successfully conducted mergers with their counties and were doing well economically. When Judge James Gordon ordered that students be bused, he had mandated the merger of the city and county school systems. Despite all of the tensions and stress it created, his order had actually helped achieve that merger.

Politically, McConnell had to be cooperative largely because his financial backers in the county favored merging. I was doing everything I could to promote the cause in the city. The difficulty we both faced was that the two communities we were trying to unify politically were deeply divided. In the city, the African-American community did not support a merger because being part of a larger electorate would dilute its political power. In Southwest Jefferson County, which was largely blue-collar, voters distrusted the East End of the city and the rest of the county—which was largely Republican (Kentucky still being a Democratic state at that point). Southwest Jefferson county residents thought that the real power in the community unfairly resided with East End politicians, and that it had so for many generations. Many residents in the southwest county felt neglected, and it didn't help that most of the large polluters in the county were located in the southwest, so residents were more exposed to pollution. They also still resented the court-ordered busing, having seen it as a solution to a racial problem that they had not initiated and were not experiencing.

McConnell and I made two city-county merger attempts. Changes of this sort had to be approved by both city and county voters, and our first try was on the ballot in November 1982. It did not succeed. The second try was the next year, during the November general election, and I enlisted the help of local planning consultant Joe Corradino to oversee the proposal and a large number of public hearings on the topic. Both merger proposals failed by small percentages in high-turnout elections. One problem was that the proposals were quite complicated, and difficult for average voters to study. The proposals involved merging not simply Louisville and Jefferson County, but also the roughly 90 independent cities in Jefferson County. Our efforts also weren't helped by the heavy support for merging in the East End of the city, which provoked suspicions in both the rest of the city and in the county.

Although our efforts to merge the city and county in 1982 and 1983 failed, they did pave the way for eventual success. When I became County Judge/Executive in 1985, I was able to craft a compact with my successor as Mayor, Jerry Abramson, to accomplish some of the things a full merger would have. In 2003 Louisville and Jefferson County finally did successfully merge. Nearly two decades later the merger is operating smoothly and is well-accepted.

*   *   *

McConnell was pleasant to work with when he was County Judge Executive. He was matter-of-fact and didn't grandstand. He did what he agreed to do. He wasn't loquacious or dishonest. But Mitch had a plan way beyond being County Judge/Executive. In 1984, he ran against incumbent Democratic Sen. Walter "Dee" Huddleston, in what was shaping up to be a tough year for Democrats with Ronald Reagan heading the GOP ticket. A Senate race meant raising money, so McConnell courted the financial interests of Jefferson County and Kentucky and looked after their interests.

He spent a lot of time campaigning around the state well beyond the confines of Jefferson County, and he tried to avoid controversy with me or my base in the city and county. He had not yet tacked hard to the right back then. He had received the AFL-CIO endorsement in his first Jefferson County Judge/Executive election. He was pro-choice on abortion when he was Judge/Executive. He would switch sides on that issue when he saw the way Kentucky Republicans were trending on such social issues. (I should acknowledge that I also changed my qualified position on abortion (supportive in cases of incest and life of the mother) to being totally pro-choice after having conversations with Kathy, Abigail, and others.) In his first campaign for County Judge/Executive in 1977, he styled himself as pro-labor, saying he would look favorably on allowing county employees to organize. That won him a union endorsement, which was practically unheard of for a Republican. Of course, once in office he opposed collective bargaining for county workers.

But Mitch had a plan and he executed it flawlessly: He won the 1984 Senate race by a few thousand votes in a year that Ronald Reagan won the state by nearly 300,000. Recently, in 2020, he was elected to his seventh Senate term. The philosopher Machiavelli would have smiled.

Today I look at congressional Republicans and am aghast at how ready most of them were to support Donald Trump's lies about the outcome of the 2020 presidential election. It took McConnell, for example, more than a month to acknowledge that Joe Biden won the presidency. Some of his colleagues still claim voter fraud. These lies led directly to the January 6 siege of the Capital. McConnell laid blame for the attack at Trump's feet, but quickly backed away from that stand, twice voting that the impeachment trial was unconstitutional. How can any self-respecting elected official act that way? I am reminded of an older gent I met during one of my walks around Kentucky for governor in 1979. He was disgruntled with the state's senators. "Jury members who are registered voters are randomly chosen and they decide pretty well on matters of life and death," he said. "Maybe we ought to pick our senators that way."

CHAPTER THIRTEEN

County Judge/Executive, "On The Job"

Once again prohibited by law from serving consecutive terms as Mayor, in 1985 I decided to run for the job which I'd passed on four years earlier—County Judge/Executive. Once again, I won handily.

The inaugural day was just terrific. Once more I took the oath of office, administered by former Governor Bert Combs, right at midnight with my family at our home. I repeated the ceremony for the public at the Southwest Government Center the next morning and then went on a tour of all points of the county on a train called, appropriately, the "Jeffersonian." This trip, organized by Cass Harris, who had arranged all of my walks, was meant to bridge the gaps between people and bring all segments of the county together. I was especially excited because it reminded me of the days I had spent riding the rails as a college student. This time, happily, I didn't have to worry about being unceremoniously kicked off in the middle of nowhere.

The politics of the trip were important for me because I was reaching out from the city of Louisville, where I had served two mayoral terms, and becoming the Judge/Executive of the whole county. "This historic inaugural day rail tour is symbolic of the unity we will bring to our community" I said. I was determined to serve the far reaches of the county as energetically as I had served Louisville.

When I was Mayor I hadn't been particularly enthusiastic about the idea of being the County Judge/Executive. There was something about being a mayor that particularly excited me, and I wasn't sure the County Judge/Executive post would be the same. One drawback of serving as chief executive in the county was that I had to clear all of my proposals with the other three members of the County Fiscal Court—as opposed to the city, where the mayor was totally separate from the Board of Aldermen/City Council. There had to be good communication with my fellow Commissioners, because I needed their approval on every major issue. To my surprise, however, the first six months were just exciting and challenging as being Mayor. A June 1986 Louisville Courier-Journal headline said, "Post may have been rated second fiddle but he's working to a tune of his own" and quoted me as saying that I had done as least as much as County Judge/Executive—maybe more—as I had in the same time span in either terms as Mayor.

My schedule was hectic. As Danny Ross, a Labor assistant who often doubled as my driver, told The Courier-Journal, I was up at 6am swimming or riding an exercise bike for 30 minutes before leaving for a breakfast meeting. I would get to the office by 8am and have a schedule awaiting me with 10 to 20 meetings or places to be. My chief of staff, Ernie Allen, who had been Safety Director when I was Mayor, told the paper: "There have been so many new groups he's dealing with, so many new people to meet. He's trying to do everything and to meet everybody. ... He's going at a campaign pace." Allen went on to say that "a very personal role has developed between Harvey Sloane and the community. In some ways—name recognition, public respect—Harvey Sloane is bigger than the office. His presence here has probably brought more attention to, and sympathy for, county government than ever before."

Because Mitch McConnell and I had previously worked on a pair of referenda to merge the city and the county governments, I had campaigned for Judge/Executive with a strong focus on the issue. The election of Jerry Abramson to succeed me as Mayor made the effort much easier. I had known Jerry for a decade, dating back to his being part of the 1975 '"Democrats For Progress" city council slate that ran during my first term as Mayor. He was constructive to work with—always upbeat, a real booster for the community and fun to be with. We had similar goals and we both had won our elections overwhelmingly, so we made our first order of business agreeing upon a city-county compact. We were able to announce it before either of us even took office.

The new agreement brought together many government functions which had been separately controlled by each entity: We shared tax revenue from economic growth, for example, allowing economic development to be a joint venture and not a competition between the city and county. Previously some city-county agencies had reported to both the Mayor and the County Judge/Executive, which effectively meant that there was divided leadership with inadequate oversight. So we divvied up most of the agencies, making city and county each responsible for certain portfolios.

*　　*　　*

The biggest immediate challenge for me in my new post was how to balance the county budget. President Reagan had terminated all federal revenue sharing funds for cities and counties, a federal program that had been extremely helpful for local governments, because it had allowed an expansion of services. The elimination of federal funding meant that 10 to 15 percent of the county budget was going to have to be cut. We were looking at an $8 million hole in the budget (which was an imposing figure in those days) and needed to act fast. So that first year was very much about cutting personnel and services—a sharp contrast with my first term as mayor, when I worked on adding new things such as an emergency medical service, new neighborhood services and saving bus service.

I appointed a managerial task force, co-chaired by banking executive A. Stevens Miles and made up of business community CEOs, to make recommendations on how to save money. They proved to be extremely helpful, particularly in reducing expenditures and merging functions of city-county government. I implemented nearly all of the roughly 100 proposals they offered. The only one I did not pursue was merging the city and county police departments, a controversial idea and an extremely difficult one to implement: Any change involving the police department usually met with a resistant Fraternal Order of Police.

It would take more than two years, but by 1988 we had the budget under control. This is not to suggest that everything focused solely on fiscal retrenchment. During this period we were able to proactively push and institute new programs to help Jefferson County residents: We set up a health-awareness program called Louisville Lite and distributed 300,000 health booklets countywide. We were also able to better coordinate primary care, especially among community health centers throughout the city and county. Building on my own experiences, and with the invaluable help of Jefferson County Board of Health Director Dr. David Allen, we opened a network of seven health clinics for poor and uninsured Jefferson County residents. Medical care for these citizens had been deteriorating for some time and snowballing downward in recent years. Uninsured County residents had traditionally gone to General Hospital in downtown Louisville for care, and as new clinics were opened around the city, General Hospital began to cater only to the indigent—a development that proved to be a money-losing proposition. This in turn triggered budget and service cuts, which eventually left poorer Louisville and Jefferson County residents without a place to receive basic, non-emergency medical care. By the spring of 1988, however, the new public health centers in the city and county were all open and running. Eventually General Hospital was closed, and between the new health centers and the new Humana Hospital University, healthcare in the region began to improve dramatically.

The summer of 1988 also marked another important milestone for both Louisville and Jefferson County as we unveiled plans for a major and desperately needed airport expansion. A friend in Washington had contacted me late the previous year to let me know that UPS, which had opened a regional hub at our airport in 1981 and accounted for roughly 40 percent of the flights in and out, needed more airfield capacity or might find a different hub. The company already employed about 4,500 people, so I paid attention.

Working with Sam Rechter, Vice Chair of the Regional Airport Authority, and Mayor Abramson, we hired Joe Corradino, now of

Schimpeler-Corradino Associates, to do an analysis. J.D. Nichols, a plane owner and pilot as well as a major land developer, provided key input. Burt Deutsch, my Deputy County Judge, worked with Corradino. Their research indicated that one way to expand the airfield was to have two parallel runways. But this would require expanding the airport's boundaries. J.D. Nichols, Deutsch, Corradino and I flew over the area to better understand how the expansion could take place. It would mean relocating roughly 4,000 residents, 115 businesses, 16 churches and two schools in three nearby neighborhoods to make room—a politically sensitive idea, to say the least.

Knowing the idea would be controversial, we developed "quietly," in many cases not briefing local officials until shortly before we unveiled the plan. We asked that *The Courier-Journal* not scoop the story until we were ready to announce it.

I announced the final plan in June 1988, along with Jerry Abramson and members of the Regional Airport Authority. The projected $300 million proposal was the biggest expansion of a business or industrial area that the city-county had undertaken in at least 50 years. After the announcement, Jerry and I walked the Highland Park neighborhood, which was going to have to make way for the expansion, to meet with the homeowners there. Some were deeply grieved, not sure of their future. We committed to do everything we could to honor their needs in every conceivable way. Eventually, we bought unused farmland to relocate a number of households.

The first new runway finally opened in 1995 and its companion two years later. In that time, cargo shipments going through the airport more than tripled, while passenger activity doubled. Not surprisingly, the project was a boon for jobs and economic development. The number of jobs associated with the airport nearly tripled between 1986 and 1997, and total annual payroll had soared from $120 million to $659 million. By the time the second runway opened, UPS was Kentucky's largest private sector employer.

It was a thrill for me to watch newscasts of UPS planes taking off to deliver the first Pfizer COVID-19 vaccines around the country in 2020.

*   *   *

During my tenure as County Judge/Executive I continued to find ways to get out into the community. Some of the greatest educational experiences I enjoyed in office were having day-long "tours of duty" at companies across the county, as part of what we called my "On the Job" program. The idea was for me to get a better understanding of local companies and their employees and figure out how government could help them. I would spend brief periods doing different jobs, giving me a chance to interact with the workers. After lunch I would spend time with the management. I made eleven of these outings in all, working as an operator at South Central Bell and unloading aircraft for UPS, among other gigs. I was clearly not suited for some of the work. Working at an assembly line at Ford's Kentucky Truck Plant, I banged a windshield into place too hard and cracked it. My stints reminded me of some of the summer jobs I had across the country in high school and college. After a morning working at Flexible Materials, I was given a check for my toil. After union dues and other deductions my net earnings for the day were $0.00! I was well-suited to at least one of the jobs, though: Humana put me to work at the Humana Hospital-University of Louisville.

The "On the Job" program really humanized the various businesses for me, driving home that these jobs were an important part of many people's lives. Once you've worked with guys on the floor of the Ford plant, you develop a certain emotional attachment to them. The biggest takeaway for me was the importance of having a business-friendly government to ensure that companies came to and *remained in* Louisville and Jefferson County, and to guarantee that the work environments were fair. We had good relationships between labor and management, and there were few strikes. We had strong worker advocacy in our government. My eleven "On the Job" excursions gave me a much better sense of how government and business could interact to be more effective. They were also a lot of fun.

Perhaps the most stimulating outing I had in the "On the Job" program was in the spring of 1989, when I served as a substitute teacher at Southern High School, a high-performing Louisville public magnet career academy. I met with teachers in the morning to hear their problems and aspirations. In the afternoon, I met with juniors and seniors and taught an American history class. I focused on the formation of the United Nations, World Wars I and II and the danger of nuclear proliferation. The students were well-informed, enthusiastic and asked piercing questions: Did I think, for example, that U.S. or U.N. troops should be sent into Lebanon to rescue Lt. Col. William Higgins, a 1963 graduate of Southern, who was heading a U.N. peacekeeping force in southern Lebanon in 1988 when pro-Iranian Muslim fundamentalists kidnapped him? The problem, I told the class, is that U.S. officials didn't know where he was and worried that a rescue attempt could lead to his being killed. A student challenged me, asking if I didn't think Higgins would want an opportunity for freedom. You're right, I said, but it won't help him if we go in and they kill him either. (Sadly, Higgins' captors would murder him months later.) The students and I bantered back and forth, and I thoroughly enjoyed it.

As it happened, I would have another wonderful experience years later, teaching public health at George Washington University in Washington, D.C. I wish I had done more teaching in my career. It requires you to really get to know your subject and I loved the interaction with the students—the thrill of feeling that you are introducing them to new thoughts, views and facts. I enjoyed the give-and-take. But teaching is not easy. You have got to be really prepared and keep the students interested if you're going to make any difference.

Throughout my term as County Judge/Executive, carrying forward a tradition from my mayoral days, I took walks through different County neighborhoods. They usually occurred in the afternoons. I would bring a cadre of county officials, department heads and neighborhood leaders along with me. As always, the point was to meet people on their own turf and to hear their complaints firsthand while proving that county government was interested in their problems and would help solve them. It also gave those of us in government a sense of neighborhood priorities. And the neighborhood walks were good politics: People remembered that I had been there and took an interest in their lives. Above all it was always enjoyable for me to meet people and get out of the office.

*　　*　　*

The most problematic issue that I faced during my time as County Judge/Executive—one I never could resolve—was jail overcrowding. I always like to remind my critics that I inherited the problem from Mitch McConnell—that he didn't resolve the issue when he was Judge/Executive! Shortly after I took office, we were placed under federal court order for having a greatly overcrowded jail system. We were told to release non-violent inmates on a regular basis. I found myself worrying about the Willie Horton issue that Democratic Presidential nominee Mike Dukakis had faced in his presidential campaign, that an inmate would commit some horrible crime after being let out early.

I did everything I could to resist building a big new jail. I greatly expanded home incarceration and halfway houses, for example. Of course, no one wanted a halfway house in their neighborhood and the constant release of non-violent inmates was not politically acceptable. It was not until the end of my administration that the County Fiscal Court finally agreed on financing a new facility, costing $63 million, even though the county was already fiscally compromised. Of course, my opponents jumped on the debt I left for the next County Judge/Executive.

*   *   *

One of the pleasures of being Judge/Executive was conducting marriage ceremonies. I performed the marriage of one couple in a hot air balloon and another at Churchill Downs Racetrack. And in November 1986 I had the privilege of officiating the marriage of

Muhammad Ali to his fourth wife Lonnie, in a small ceremony in my home. That marriage would endure for the next 30 years until Ali's 2016 death, and to this day Lonnie remains an active figure in various charitable and community causes in Louisville. At the time of his 1986 wedding to Lonnie, Ali was already starting to display the first tremors from the Parkinson's that would ravage him, but he remained indomitable for years to come. As he joked around with us before the ceremony, I was reminded of the time an old family friend—Edith Munson, who was married to my godfather, Curtis Munson—was staying with us in Louisville when the Champ stopped by. We had invited Ali over but had forgotten to let Edith know we were expecting a guest. We were at church when Ali arrived, wearing shorts and a t-shirt. Edith answered the door, and politely explained that we were not home and asked his name. "I'm Muhammad Ali," he told her. Without missing a beat, and slightly annoyed at her leg apparently being pulled, Edith looked up at him said: "And I'm Santa Claus!" (Edith was herself an athlete of some renown—an amateur golfer and, in 1924, the first female athlete to appear on the cover of Time magazine.) It fell to Mattie Lewis, our housekeeper, to explain that yes, this was, in fact, the famous boxer standing at the door.

As irrepressible as ever, after his wedding ceremony with Lonnie, Ali took my sons Patrick and Curtis, ages eight and nine, aside and showed them his levitation trick. It really did look like he was floating.

Ali certainly said some controversial things over the years, but I never got the sense of his having any racism or hostility. He was married by a white man, after all, and buried in predominantly white Cave Hill Cemetery in Louisville. His first trainer, Joe Martin, was a white police officer. Representatives of a dozen religions spoke at his funeral service and the final eulogy at his funeral was delivered by a white man, former President Bill Clinton. Speaking of Ali, Clinton said, "before he could possibly have worked it all out, and before fate and time could work their will on him, he decided he would not be ever be disempowered. He decided that not his race nor his place, the expectations of others, positive, negative or otherwise would strip from him the power to write his own story."

CHAPTER FOURTEEN
All Politics Is Personal

I finally squared off against Mitch McConnell in 1990 as he sought re-election to the Senate. It promised to be a brutal and dismal race and several people that I admired counseled me against running. Barry Bingham Sr., for example, said before his death that he thought it would be a very rough campaign and difficult to win. He had supported his close friend Wilson Wyatt's runs for governor in 1959 and against Thruston Morton for senator in 1962. He saw then that a former Louisville Mayor would have tough going in the rest of the state. A predominantly rural state, Kentucky has always viewed cities—even its own—with great skepticism. He also knew that McConnell's espoused conservatism would resonate better in Kentucky. In addition, Mitch was a vicious campaigner with a lot of money. He suggested that I consider going to the University of Louisville and teaching nutrition. I thought about it for a long time, but it just wasn't where I wanted to be.

As he approached the end of his first term in the Senate, our polling indicated that McConnell was vulnerable. But he had the backing of a popular administration. In early August of 1990 Iraq invaded and annexed Kuwait, prompting President George H.W. Bush to rally an international response. "This will not stand, this aggression against Kuwait," he declared just days after the invasion.

And while the Persian Gulf War would not begin until the following January, troops and equipment were already pouring into Saudi Arabia, putting Bush onto a wartime footing, politically. His approval ratings soared.

McConnell had been the first sitting Senator to support Bush's 1988 bid and had raised a great deal of money for the Republican ticket. As a thanks, Bush had made a McConnell fund-raiser the first campaign event he attended in the 1990 election cycle. Bush and practically all of his cabinet came down to campaign for Mitch and, of course, raise a lot of money. Nonetheless, I thought we could win. I came with a significant base of support from Louisville and Jefferson and Fayette Counties. I was recognized in the state after my two attempts for the Democratic nomination for governor, the second of which I had only lost by a half-percentage point. But there were some unanticipated challenges that would come my way.

*   *   *

My problems started during the primary, with a feud that dated back years. Wallace Wilkinson, a successful businessman who had done a good job as the finance chairman of my 1983 gubernatorial race, had asked for my support when he ran for the same office in 1987. We were on his private plane, flying from Florida to Kentucky when he made me an offer and a threat. If I supported him for governor, he would help me beat McConnell in 1990. "But if you do not support me, I will do everything to cut you down at your knees and see you defeated," he said. This enraged me and we nearly got into a fist fight at 30,000 feet before Kathy intervened. This might have been a political mistake, but it wasn't a moral one: Wallace won the governorship in 1987, and his administration was marked with political scandal as he had no compunction with mixing his public office and his private business, to his own benefit. In hindsight, I'm glad I followed my instincts.

Tip O'Neill famously said that all politics is local; in Kentucky, all politics is personal—and memories are long. As Governor Wallace was true to his word: He pointedly recruited John Brock, the Kentucky Superintendent of Education, to challenge me in the Senate primary, undercutting me politically and keeping big Democratic donors on the sidelines. I won easily, with a great deal of help from Andrew "Skipper" Martin, my campaign chairman, but the win came at a cost, both in terms of fundraising and having to spend important dollars to win that race—dollars I would need later on.

Raising money proved to be a problem for the entire campaign. Kentucky contributors were much more interested in the governorship and local offices than national offices, especially challenging an incumbent. McConnell also had the support of some especially potent special interests, including the American Israel Public Affairs Committee. AIPAC adopted the philosophy that if an officeholder voted right on Israel then it would back that candidate no matter his or her domestic views and regardless of their opponent's positions. How seriously they took this was illustrated for me when an AIPAC member approached me about being my fundraiser. He recalled that in 1985, as mayor I was asked to lead a delegation of American mayors to visit Jerusalem to study and witness what the great Mayor Teddy Kollek had done to reduce religious conflict in that historic city as well as its restoration. I left firmly supportive of the city and Israel.

But an AIPAC official called my would-be fund-raiser and warned that crossing McConnell would get him black-balled among Jewish donors. In addition, AIPAC officials got the word out to all the state Democratic finance committees across the country that they would not support me and that the committees should not fundraise too aggressively for me.

I spent a lot of the first six months of 1990 dialing for dollars, as fund-raising is often called. There is nothing more frustrating and demeaning than making a cold call, when you phone a total stranger, and ask for money. My daughter Abigail, then 19, spent the summer egging me on to make phone call after phone call and use that time as effectively as possible. It was the closest I've come to agony in seeking a public office. Kathy helped raise money, particularly out of state money, through our contacts in Florida, California, New York and other states.

Since 1990 the role of money in politics has only worsened. The Supreme Court's 2010 Citizens United decision that corporations are essentially people and enjoy free speech rights reversed century-old rules prohibiting them from spending money directly on campaigns. I've been involved with medicine all of my adult life, and a person bleeds and thinks. To suggest a corporation is a person is just an abuse of language. Instead, these corporations, and also wealthy individuals, can give unlimited amounts. It has made achieving significant levels of political office an almost impossibility without a lot of wealth. The incomes and net worth of Senators is astronomical—members worth under $1 million are now the exception. According to Open Secrets, a website that tracks money in politics, McConnell's net worth in 2022 was about $34 million, much higher than when he came into the senate and making him one of the ten richest members of his chamber. More than half of all members of Congress are millionaires, according to Open Secrets. Congressional candidates in the House and Senate spend enormous amounts of time raising money instead of doing public business.

In addition, members of the House and Senate work on Congressional issues about three days a week. They come to Washington on Monday, they're working Tuesday, Wednesday and Thursday, and then Friday they usually head back home, often to raise more money. This is one of the reasons that members of Congress have reached such low esteem with the American public: Their approval ratings linger in the 20s with disapproval in the 70s.

It is a disgusting system—and McConnell has been perhaps its fiercest defender, fighting every campaign finance reform which has been proposed, including a 1990 proposal (which he filibustered to death) and the 2002 McCain-Feingold campaign finance law, which he tried but failed to stop. Not surprisingly, he hasn't always been consistent on the issue: He published an op-ed in The Courier-Journal long ago in 1973 calling for *more* regulation of money in politics. He later argued that the solution to the problem of fundraising as legalized bribery was disclosure: give a public accounting for every dollar raised and let voters decide. He believed in disclosure until he didn't, though—now he sees publicizing such information as an invasion of donor privacy. The bottom line is that once Mitch spent time in politics, he realized that money was power—and he has always craved power. The philosopher Machiavelli would smile again.

Recalling the 1990 Senate race in his 2016 memoir, McConnell wrote: "I never would have been able to win my race if there had been a limit on the amount of money I could raise and spend."

*　　　*　　　*

Another problem I encountered during my Senate campaign against McConnell was that I had made an enemy of the National Rifle Association by advocating for an assault weapons ban. In September 1989, a 47-year-old named Joseph Wesbecker had brought a cache of semiautomatics and other guns to Standard Gravure where The Courier-Journal had been published and where he had worked. He was evidently angry at the president of the company, who had fired him. The president was not there but Wesbecker sprayed the large print and operations room with bullets, killing six and wounding 12 others. It was the largest mass-killing in Kentucky history and the first such assault to capture national attention.

Assault rifles are weapons of war and serve no legitimate domestic purpose. Every hunter knows that if they used a semi-automatic to bag a deer there wouldn't be much left to eat or mount on the wall. Some warned that I could cost myself the race given that Kentucky is a conservative state with many hunters. I was fine with that: Some issues are worth losing over. Late in the campaign, Kathy was on the radio defending my position on assault weapons. People would call in and say, "We like your husband, but he wants to take away our guns." This is a tactic the NRA has used over and over again on many races and unfortunately, it's effective.

The politics of guns have shifted dramatically over the years. Four years later, in 1994, President Bill Clinton was able to enact an assault weapons ban but Republicans used the issue to bludgeon congressional Democrats in that year's midterm elections. For years afterward the issue gained a reputation for being politically radioactive—it wasn't worth crossing the NRA, the thinking went, because gun activists were more likely to vote on the single issue than were gun control proponents. By the time the 1994 ban was up for renewal it enjoyed little support in Congress and an opponent (George W. Bush) in the White House. In recent years the pendulum has begun to swing back as the number of mass-shootings—including at schools—has steadily mounted. The NRA is now is now facing deep financial challenges and filed for bankruptcy, while polls show the public overwhelmingly supports sensible gun safety measures. Maybe we'll make more enduring progress this time.

*   *   *

Although many things seemed to be working against me, my real base of support in my 1990 Senate campaign was labor organizations. They were unwavering, even though I had had to fire the striking sanitation workers during my first term as Mayor, and we had split in 1983 over the right to work. I went to the United Mine Workers executive committee to seek their support. A couple of members were still very disturbed that I had fired employees just because they were striking. They argued that every labor member in the country ought to have the right to strike and that it was the basic right of all workers. My response that it was against state law didn't seem to carry a lot of water. "If you are against the right to strike, I am against you," one member told me.

But while unions sat out the primary, they did support me aggressively in the general election. Kathy and I went to an outdoor meeting in Eastern Kentucky that summer which felt like a religious revival. We sang labor songs such as "We Shall Overcome" and "Which Side Are You On?", discussed the history of the mineworkers and what they sacrificed to provide energy to the country, and why this marvelous tradition still needed support. After that meeting the president of the Mineworkers approached me and said that he had seen an energy company in my financial disclosure that wasn't supportive of miners and wasn't unionized. He asked me to sell my shares in the company, which I did—and lost a lot of money.

McConnell uncovered another self-inflicted wound in the primary: I had not renewed my license to prescribe controlled substances but had still renewed a prescription for myself. My physician had prescribed me Amitriptyline for painful hips, back and osteoarthritis conditions and I had renewed it myself out of convenience. Mitch made a big issue of this, branding me a drug addict. I eventually took a drug test to dispel the issue and submitted all the relevant information to the Kentucky Medical Society, which agreed the medicines I was taking were appropriate. But McConnell hammered me relentlessly on it, running ads accusing me of relying on "powerful" and "mood-altering" pills. A week after the election I had the hip replaced, which finally resolved the hip pain.

McConnell demonstrated his personal cynicism in the way he seized upon my central campaign issue, the importance of dealing with healthcare. This was an issue he'd never addressed before, but he introduced a healthcare bill just in time to cut an ad about his "plan." The bill was never heard of again, but it had served its purpose for Mitch: He could pretend to be addressing my campaign's raison d'etre.

McConnell is a calculating politician whose quest for power overshadows anything else as he would later demonstrate in his despicable treatment of Merrick Garland, President Barack Obama's last Supreme Court nominee, whom McConnell refused to accord a vote during a presidential election year. (Four years later, he made sure that Amy Coney Barrett was hastily added to the court mere weeks before an election). Obama tells an illuminating anecdote about McConnell is his presidential memoir, "A Promised Land." The story was related to former President Obama by his then-Vice President Joe Biden, and involves an incident when McConnell was blocking a piece of legislation. When Vice President Biden tried to explain why it was a good bill, the GOP leader responded: "You must be under the mistaken impression that I care." It's never been about policy for Mitch, just power. The policy shifts he has made over the years, becoming a more pronounced conservative as the state drifted to the right, illustrated his understanding of how Kentucky politics and the South more broadly were changing. He knew how to adjust his beliefs to the public's mood and as Kentucky has moved steadily rightward so has Mitch.

The whole Senate election season of 1990 was rough and tumble. But Mrs. Barry Bingham Sr. helped my campaign by funding $250,000 worth of ads with a series of clips about the FDR, Truman and JFK year years, stressing how in the era of Reagan-Bush many important Democratic achievements had lost their momentum. The country needed to give more support to the working person. These ads, along with my campaigning—Mrs. Bingham's grandson Rob, son of my late friend Worth Bingham, was a campaign spokesman—helped me close the gap with McConnell. On the last Thursday of the campaign, ABC News anchor Peter Jennings called to give me a heads-up that he was going to report that evening that according to Republican polls I was even with McConnell. Over the next four days, McConnell, guided by his campaign consultant Roger Ailes (who later would start the Fox News Channel), unleashed hellfire: a barrage of letters, radio spots and ads highlighted my liberal stances on issues such as the assault weapons ban and suggested that I was a drug addict.

We couldn't withstand the onslaught. We had no money for polling, and barely enough to keep us on the air and advertising. On Election Day McConnell squeaked past me by a little over four percentage points. (Believe it or not, six years later he called me and asked for my endorsement against his Democratic opponent! Incredible.)

We had come so close, and it was a disappointment to lose to such an unscrupulous opponent. Kathy suggested that I run for County Judge/Executive again. But I was mentally and financially drained. I was done with politics—but not with public service.

CHAPTER FIFTEEN

D.C. Commissioner
For Public Health

After the letdown of the Senate defeat, Kathy and I got a call from Pamela Harriman inviting us to visit her in Barbados to recuperate. We had become friends with her and her husband, Averell Harriman, and they had come to the Derby as our guests. Pam had met Averell in England during the Second World War, when she was married to Randolph Churchill. She was dedicated to the Democratic Party and particularly to the Senate—she had set up a political action committee, PamPAC, to help Democrats win. We relished the opportunity to think through next steps in the warm breezes and waters of the Caribbean.

During the campaign against McConnell, I had worked very closely on my healthcare policy proposal with Massachusetts Sen. Ted Kennedy's top aide on the issue, David Nexon. David was the staff director of the Health subcommittee of the Senate's Health, Education, Labor and Pensions Committee and had very patiently made time to work with me on what proved to be a fairly detailed campaign proposal. The fax machine was in widespread use back then, and we went back and forth sending faxes, making corrections and alterations. After the campaign and my loss to McConnell, I told

David that I really wanted to come to Washington to work on national health issues. I wanted to be in the heart of the action, and I couldn't see a position in Louisville that would allow this. David told me that Phil Johnston, who had been Massachusetts's Secretary of Health and Human Services under Gov. Michael Dukakis in the mid-1980s, was interested in promoting universal health coverage. When I met with Nexon and Johnston in Washington, we all immediately clicked. Phil and I decided to form a 501(c)3 nonprofit called Healthcare for America, to advocate universal health care coverage through the healthcare reform bill which Senator Kennedy was sponsoring.

I had gotten to know Ted during the early '70s through the Committee of 100, which I had been asked to join in 1969. Believing that labor shouldn't just concentrate on organizing and negotiating with employers but should also serve as the voice of progressive change in the United States, the great union leader Walter Reuther had established the Committee—for the specific purpose of advocating for universal healthcare—shortly before his untimely death in a plane crash in 1970. The Committee consisted of a mix of distinguished health professionals, including the pioneering heart surgeon Michael DeBakey, who helped develop the artificial heart. Max Fine was the Committee's brilliant executive director.

In the 1970's the Committee of 100 had helped develop Kennedy's single-payer program, and in 1970 I had been sent to testify about the program before the House Ways & Means Committee. At the time, Wilbur Mills, a potential 1972 presidential candidate, chaired the House Committee. Sitting at a podium much higher than the testimony table, he grilled me with various questions about coverage and feasibility. Mills proved to be a tough opponent of a single-payer health plan, and the bill never really got off the ground. (Mills' presidential bid did not go anywhere, and his national profile never recovered from a highly publicized incident in 1974 in which he was caught driving under the influence while in the company of an Argentine stripper known as Fanne Fox, who famously jumped into the Tidal Basin trying to avoid police.)

Over the years I had also interacted with Senator Kennedy through Democratic politics. Ted was always jovial and fun, and you generally felt good after being with him. He and his family had helped me raise money for the 1979 governor's race, and I had supported him in the 1980 Democratic presidential primary. Kathy and I were sitting in the balcony behind the rostrum when Ted gave his famous stemwinder at the 1980 Democratic National Convention. It was the most incredible political speech I've ever heard. He talked about true Democratic values and what Democrats have done for the country, particularly in the 20th century. Bob Shrum, Ted's longtime political adviser and speechwriter, had penned the speech for him. The whole convention went wild. President Carter then joined Kennedy on the stage and tried to get a picture with him to unify the party, but Teddy kept evading him. He was angry that Carter had failed to follow through on his campaign promise to push for national health insurance.

Ted came to Louisville during that Presidential campaign, and Kathy and I met him at the airport—as did a crowd of protestors carrying signs decrying his pro-choice position on abortion as well as his accident at Chappaquiddick eleven years earlier. "Well, I see some of my friends are greeting me here," he quipped. He had separated from his first wife, Joan, at that time (they would divorce in 1982), and I noticed he was wearing different colored socks. "Yes, that's the problem with not having a wife," he remarked when I pointed it out to him. A dozen years later, Ted would marry Washington lawyer Victoria Reggie. Vicki was really a breath of fresh air and is credited with helping Ted tame his womanizing and drinking habits. She has an effervescent personality and I always enjoy talking with her, especially because of her deep political values.

By the time I moved to D.C. to set up Healthcare for America with Phil Johnston, Ted had laid his presidential ambitions to rest and had settled into his role as master legislator. Phil and I set up an office near Capitol Hill, and over the next two years we developed a coalition of about twenty-five different health interests, from health providers to seniors' organizations to labor groups and church groups. Working so closely with Kennedy's office gave us a lot of credibility. The bill Kennedy sponsored in 1990 would require corporations and employers to either pay a certain amount of money for public health insurance or provide coverage for their employees. It was the most progressive piece of legislation at the time and even though George H.W. Bush was president, it seemed to have a chance of being enacted. But once again the bill never got off the ground because of opposition from insurance companies and conservative forces.

It is amazing to me that the idea of universal health care has advanced in such halting fits and starts in the United States over the years. Otto von Bismarck successfully established the first universal healthcare program generations ago in Germany in 1885, but the U.S. just can't seem to get there. In his 1912 Bull Moose campaign, Teddy Roosevelt introduced the concept of universal health insurance coverage, and his cousin Franklin Roosevelt also thought about pushing the issue—but he was concerned that politically it would compromise his beloved Social Security program. In his 1948 campaign, Harry Truman made a national health insurance plan his number one domestic program. In 1965, under President Lyndon Johnson, Medicare and Medicaid were established—but still no universal health care.

Senator Kennedy's single-payer program became the healthcare dream of progressives in the early 1970's, and seemed a realistic possibility back then. In 1970 even Richard Nixon had made what was, in retrospect, a reasonable proposal, which included an employer mandate—a so-called play or pay initiative not unlike the bill that Kennedy sponsored twenty years later in 1990. Liberals such as myself and Kennedy did not support Nixon's proposal at the time because we felt it wouldn't have achieved enough—so that opportunity was lost. Years later, Kennedy would rue that decision, realizing that he should have taken the limited success and fought to build on it later.

In 1992, when Bill Clinton was elected president largely on a universal health insurance platform, those of us at Healthcare for America thought the best strategy would be to fold our efforts in with whatever his new administration produced. Working with Ira Magaziner, Hillary Clinton took over developing healthcare legislation. Unfortunately, the proposals she and her advisors developed were so complex and confusing, they had very little support even among congressional Democrats. Hillary really tried, dedicating her first two years as First Lady to the issue, but her plan was never voted upon. Healthcare reform remained an unrealized dream from Truman through Nixon through Clinton and beyond. It would not be until 2009, with the Affordable Care Act (also known as Obamacare) that any progress was made. In the years since its initiation, Republicans in Congress have tried to repeal the ACA well over 50 times.

I feel it is important to stress that over the years not one of these health-care proposals—not Teddy Roosevelt's 1912 Bull Moose campaign proposal, not Ted Kennedy's single-payer program proposal, not Hillary Clinton's complex health plan proposal—has ever been pushing "socialized medicine", as so many conservatives and insurances companies have claimed. Socialized medicine is when the government owns and operates hospitals and health care facilities and employs doctors and other providers. This was not the case with any of the proposals mentioned above, all of which are more comparable to a Medicare for all plan.

To me it is unimaginable that a country of such affluence and development as ours has not yet achieved universal health coverage. No other industrialized country denies universal health coverage to its citizens. For instance, Texas is one of 11 states that have not adopted Medicaid expansion under the Affordable Care Act which would provide care to more low-income Texans. At the same time, Texas has no income tax and the highest number of uninsured citizens. These deficiencies became even starker in the COVID-19 epidemic.

*   *   *

I first met Malcolm "Mike" Peabody when I came to Washington in the early 90s. Mike descended from the Endicott Peabody family in Massachusetts. His father Endicott founded the prestigious Groton School and his brother Endicott served as Governor of Massachusetts.

Mike came to DC to work on public housing but identified public education as the most important civil rights for young students in Washington. He founded the charter school movement as the most important educational reform to the consternation of some of the traditionalists and the teacher unions. Mike persisted in having choice available for Washington students. In 1996, he helped found Friends of Choice in Urban Schools (FOCUS) which is the primary advocate for charter schools in Washington, DC. He asked me to serve on a board that advised and advocated for mental health and ancillary services at charter schools in DC - and it was an honor for me to do so. Today over half the schools in the district are charter schools and most are located in low income neighborhoods. The charter schools have challenged the traditional public schools and I think to the benefit of both of them though even today, the large majority of third through eighth graders have scored below grade level in reading and in math for many years, with a notable drop after COVID.

* * *

One of the joys of Washington has been meeting people like Johnny Allem. After a distinguished career in politics nationally, Johnny decided to get involved in politics and policy locally, serving in Marion Barry's administration as the Deputy Commissioner of the DC Mental Health system. A recovering alcoholic himself, he has dedicated his efforts to addiction health advocacy, founding Faces and Voices of Recovery and the Aquila Recovery Clinics. Johnny organizes a monthly roundtable of local figures involved in Washingon, DC politics and policy. I have been fortunate enough to be included, along with impressive figures such as Bernard Demczuk (a professor of African American history at George Washington University who worked in the administrations of two DC mayors and was a labor leader before that), and Tom Lindenfeld (a Democratic political consultant). We discuss many issues impacting the lives of Washingtonians, and one thing upon which we all agree is that Washington, DC should no longer be subject to taxation without representation and should be made a state.

I was fortunate to reconnect with my cousin, Abby Trafford, when I moved to DC. Abby was a health journalist at the Washington Post and a fellow dedicated liberal. We have enjoyed many conversations and commiserated over the need for policy changes in health in this county. We fondly remember singing Christmas carols at her home at Christmas.

*   *   *

I left Healthcare for America in 1993 in order to serve first as President of the Leukemia Society of America Research Foundation, and then as a Project Director at the National Association of Community Health Centers. Then in early 1995, I read a report that the District of Columbia had spent $1.6 billion on healthcare the previous fiscal year. That worked out to $3,000 for every man, woman and child in a city that had one of the country's worst mortality rates for infants and adults with ailments like cancer, AIDS and heart disease.

I went to my newly elected City Council member, Kathy Patterson, told her about my background and asked if I could help in any way. She said to go down to the Mayor's office because they were looking for a new Commissioner of Public Health. The Mayor at the time was Marion Barry.

I did as Patterson had suggested. I went down to City Hall and met with Mayor Barry. There was not a long line to see him. He and Mike Rogers, the City Administrator who functioned as his chief of staff, interviewed me—asking questions not only about my medical background and approach to public health but probing me about my experience working in a racially diverse community in Louisville. Apparently, I gave the right answers, because in short order Barry hired me as Washington's Commissioner for Public Health.

Marion Barry Jr. was a charismatic, compelling and colorful character who would become the most powerful D.C. politician of his generation. The son of a Mississippi sharecropper, Barry was a bright guy who got a master's degree in chemistry from Fisk College in Nashville before coming to Washington to become a civil rights leader and a political player. In 1977, when he was a member of the D.C.'s City Council, his mystique was enhanced when he was shot during the siege of the District Building by members of the Hanafi movement—a small group of Muslims that had splintered from the Nation of Islam. His wound was serious, but he recovered, and the experience, but it enhanced his mystique, and by 1978 he was running for Mayor of the District. In that first run for Mayor, The Washington Post gave Barry a glorious endorsement, saying "we think that the hard problems and bright opportunities now before the District demand exactly the qualities and talents that Marion Barry will bring to the job." Barry won that election and would go on to serve three consecutive terms as Mayor.

When I first met Barry at the U.S. Conference of Mayors in the '80s, he had a great reputation for having accomplished many things and in general was considered a good progressive. He had brought black and white people together, created jobs for young people in the summer and provided housing for middle income individuals. His administration advocated for and employed a lot of black citizens. Although he wore fancy clothes and drove an expensive car, he lived in Ward 8, the city's poorest community. African Americans in particular believed that he understood their plight and would never neglect them, and they identified with him strongly. He was a champion for the poor.

By the time I arrived in Washington in the mid-1990s, however, Barry's image had been badly blemished. In January of 1990, during his third term, the FBI and the D.C. police had caught Barry in a drug sting set up by a former girlfriend. A devastating video that went viral globally shows Barry in a room at D.C.'s Vista International Hotel at a rendezvous with his former girlfriend taking a long drag on a crack pipe. The room is then stormed by FBI agents who throw the Mayor against the wall with outstretched arms and read him his rights. "Bitch set me up—I shouldn't have come here," the Mayor famously mutters.

Although Barry was sent to rehab and then served six months in federal prison, in the black community he remained quite popular and was still widely seen as a great leader. When he was released from jail, he returned to public life, winning first a seat on the City Council in 1992, and then in 1994—just four years after leaving office as Mayor amidst great scandal—a fourth term as Mayor.

Working with Barry was a tumultuous experience, to say the least. Shortly after we came to D.C. Kathy and I had dinner with Kay

Graham, the publisher of The Washington Post, and she bemoaned the fact that the Washington Post had endorsed Marion so effusively in his first run in 1978. The Post had reported on his subsequent erratic behavior and drug addiction. But worse than his personal failings was the general perception of a dysfunctional urban administration. In fact, when I joined the administration in 1995, the departments which oversaw public housing, foster children, prison inmates and the mentally ill were all in court receivership for basically malfunctioning and inadequately caring for their constituents. Barry had run the city and its budget recklessly, and the deficit was over $700 million. In an attempt to remedy this, Congress under Republicans had just created the DC Financial Control Authority, which essentially took total control over the city spending.

My first day on the job gave me a taste of what I could expect. The Department of Health was located in D.C.'s Chinatown neighborhood, which today is a vibrant commercial area but in the mid-1990s was rundown. There was a DJ broadcasting from outside the building's front door to raise money—for the Health Department employees, it turned out. What do they need, I asked? Toilet paper—the city hadn't finalized the maintenance contract for the building. Oh.

Upon entering my new office, I asked how to call someone in Maryland—I had a friend there, Dr. Mohammad Akhter, who had been my predecessor as Commissioner. I'd met him a few times at national meetings and wanted to consult with him about the new job. The answer: If you want to call long distance, use the payphone on the street. Oh.

When I was able to get him on the phone, Dr. Akhter gave me some useful advice. First he said that the Health Department problems—inflexibility, bureaucracy, slowness—were endemic to the city government generally. Second, he told me never to try to fire someone; it would lead to litigation, any problems you'd had in life would be dug up—and you wouldn't be able to fire the person in any case. Oh.

Next came a telephone call from a congressman: *A constituent of mine died in D.C. six months ago and the family can't collect life insurance because you guys haven't done the autopsy report.* A call to the medical examiner's office brought the news that the District of Columbia was 500 autopsies in arrears. Worse: The crematorium had broken down, so bodies were accumulating. Oh my.

Before my first day was through, I found myself in federal court because the U.S. Justice Department had sued the District over its administration of D.C. Village, a 75-year-old nursing home. The suit included allegations of recklessly poor care—things like patients having their legs amputated because of chronic bed sores. Wow— horrific. Clearly my new job was not going to be dull.

*   *   *

The budget for the entire city of Louisville in my last year as mayor in 1985 was a third less than that of D.C.'s Department of Health when I started (though congressional budget-cutting quickly changed that). I had to deal with an impenetrable and intractable bureaucracy and, seemingly, a new crisis every day. Most of the city's health services were compromised by equipment failures: air-conditioners wouldn't work in patient settings; city vehicles, necessary to follow up on infection contacts or to transport lab specimens, didn't work; some clinical areas still used rotary phones, and e-mail use was not even a dream. It was hard to believe that a city could be so dysfunctional, let alone the capital of the United States.

Running Louisville had nothing on working in city government in Washington, D.C. New treatments were coming online to help manage HIV/AIDS, a serious problem in D.C. We had to get approval from 60 offices in the city government before we could apply for federal aid to help the afflicted residents. Dr. Akhter commented that trying to improve the system while it was operating was like flying a plane and fixing it at the same time. It was bound to crash.

Part of the problem was that just before I became the Commissioner of Public Health, the new Republican Congress had created the D. C. Financial Control Authority to oversee the city government and its operations, impinging on District home rule. Congress rightly felt that D.C. government was not being run efficiently or appropriately, and every contract was scrutinized carefully, which of course slowed everything down.

I did my best to find creative solutions. I contracted with the U.S. Department of Defense to wipe out the autopsy backlog. They took over the contract for this service and almost immediately cleaned up the problem. The Defense Department claimed that this was the highest number of deaths that they'd seen at one time since Vietnam. The regular contracting services for HIV/AIDS and other health issues was another problem. I had good connections with the Clinton Administration, and I was able to get many of these services contracted through the federal Department of Health and Human Services (which unhappily required payment of 5 percent of the total grant).

In the summer of 1996 it was very hot, and the power went out at D.C. General, including the morgue. And, of course, the crematorium had broken down. There were many unclaimed bodies in the large refrigerators, and the morgue had to keep unclaimed corpses for six months. With the power out, bodies would start to decompose. We had only two refrigerated trucks to pick up deceased bodies, so we rotated bodies through the two trucks, putting them in for a number of hours and then bringing in other bodies that hadn't been refrigerated. This process went on for days.

*   *   *

HIV/AIDS had begun to appear in Washington in the '80s, shortly after the epidemics emerged in San Francisco and New York. There was a lot of IV drug use in D.C., and sexual transmission became widespread. By 1996, Washington had the highest HIV rate of any American city, meaning that an enormous number of its citizens were immuno-compromised. In 1995 and '96 the so-called "cocktail" of drugs which would convert AIDS from a death sentence to a chronic disease, were just arriving on the scene. But the city government, with its inflexible bureaucracy, was ill-equipped and unwilling to deal with this health crisis.

Once again the incredible backlog of work required to pass the contracting procedures of the District government under the newly established Financial Control Authority complicated everything. I hung a huge chart on the wall of my office to keep track of the contracts and the different approval processes. Working with Mel Wilson, who was the director of the city's Agency for HIV/AIDS, I would call the unit—usually in the D.C. Department of Human Service—where the contract appeared to be held up. The conversation would go like this; "Hello Mrs. W_____. This is Harvey Sloane and I'm wondering why the contract numbered 4004 has not been approved." Often this person would respond by saying "I never got that proposal." Then I would say that "Mr. Wilson of the HIV/AIDS department says that he delivered it to your office a week ago." And then the response was "Ok, bring me up another." At that time everything was on paper—not electronic—and it was all filed haphazardly.

Barry's administration was too timid about making reforms to the system. Since the contract system was dysfunctional, I advocated for turning all the contract arrangements over to a private firm—pay them a fee and then fix our system in government. When it was functional again, we could bring the contracting back in-house. Paul Offner, who had come in from Wisconsin to run the D.C. Medicaid program around the same time I started as Commissioner, joined me in pushing for this, but we never got anywhere.

Another amazing friend I made was a somewhat hunched over and very intense man who came up to me early on in my tenure. Freeland Henry Carde III, or Hank as his friends called him, was a tremendous figure. He had grown up in a Navy family, and he signed up himself in 1968 after graduating from Yale. During a twenty-year Navy career, he became a SEAL and did three tours in Vietnam. Along the way he got a master's degree from the Naval Postgraduate School and also graduated from the Army War College. He received two Bronze Stars.

Hank was gay. He had retired in 1988 from a strategic planning position with the Joint Chiefs when he learned that his partner, Ben Hartman, was ill with AIDS. Hank took care of Ben, but he died later that year. Infected himself, Hank then volunteered with the Whitman-Walker clinic in Washington to be a personal care assistant for AIDS patients. He gradually saw that the money the federal government allotted D.C. through the Ryan White legislation (named for a young boy who contracted HIV through his dentist) was not getting to various private treatment centers like Whitman-Walker. Hank developed a newsletter, called A Letter to Friends, which he faxed out most mornings at 3 AM to the national and local government leaders and HIV/AIDS activists that were working to bring medications and care to AIDS patients in the District government.

The same steely determination that had earned Hank his SEAL trident and those two Bronze Stars informed his activism. In 1991 he became exasperated with the employment office in the District since the office had not filled a federally funded position for the HIV/AIDS department for a number of months. He was frail, having lost about a third of his body weight from his illness. But he held a three-day hunger strike outside the office of then-Mayor Sharon Pratt Kelly. They didn't want a picture in The Washington Post of Hank dying in front of City Hall, so the HIV personnel slots were funded and filled in short order.

I had Hank come in and talk about the importance of a functioning healthcare delivery system to a class I was teaching at the George Washington School of Public Health. He preached advocacy.

He obviously sparked the students' imagination and wonder. He was only able to stay about a half hour because of his illness.

Hank kept sending out his newsletter right up until his death in 1998. Dr. Patricia Hawkins, who was the Associate Executive Director of the Whitman-Walker clinic, remembers that Hank would get exasperated but never discouraged—and he never gave up. Whitman-Walker eventually renamed their AIDS foundation The Hank Carde AIDS Foundation.

Hank asked me to be sure that when he died his Yale obituary would note that he was not a "wimp." He was definitely not that. He was truly a servant of the Lord.

*   *   *

About a month after I became Commissioner, I confronted problems with D.C. Village, a city-owned nursing home. It had over 100 totally indigent patients, many of whom had suffered gunshot wounds and were crippled because of spinal injury or other debilitating assaults. Many were chronically ill with diabetes or senility.

The healthcare financing administration of the Federal Department of Health and Human Services visited D.C. Village, prompting a federal judge to issue a consent decree requiring that the city close the nursing home because of its terrible conditions. The three main areas of public concern were: patients being restrained, the decubitus ulcers—more commonly known as bed sores—and the fact that Foley catheters for incontinent patients often were not clean.

In 1995, The Washington Post ran an editorial asking, "What kind of workers leave patients restrained in beds gathering bedsores, confined to wheelchairs for hours without being taken to the bathroom? Who would leave curtains stained with feces next to their patients' beds? What kind of employees would use dirt-encrusted tubes to feed disabled residents unable to eat solid food?" I started to make daily rounds at D.C. Village to get my own answers to these good questions. What I found was that the staff was deeply embarrassed and demoralized--they had neither adequate staff nor basic supplies such as liquid soap and appropriate garments. We had to scrounge around to get soap for the facility. Soap is obviously the first line of defense against infection. To make things worse, the District was out of cash.

After two-and-a-half weeks of working on the problems at D.C. Village I was able to report that it "had really come together." The staff was working diligently to make improvements. Restraints on patients had been reduced from 59 to 10. Decubitus ulcers had been reduced and were better managed. (But an ongoing problem was that when a resident went to a hospital, they often got a pressure sore, which he or she then brought back to D.C. Village.) The staff had the Foley catheters cleaned for incontinent patients. Cleanliness throughout the facility improved, and it no longer smelled.

During this makeover campaign we also started moving patients to other, private facilities. Ironically the patients had a demonstration about not wanting to leave D.C. Village, and the court-appointed monitor, Dr. Harriet Fields, told us that some of the nursing homes to which the patients would be moved were definitely of poorer quality. Meanwhile, the nursing staff were all diligently putting together systems for continued improvements.

Despite all these efforts, in July the Financial Control Authority mandated that D.C. Village be closed in a week. On receiving the order to close D.C. Village, our major problem was where to outsource the patients, some of whom were very sick. Some private facilities would have to accept these patients, who were not easy to care for. Many of the nursing homes were reluctant to take on severely-disabled patients, especially since the only remuneration they would get was Medicaid—which was not enough to cover expenses.

I spent July 3rd going around to these different private facilities trying to get an agreement from them to take care of our D.C. Village patients, with mixed success. Sister Eileen Egan, the wonderful kind-hearted Administrator of Providence Hospital, was willing to do whatever possible for the public good. Providence had a nursing home and she agreed to take a number of the patients. Other facilities were less good-hearted.

That same day, another bombshell dropped. A Washington Post reporter called and informed me that the E. Coli count in the D.C. water was dangerously high. This meant human or animal waste could have been in the water. One of the frustrations of being the Commissioner of Health was that environmental information was not sent to the Health Department, but to the Department of Public Works—which was why I only heard about the outbreak from the press.

So how to handle the water problem? You've got to give people a warning about this kind of risk—the city had a high number of immunocompromised residents and E. coli could indicate potentially deadly contamination in a water supply. So I told the Post that people should boil their water before drinking it.

I was thinking of public health for the whole community, but I made one critical mistake: I forgot to tell Mayor Marion Barry.

The next day, in the middle of the Fourth of July parade, Barry went berserk, demanding water to drink on television to prove that the city water was safe. Our relationship never recovered.

Kathy and I were at a lunch at the home of Peter and Florence Hart when the Mayor's office called me. As Kathy and I left for a chaotic news conference, Peter yelled: "There you go again, Sloane! Thinking public health over public relations!"

It didn't help that Congress stepped in as well: During an unrelated hearing with an EPA official, Congressional members started asking the agency to test the D.C. water—we drink the water too, they said. (Never mind the hundreds of thousands of people who were exposed to it by mere fact of D.C. residency.) Responding to Congress, the EPA took control of testing D.C. water.

While the event did nothing to improve my relationship with the Mayor and his staff, I hope that it did save the lives of some of our elderly or otherwise immunocompromised citizens.

*   *   *

My crowning debacle with Barry's administration came in mid-1997 when I attempted to contract out to the federal Department of Health and Human Services the process of hiring new staff for the Health Department. We had tried to hire a White House staffer during the Clinton administration, an African American physician who wanted experience in D.C. government, but even with an intercession from Barry himself the process had dragged on interminably. The physician eventually withdrew his application. Firing anyone was also next to impossible.

Barry really didn't like my trying to enlist the federal government. He claimed that we were not a subsidiary of theirs and declared that the District was going to run its own affairs—and then he fired me. (This backfired on him: Congress put in a stipulation after my termination that he could no longer hire or fire anyone without its approval.)

Barry was a bright guy and had been a key civil rights leader. In 1996, during my tenure, he handled the Million Man March to Washington without incident because he had the respect of African Americans around the country. He was for many years a good mayor, but by 1997, especially having to deal with a suspicious Congress, he was out of his element, events were out of his control and the city was deeply in debt. He and his team were perversely conservative in the face of a massive failure of city government; they were too tepid when bold action was required. The inability to handle city matters directly—as a result of the newly established federal Financial Control Authority —only made things worse.

My whole experience as Commissioner of Public Health for D.C. had been astounding. When I was Mayor of Louisville we had difficulties on occasion and sometimes getting things done took longer than I would have liked. But the Louisville's city government was functional, and we were able to handle crises. The D.C. government was really dysfunctional and just couldn't operate as a normal local government should.

This unfortunate state of affairs would not be rectified until after Barry's last term, when Anthony Williams, the chief financial officer of the D.C, Financial Control Board, was elected mayor. Gradually, in a tough slog through his eight years in office, Mayor Williams was able to bring stability and operational efficiency to the District.

Unfortunately for Barry, his personal habits of drinking and using drugs affected his health, and as he approached the end at age 78 he had cardiovascular disease, diabetes, prostate cancer, and kidney failure. Despite all the dysfunction of city services during his tenure as Mayor, and despite his scandals and instability personally— in addition to his problems with drugs he was married four times— over the years Marion Barry maintained his popularity with many, and he now ranks as a legendary political figure.

*   *   *

Years after my job as Commissioner of Health for the District, when Muriel Bowser was nominated to be Mayor of the District in 2014, I took it upon myself to be a minister without portfolio for the city and to make recommendations about the emergency medical service in Washington, which was famously a disaster. The highest-profile example occurred in 2006, when 63-year-old former New York Times reporter David Rosenbaum was found semiconscious on a sidewalk near his home. He had been beaten with a metal pipe and robbed but the ambulance technicians who treated him assumed he was just drunk, and he was not treated with the required urgency. He died two days later. Another terrible event occurred in 2014 when an African American man collapsed across from a fire house and none of the firefighters helped him with cardio-pulmonary resuscitation.

The city of Seattle is regarded as having the best EMS service in the country. It is the best because it is medically-driven: Every activity—such as the time of call, the paramedic's arrival time at the hospital—is recorded and the actual service detailed. Then each run is carefully analyzed. Seattle has been able to reduce its deaths from cardiac arrest by over 60 percent. Washington D.C. had an 18 percent survival rate. Also, Seattle had a very active CPR education program for its citizenry to give immediate lifesaving support before medical personnel could arrive.

As part of my volunteer crusade, I shared all of these incidents and suggestions with Mayor Bowser's staff after she took office. I was able to get the administration to have the Fire Dept start a CPR program for the citizens of the District. And Mayor Bowser hired the head of the Seattle EMS to come and run the service in Washington, which has greatly improved.

CHAPTER SIXTEEN

Zero To Three—
Reach Out And Read

After my abrupt dismissal from my chaotic duties as D.C.'s Commissioner of Health, I was casting about for new ways to pursue my on-going work in the fields of public health and public service. One area I have remained committed to ever since my classes with Dr. Benjamin Spock at Case Western Medical School back in the 60s is the crucial matter of children's development from age zero to three. The national child poverty rate in the U.S. has lingered at around 15 percent for decades. This is not acceptable in an affluent society such as ours. Poverty damages children for life, and the issue is complicated by the fact that these children are often from single-parent families. The COVID relief bill which President Biden signed in March 2021 was a good first start in addressing this issue, and I'm hopeful his new childcare tax credit will be continued because it could reduce the child poverty rate by as much as 40 percent. But these measures will not resolve all the problems parents face in the very difficult years of zero to three.

Physicians and child development experts agree that there are four essential guidelines for the first three years of life: DO: NUTURE and STIMULATE. DO NOT: ABUSE or NEGLECT. If a child is not nurtured and stimulated in those first years, she just won't reach her potential intellectually or emotionally. A child that is abused or neglected certainly won't reach his emotional requirements for adulthood. The Nurse-Family Partnership program, started by Dr. David Olds in Denver, has targeted this important span of life to great effect, fostering supportive relationships through home visitations of trained nurses with at-risk mothers. What started as a pilot in a handful of small communities has grown and 40 states now have such a program. But ultimately the parents are the first teachers. They need to have an understanding of how to bring a child through those formative years. The most significant brain development occurs from zero to three. A child learns how to walk, talk, interact with others at that time. In many ways being a parent is the most important and demanding job for adults who have children. Unfortunately, many young parents are not themselves equipped emotionally, and they need support.

Presidents Clinton and Obama acted on early child development. But there hasn't been a concerted effort focused exclusively on that very crucial period from age zero to three. There have been many studies about improvement in behavior and learning from appropriate early child stimulation and literacy. Economists have shown it's not only important from a sociological standpoint but also from a financial one. Children don't repeat grades, there's less incarceration and crime, there's more stability in jobs and generally less low-productivity and poor performance. Indeed, the Nobel laureate economist James Heckman of the University of Chicago has demonstrated that quality early development programs can have ripple effects which not only benefit the children involved but their children as well. None of this is rocket science. As I said, I learned these principles in medical school at

Case Western when Dr. Benjamin Spock taught us about child development in 1960. But as a country we have consistently failed to step up and focus on this issue effectively.

One evening not long after I had left my job as D.C. Commissioner of Health, Kathy and I were having a drink with our friend Hodding Carter and his wife, Pat Darian. Hodding came from a Mississippi family steeped in journalism and civil rights, and when I first got to know him as a fellow board member of The Century Foundation, he was the President of the Knight-Ridder Foundation, which was funded by the Knight-Ridder media empire. The foundation had a long practice of financing educational programs in the communities where it owned newspapers. During the course of that evening I talked about my interest in early child development and education, and in the course of our conversation Hodding mentioned that he was having trouble getting educational programs going in Camden, New Jersey and Gary, Indiana- two challenging cities in the mid-'90s. I suggested that I could help set up a program called "Reach Out and Read". This was a program for young infants and children to help them make the associative connections needed for reading and increase their vocabulary. The basis of the program was that the mother or father of the newborn child—or both—would be prescribed by the pediatrician age-appropriate books for the parent to read or show to the child. The American Academy of Pediatricians had endorsed it very positively.

The mere act of speaking around children can have profound effects. A study conducted at the University of Kansas in the 1990s— a very complex study which involved recording the dinner conversations of two groups of families for three years—estimated that by the age of four, the children whose families received public assistance had heard 30 million fewer words than their peers in families where the parents were professors at a university. That gap shapes the rest of their lives, with the kids who were exposed to more words at a young age developing greater facility not only for language but better cognitive processing and self-regulation skills.

"Reach out and Read" not only helped parents bond with their children, it also helped the children develop to their potential more fully. It was in keeping with the emerging research about the importance of a child's first three years of development. During the years a child learns to read, talk, walk and socialize, she or he develops vocabulary by hearing and seeing words. If a child doesn't really get a grasp of words at that stage, she or he will probably be limited in school and life.

To set up a viable "Reach Out and Read" program you have to get the community backing to contribute books, have volunteers help parents read to their infants and have buy-in from a hospital with pediatrics or a group of physicians. After talking with Hodding, I got to work and set up "Reach Out and Read" programs in both Camden and Gary, and I also helped start one in Washington, D.C. I found this work both interesting and satisfying—but the fact was I was itching to return to my public-health roots in some more intense, full-time capacity. When a former professor of mine at the Cleveland Clinic, Richard Farmer, called me up and asked if I wanted to go to Russia to work on HIV/AIDS and tuberculosis for the European Medical Education Program (EMEP), a non-governmental organization, I immediately said yes.

CHAPTER SEVENTEEN

To Russia—
To Fight HIV and TB

I have been intrigued by Russia ever since my 1965 trip there with Paula Steichen, during which we visited Lenin's tomb. Upon returning from that trip, I had read *Ten Days That Shook the World,* the 1919 book by American journalist John Reed, who was himself a communist. The book chronicles Reed's eyewitness account of the October 1917 Bolshevik Revolution. He got to know many of its leaders, especially Vladimir Lenin. Reed died of typhus in 1920 and is buried in the Kremlin Wall Necropolis in Red Square, one of only three Americans honored in such a way.

In the late 90's my former professor Farmer and his colleague Dr. Ed Burger—whose career had included stints with the White House science office and with the U.S. delegations to the Organization for Economic Cooperation and Development—had jointly developed the EMEP (Eurasian Medical Education Program) to bring American physicians and specialists to Russia to train Russian doctors on the treatment, prevention and control of tuberculosis, HIV and cardiovascular disease. The Russian government required that Russian physicians get continuing medical education in their respective fields of expertise in their home country, but their approach to medicine in general was radically different than that of the U.S. Russian physicians, for instance, were not allowed to attend international medical meetings or read medical journals—not exactly conducive to keeping up with new medical discoveries and treatments. Farmer, with the help of Burger and another EMEP associate Roberta Wirth, had managed to recruit the American College of Physicians (ACP) to join in the EMEP in its continuing medical education for Russian physicians. With 152,000 physician members from 145 countries, the ACP, which was founded in 1915, is the largest organization of medical specialists in the US, and its ongoing education programs with American physicians are highly respected.

Having the ACP join the EMEP in Russia gave the organization great credibility, and also allowed us to recruit talented specialists in the fields we were targeting—TB, HIV, diabetes and cardiovascular disease. Russian physician-specialists were also invited to come to the U.S. to witness our methods for treating these diseases. The support for this unusual program truly took a village, as they say. United States Aid for International Development (USAID) funded the EMEP program throughout its years, and in 2008 I was able to get the National Institutes of Health's Office of AIDS Research to support our HIV component. In 2003 the Gates Foundation contributed a generous grant to support the tuberculosis program. And in the U.S. Senate, Vermont Sen. Patrick Leahy, then the top Democrat on the State, Foreign Operations and Related Programs subcommittee of the Appropriations Committee, would be an invaluable ally.

During my time with the EMEP, I would make 40 trips to Russia over 12 years and grow to admire the Russian people, if not its authoritarian and discriminatory political leadership.

*   *   *

Russia is the largest country in the world geographically, spanning eleven time zones, and is a powerful player globally, particularly on the nuclear front. But when it comes to health care, Russia is essentially a developing country. The country's general health problems date back at least to the Bolshevik Revolution in 1917. Prior to the revolution, medicine was viewed as a prestigious profession and physicians were well compensated. But after the 1917 revolution, Lenin and his followers felt that clinical medicine was *too* prominent, and it was deliberately downgraded in importance. Public health and personal medical care were deemed state responsibilities, and doctors were prohibited from engaging in international meetings and publishing papers. Then in the '30s, under Soviet rule, there was an enormous increase in the number of physicians and hospital beds. Patients who were hospitalized were kept for much longer than in Western countries—not an economical way to treat disease. Since physician salaries were kept low, there was a lot of what they called "envelope-passing medicine"—referring to off-the-books payments doctors would get in return for preferential treatment. The low compensation meant the field became dominated by women, as men sought careers in which they could make more money. While in Russia, I would often hear that approximately 85 percent of Russian physicians are women.

Between 1992 and 2010 the Russian population was either stagnant or shrinking. One of the reasons was that Russian women were not having babies because it was too expensive. In addition, for the last three decades the principal causes of morbidity in Russia have been cardiovascular and cerebral vascular disease. Premature death in turn has caused decreased fertility, which has led to population loss. This level of population decline—a net yearly loss of 4,000 to 9,000 people—is without precedent in Russia outside of wartime. By the middle of the '90s, life expectancy for Russian men had dropped to 59 and for Russian women to 72. This differential between men and women was largely due to cardiovascular disease, alcohol consumption and accidents.

Through EMEP's efforts we were able to get permission to bypass the central government in Moscow and St. Petersburg, and instead offer assistance directly to regional Russian authorities in the Russian Far East and Siberia. To help overcome 70 years of isolation from Western principles of treatment and research, EMEP provided continuing medical education to Russian physicians. This was a good fit with the existing Russian medical system, which requires physicians to get re-certified every five years. We brought Russian specialists in the fields of cardiovascular care, tuberculosis and HIV over to the U.S., and they studied at Georgetown University, Johns Hopkins University and the New Jersey Medical Center. A very effective Russian physician and friend, Ioulia Vvedenskaya, served as organizer, interpreter and coordinator for the trips. The most significant visit was always to the National Jewish Medical Center in Denver, because two of the top TB experts—Drs. Michael Iseman and Leonid Heifets, a Russian physician who had come to the U.S.—were based there. These residencies typically lasted one to two weeks and included clinical experience and laboratory diagnosis.

*   *   *

In general, our EMEP teams met with great cooperation from the Russian physicians. At times there could be some disconnect between the Russian and American cultures, but I found that all the *individual* Russians with whom I came into contact, both in the medical field and in everyday life, were as friendly and concerned as any neighbors I have had here in the United States. They are a good people whose leaders do not measure up to them.

One example among many: Our coordinator and interpreter in Ekaterinburg was Maria Syrochkina, a woman in her early 30s with three children. She was a pediatrician, spoke English well and even published a book with her grandmother about female diseases. Her husband, Boris, would drive for us. Our American lecturers would write up the lectures and slides in English and Maria would translate them. She would be the translator as well as a physician specialist who answered questions. Maria had academic standing with the Ural State Medical Academy, and a keen sense of the medical and political politics of her region, which was Sverdlovsk.

She and her family lived in an apartment building and on special occasions treated us to a dinner. On occasion she would invite us to the school musical performances by her children. She had a great sensitivity about the welfare for her children, especially her boys, and vowed if they were to be inducted into the army where extensive abuse took place, she would take her entire family out of the country. Maria and her children now live in Israel.

*   *   *

The U.S. and Russia have more of a history of partnership than most people realize. It dates back at least 100 years. As described in the book *The Russian Job; The Forgotten Story of How America Saved the Soviet Union from Ruin*, by Douglas Smith, in 1921 Russia faced the worst famine in its history. Three years of drought, the First World War and the Bolshevik Revolution had caused disastrous hunger and despair among the Russian people. The Bolshevik government feared that the populace might rise up against it in desperation. There were terrible stories in the Soviet press, such as the one about the mother of four children who had to cut up her fifth child, their dead sister, and use her to feed the others. There was another report of a woman who refused to let her dead husband's body go. "We won't give him up," she screamed to the authorities who came to take it away. "We will eat him ourselves, he's ours!"

Vladimir Lenin understood the connection between food and power, and he feared that the Soviet revolution would fail if relief did not come to the people. He found his rescue plan in the most unlikely place: Herbert Hoover, the future American President, had headed the American Relief Administration (ARA) during the First World War, an organization which had helped seven million Belgians escape starvation after the war by bringing a massive amount of food from the U.S. Lenin approached Hoover about bringing food to the Soviet Union, where ten million people were starving. Hoover and the ARA agreed and over the next two years arranged relief for ten million men, women and children across an area that ranged from the Baltic Sea to the Ural Mountains to the Siberian border—over one million square miles of territory. This was at a time when the Soviet transportation system was in post-war shambles. It was the largest humanitarian operation in history and prevented a catastrophe of incalculable proportions.

Few Americans or Russians knew of the American relief effort. Hoover didn't dare advertise it in Red Scare America, especially as he was heading back into the Harding administration. Lenin did not want to propagate the knowledge that America had largely saved the Soviet state.

Decades later, in March of 1941, President Franklin Roosevelt used the Lend-Lease program to deliver $12 billion worth of supplies to the Soviet Union between 1941 and 1945, to support the effort against Nazi Germany. The supplies included 15,000 planes, 9,000 tanks, 362,000 trucks and 15.4 million pairs of army boots. We were acting in our own self-interest at the time—if Russia folded as they did in the First World War there was a little doubt that Hitler would overrun Great Britain. In 1942 the Soviet Union, in a campaign that suffered one million casualties, finally stopped Hitler's advances at Stalingrad. When the allies launched D-Day—the largest seaborne invasion in history—in 1944, most of the German army was fighting the Soviets in the East. The Soviet Union lost 27 million people, and we lost 400,000. This American-Soviet alliance was both a noble and a successful one. It is tragic that there is so little in common between our countries now, as exemplified by the current crisis in Ukraine.

One of my first trips for the EMEP was in 2000, to Ekaterinburg in Siberia, the city where the Czar's family had been murdered after the Russian Revolution. I was walking the streets one evening when an older man approached me and asked, "Are you American?" I nodded and then he said, "Uncle Joe [Stalin] and FDR were partners and now we're partners again." He clasped his hands and smiled. It seemed a promising omen and illustrated where things stood after decades of Cold War. After the breakup of the Soviet Union in 1990, European states and the U.S. had sought a partnership which would benefit both sides. USAID contributed to Russia to help with specific problems; Russia also received private support from the Gates and Soros Foundations. It was a moment of promise.

Siberia is one of the biggest and least-populated parts of Russia. In the American lexicon it's associated with prisons—to be sent to Siberia is to be exiled to somewhere hopelessly bleak. "The Gulag Archipelago," Aleksandr Solzhenitsyn's masterwork, highlighted the immense number of prisons Stalin set up, largely for people who were political opponents.

Although only around 36 million people live in Siberia, it provides the country with a wealth of natural resources: gas, oil, diamonds, gold, zinc, nickel and cobalt. And it is often unimaginably cold. In my work with the EMEP I went to Yakutsk on the upper Lena River, just a few hundred miles south of the Arctic Circle. The temperature was 30 degrees below zero centigrade, but the town activities carried on as usual and children went to school. The Lena River was frozen over so cars drove directly over it to the other side. The whole community was encased in permafrost. The residents dealt with the weather as routine. Some even ate ice cream in spite of the oppressive cold outside. Our physician host sometimes braved the weather without an overcoat.

I went to Ekaterinburg with the EMEP again in 2003. We had a wonderful coordinator there, Alexi, who was Russian and spoke good English. In the early morning of January 14th, he drove me to Nizhny Tagil, a highly productive metallurgical and militaristic city of about

350,000 where the Soviet T-34 tank, which beat the Nazis in the "Great Patriotic War", was made. The sun does not really come up until about 10 o'clock in the morning at that time of year in Russia. Alexi and I left around 7am and arrived at Nizhny Tagil just as the sun was rising in the East. It was spectacular. However, as we were approaching the city, I saw smokestacks belching yellow and orange plumes all over the city. I asked Alexi if the residents ever demanded cleaner air. Yes, he said, on one occasion they all stopped work and demonstrated in the streets. The owners of the plants told the citizens that if that's how they wanted it, the factories would close. The workers needed the work and couldn't move their families to another city because the government made it almost impossible to change residences. So the factories belched on.

Nizhny Tagil produced a lot of weapons for the Russian wars in Afghanistan and Chechnya as well as for buyers from areas like the Middle East. The city hosts an armament exhibition every summer. Our team attended one: Buyers came from all over the world to purchase everything from AK-47s to tanks and missiles. Exhibitors shot shells off periodically which landed on a mountain about a mile away to demonstrate their destructive power.

My reason for visiting was Nizhny Tagil's "tuberculosis prison", a jail with nothing but tuberculosis-infected inmates. The Russian prison system had become a breeding ground not just for the disease (in 2002 more than 79,000 inmates had active infections) but for its drug-resistant forms. It was about 25 degrees below zero centigrade as we approached the prison. The building had ice on its roof and every window was shut. I knocked on the iron door, which was iron and seven feet tall, and the guard let us in. He then proceeded to take away our passports and everything else in our possession, including pocketknives and cellphones. He then let us through the iron gate, which clanked as it was turned. One had the feeling that this could be a long stay.

Dmitri, the head of the prison, came to meet us and was dressed all in black. He was well-built and had a gruff air about him. The prison's head surgeon, who spoke English, acted as translator and introduced everyone. Dimitri had fought for the Soviet Union in Afghanistan in the late '70s and early '80s. I explained to him what our program was about and that we wanted to see if we could be of any assistance to him and his TB physicians. Wearing protective masks, we went up to the floor where TB surgery was done and found some very friendly surgeons, one of whom spoke reasonable English. He explained that they didn't have any TB drugs to treat the disease, so they dealt with infection through surgery. He would open up men's chests and take out the TB-infected lobes in the lungs. In those who had spinal TB, they did a miraculous job of fusing the spinal column at various levels, after removing the infected vertebrae. They did all of this without adequate protective equipment such as surgical gloves. I asked the prison director if there was a problem with TB among the staff. He said that 27 of his staff had contracted TB in the last year; there could not have been more than 100 people total on staff, so 27 was a large number.

The head surgeon took me into the room where the TB patients were sequestered. It was about 30' by 30' and the 32 men in it were triple-bunked. The one window was frosted shut, and there was no ventilation. The men looked anxious and scared—I'm sure wondering about what was going to happen to them. It was a sight that I will never forget for the rest of my life.

The commander of the prison warmed up to me after he saw my interest was genuine and said that they would be grateful for any help. I said I would do everything I could to encourage not only the provision of tubercular medications but also adequate beds and protective clothing for the staff.

I left the prison really shaken by the experience. It was truly the most daunting—and haunting—of all my experiences in Russia. I vowed that I would do everything I could to get them equipment, but most importantly tubercular drugs. I petitioned the regional health authorities in Russia and brought them the information I had gathered. I didn't know what the outcome would be, but when I returned to the prison in the summer of 2006 it was a bright day and we were met by the same commander—although this time he was smiling. "I want you to see what we have done," he told me through an interpreter.

The same surgeon took me through the wards. Each patient had an individual bed and the windows were open, the patients actually were alert and smiling. Outside in the courtyard the patients had constructed a chapel which they regularly used. It was a far cry from what I had seen in the dead of winter in 2003.

*   *   *

Tuberculosis has a long, grim history in Russia. It was associated with the death of artistic geniuses during Russia's romantic era and was often a plot point in opera and literature between 1890 and 1940. In fact, it was the most common reason for death in Russia during that period. Caused by a bacterial pathogen and transmitted by air, historically TB was also been associated with poverty and overcrowding and afflicted the elderly especially.

Historically Russians typically treated tuberculosis in hospitals and sanatoriums, as the United States had before the introduction of the antibiotic therapy that made tuberculosis curable. My experience at Nizhniy Tagil was standard procedure in Russia: Because surgeons are in charge the therapy and treatment of tuberculosis, there's a tendency to use surgery to deal with the disease.

Two great tuberculosis leaders from the National Health Center in Denver—Drs. Iseman and Heifets—joined us on our EMEP tours of Russian TB hospitals. We emphasized using the best practices recommended by the World Health Organization: directly-observed therapy with antibiotics rather than surgery. Competent laboratory diagnosis established the antibiotic-resistant pathogen. This required patients to receive TB medications in the presence of medical personnel in order to reduce the possibility of noncompliance. One of the great difficulties of TB treatment is the need to follow up and ensure that patients have completed their six-month treatment: Often because of side-effects patients would cease taking their medication, which led to resistant strains developing. Many in Russia are lost because they are not followed up on in their home oblast (state).

New York City's experience in the late '80s and early '90s demonstrates the need for eternal vigilance regarding tuberculosis—and tactics for how to handle an outbreak. In the late 1980s the city only had three percent of the U.S population but fifteen percent of its

TB cases, largely because measures such as following up to ensure completion of therapy had been loosened. At that time Margaret Hamburg was Commissioner of Health for the city, and thanks to her and Mayor Dinkins, resources were mobilized in response: Staff was added to monitor and ensure follow-up compliance and to perform what we now refer to as contact tracing. The New York City Council passed a law that if an infected tubercular patient refused treatment he or she would be taken to the hospital, put into solitary confinement and treated until the patient was no longer infectious.

Because many of the tuberculosis patients were homeless and were not coming in for treatment, outreach workers went under bridges or into abandoned houses to find these people and ensure that they take their medication daily. Since some of the homeless shelters had as many as 800 people, they were closed and much smaller shelters were erected, which mitigated against faster communal spread. As patients with active tuberculosis were brought into hospitals, rooms had to be remodeled to have negative pressure (which meant essentially that the air would be sucked into the room from the hospital and then blown outside of the building).

Thanks to these actions, the incidence of tuberculosis and multidrug-resistant tuberculosis declined dramatically in New York City. HIV patients were no longer dying of tuberculosis. The total effort, which took less than a year, cost around $1 billion. This would be hard to scale up for a country the size of Russia, not simply because of the financial cost but also because they have never displayed that level of commitment to public health.

For Russia in the 1990s, the problem of TB was compounded by the rise of AIDS. The compromised immune systems of HIV patients make them much more likely to develop tuberculosis. And TB, in turn, cannot be adequately treated in those instances because of the HIV-positive patient's compromised immune system. Fifty percent of HIV deaths in Russia came from TB.

Russian authorities have been characteristically slow to grapple with this. I visited a TB hospital in Irkutsk, Siberia in 2012 and while all the TB patients were being tested for HIV, those who tested positive weren't being treated for it. We had to point out that tuberculosis can kill an HIV-positive patient because the patient does not have an adequate immune system.

*   *   *

AIDS came later to Russia than to the U.S. It metastasized as a problem for Russia, ironically, only after U.S. forces displaced the virulently anti-narcotic Taliban in Afghanistan after 9/11/2001. Heroin from that country started to flood into Russia, and with users sharing dirty needles the disease spread rapidly. The growing number of those affected has been abetted by various forms of Russian prejudice—against homosexuality, against drug-users, against needle-exchange programs and methadone programs—and have created another burgeoning health crisis for the country.

Perhaps the level of denial and prejudice is best illustrated by an excerpt in my friend, Dr. Ed Burger's book, that cites a letter a group of 16 young Russian medical graduates wrote to the director of Russia's central epidemiological research institute in 1987:

Dear colleagues,

We are graduates of a medical institution categorically opposed to combating the new disease "AIDS." And we intend to do everything in our power to impede the search for ways to combat this novel epidemic. We are convinced that within a short time AIDS will destroy all drug addicts and prostitutes. We are confident that Hippocrates would've approved of our decision. Long live AIDS!

In fairness, President Ronald Reagan didn't even mention HIV/AIDS in the U.S. until 1985. But Russia didn't start to address the epidemic until the early 2000s, and by 2007 they were spending $300 million annually to try to handle it. The Russian government formed a commission on AIDS in 2006 and then started to work with the regional authorities to set up separate departments for the study of HIV epidemiology, treatment and prevention.

Russia is officially reported to have approximately one million people living with HIV. But that statistic misses many Russians because they have not been tested. Experts say the real number is somewhere over 1.2 million people. Many HIV-infected people are afraid to go to the hospital to be tested for fear of being stigmatized. As a result, by the time people get into the medical system, they are often in the advanced stages of HIV and tuberculosis.

Tuberculosis, which kills the majority of HIV/AIDS patients, brings another complication. The World Health Organization lists Russia as one of the 22 countries where TB takes the highest toll. What is more alarming is that Russia, China, India and South Africa have almost 60 percent of the world's multidrug-resistant TB cases. Multi-drug-resistant TB is difficult and expensive to treat, often requiring 24 months of antibiotic treatment. Murray Feshbach, the senior scholar at the Woodrow Wilson Center in Washington, has studied Russian health and population trends for years. He notes that the United States, with a population of 314 million, has 500 to 600 TB infections a year. Russia, which has 143 million people, has more than 20,000 a year.

Along with malaria, HIV/AIDS and TB are the three major diseases for which we still do not have a preventative vaccine.

Homophobia remains the official position in Russia under President Vladimir Putin. At the end of a prison visit in Vladivostok, I asked the director if condoms were provided to the prisoners upon request. He turned to me and very sternly said, "We won't promote homosexuality." This prejudice also blinds them to the changing vectors of HIV transmission: In 2008, 80 percent of HIV infections were connected to intravenous drug use; since 2012 the main route has been heterosexual transmission among drug users with their partners.

Other countries work to prevent HIV infection by establishing needle exchange programs to keep users from sharing dirty needles. They also use substitutes such as methadone to help users to get off of addicting drugs. But methadone is illegal in Russia because officials insist that substitutes will only perpetuate dependency and disease. In fact, the only drug-treatment programs offered in Russia are privately funded ones such as "farms" where patients go cold-turkey, often under harsh circumstances, including restraining patients going through withdrawal, sometimes chaining them to trees.

My EMEP colleagues and I brought professionals from many areas of the United States, but the most consistent AIDS expert was Dr. Donna Sweet from the University of Kansas Medical Center in Wichita. Dr. Sweet has chaired the Board of Regents of the American College of Physicians and maintains a highly active practice at the University of Kansas. She traveled throughout the state of Kansas treating AIDS patients. She repeatedly returned to the Russian Federation to lecture and meet with infectious disease specialists. She was our most popular lecturer, emphasizing the need to decrease the mother to child transmission as well as the actual treatment of HIV/AIDS.

In 2012 the head of the Russian federal AIDS center said that he hopes "minds will change, and HIV prevention will be a priority." Unfortunately, this optimism seems misplaced.

*   *   *

Despite our efforts I watched with great distress as Russian public health deteriorated, especially with regard to TB and HIV, over the dozen years I spent traveling there. The overarching problem for Russia is that the prejudice and ignorance which have allowed these health problems to grow is fostered from the top. The government does not have any kind of aggressive or dynamic response to these deadly diseases. Instead, its approach to public health is uncoordinated and uninformed.

After being appointed President by retiring President Yeltsin on December 31st, 1999, Putin ordered his government to make improving health and life expectancy a priority, but the follow-through has been ineffective at best. His government has started campaigns to encourage people to cut down on tobacco and alcohol, a formidable challenge in a country where 60 percent of the men smoke and where, until recently, vodka was classified as food. The country's Finance Director actually encouraged smoking because it increased Federal Revenue. But the government response remains woeful when it comes to TB and AIDS.

In the past Russian leaders have occasionally made real public health efforts. When Mikhail Gorbachev was president of the Soviet Union, he initiated a vigorous campaign against drinking. He made it more expensive and harder to get alcohol, especially vodka. International health authorities credit him with reducing yearly death rates by 700,000. But vodka proved too popular and the drinking death rates crept back up.

Russia no longer accepts help from the USAID and other international organizations because it sees itself as a donor of health expertise rather than a recipient of help.

*   *   *

To this day I am haunted by many of the things I saw in my twelve years visiting Russian health facilities. But in 2007 I visited an AIDS clinic in Khabarovsk, a beautiful city of around 600,000 in Russia's eastern reaches, near the Pacific coast. Our team had been regularly visiting there since the early 2000s. Khabarovsk is situated on the Amur River, which borders China to the southwest. We would often combine a trip to Khabarovsk with one to Birobidzhan in the Jewish Autonomous Oblast, which Lenin had created, and Stalin reinforced as a place to send Russian Jews. These days only about one percent of the population of the old Oblast is Jewish.

When we landed at the airport the head of the clinic greeted us. She was excited about a new HIV facility which they had opened since our last visit. She insisted that early the next morning we go and visit. The clinic was separate geographically and professionally from any hospital and obviously of relatively new construction—the exterior wasn't even fully painted yet. As she led us into her new facilities, I looked to see who was on the wall: Lenin? Stalin? Putin? The walls were bare but the patients' waiting room had a 7-foot bas relief of the Statue of Liberty. This was soft power on display. The HIV specialists did not relate to Moscow and its conflicts with the U.S. but instead to the knowledge we brought them on this disease.

At that time, Presidents Putin and George W. Bush were at loggerheads over missile sites being set up in Poland and Czechoslovakia. But that was 5,000 miles away from Khabarovsk. The major concern at the clinic was not geostrategic gamesmanship but how we could contribute to their doctors' HIV/AIDS education. This was really soft power!

It was a telling reminder that the U.S. has a role to play in the international arena of public health. Our political leadership should never discount the importance of demonstrating leadership to the world in matters of health, whether that means helping Haiti after its hurricanes or people contracting cholera and other diseases or helping Africa with Ebola and AIDS.

In 2003 Bush initiated a program to fund the fight against HIV/AIDS in Africa. The program mainly focused on African countries that had high HIV rates, and was called The President's

Emergency Plan for AIDS Relief, or PEPFAR. Sub-Saharan Africa was being ravaged by HIV. More than 20 million people there were infected by 2000, accounting for more than two-thirds of the global total and it was spreading unchecked. As he would with the COVID-19 pandemic, Dr. Anthony Fauci was the leader in NIH who worked with pharmaceutical companies to develop life-saving therapies. Fauci worked with physicians such as Dr. Paul Farmer, who has done work in Haiti, and Dr. Mark Dybul, who has done work in Africa, to develop the initial plan, which was slated to cost $15 billion over five years. The money was to not only treat and rehabilitate AIDS patients but to also prevent the disease. When President Bush announced this initiative to Congress it was applauded by such diverse people as prominent evangelical Franklin Graham, a son of Billy Graham, and conservative senators as Jesse Helms of North Carolina, as well as liberals and health experts. It was the largest commitment ever of a nation to fight a single disease.

According to official sources, 2.6 million babies were saved from contracting the disease through the interruption of maternal to child transmission. Twenty-three million men were circumcised, and massive education was provided about how the disease was contracted through sex and injected drug use. Eighteen million lives were saved. The first five years of the program proved to be such a success that in 2008 Bush asked Congress to double its funding to $30 billion. Joe Biden, then the Chairman of the Foreign Relations Committee, said that PEPFAR was the most successful bipartisan effort he had ever seen and pushed the figure to $30 billion. In the end, even more was appropriated.

This commitment was on a par to what happened in the Marshall plan after the Second World War, though it was focused on sub-Saharan Africa which, unlike the European countries in the Marshall Plan, had little to give back to the U.S. Working in Russia, I was particularly aware of the program because Russia, China, India and other countries not in sub-Saharan Africa were considered for inclusion. But in the end it was decided that Russia, China and India had enough resources to fight the disease on their own—which certainly was not the case in Russia.

PEPFAR helped many low-income countries develop their public health efforts not just in Africa but as far east as Vietnam. Specifically, what it did was purchase many expensive anti-retroviral drugs and set up a process of distribution. The Clinton Foundation also provided an enormous number of lower-priced drugs to help countries struggling with high HIV rates, significantly augmenting PEPFAR. Many of these countries can't afford what our drug companies are charging for the medications. The Obama administration continued funding for the PEPFAR program. We should also not overlook that private foundations like the Gates Foundation put enormous resources into the research for the best treatment and prevention of HIV worldwide.

The episode of HIV/AIDs in the United States and worldwide is a remarkable story of the mobilization of public and private resources, mainly in this country, to convert HIV from a death sentence to a chronic disease; and hopefully one day in the future to develop a vaccine to eliminate HIV, as we've done with smallpox. In 2008 Bush awarded the Presidential Medal of Freedom, the nation's highest civilian honor, to Dr. Fauci, for his work bringing "hope and healing to tens of millions" around the world.

People often deride ideas like soft power, but programs like EMEP and others made important differences. The U.S. benefits doubly from the kind of victories we won, first from intangible goodwill and second in our own homeland defense against disease in a shrinking world.

*   *   *

I was able to mix some pleasure travel in with my business trips to Russia. On my trips to Siberia many people had talked about Lake Baikal, referring to it as the "Pearl of Siberia." The great poet Anton Chekhov once said of the lake that everything before he saw it was prose and everything after was poetry.

I was able to verify that observation myself in the summer of 2006. My old friend Peter Berle was then the President of the Audubon Society and had expressed an interest in visiting the lake. I was scheduled to travel to Siberia that July, so we agreed to meet at the lake. Peter enlisted as guides two professors from Buryatia, a Russian province situated on the lake's eastern shore. The Buryatian people originated from Mongolia and are the heirs of Genghis Khan. They had fought with the Whites against the Red Army during the Russian Revolution and were persecuted by Stalin because of it.

I told Peter I would fly into Irkutsk, the nearest major airport. A flight from Moscow had crashed there three days earlier, killing 25 people—not, unfortunately, an unusual event in Russia. The airport itself was chaos and the luggage pickup area was a small room jammed with hundreds of people. I didn't see Peter at first but heard his voice from the other side of the crowd: His wife had told him to make sure

I knew he was diabetic, he yelled. I'd never realized this strapping man suffered diabetes. "Please get some food," I yelled back and after two hours we finally got together and were able to get on a bus for Ulan-Ude, the capital of Buryatia.

Peter and I got to Ulan-Ude, met up with the two professors, who were Buddhists, and a knowledgeable woman who would be our translator. We toured the city and then went to the Great Lake Baikal. The citizens around Lake Baikal were very protective of it. When the government wanted to put a pipeline across its northern base, they rejected the idea with such vehemence that the Kremlin had to capitulate. A paper mill at the southern base of the lake was shut down at the first sign of pollution.

Lake Baikal is the largest freshwater lake in the world, holding more water than our five Great Lakes combined. With a depth of one mile, it also qualifies as the deepest lake in the world; and it is the oldest lake in the world, having existed for 25 million years. It holds 23 percent of all of fresh water in the world. There are 3,500 species of plants and animals and about 80 percent of those are indigenous.

These are impressive statistics, but nothing matches the clear blue water of the lake. When it is calm you can see down 130 feet. The water is cold and in the winter it can have up to six feet of ice on it. Cars and wagons drive across its 16-mile width and 47-mile length. Roughly 300 streams and rivers flow into the lake and it drains into the Arctic Ocean. It's bordered on the west by the Irkutsk Oblast and on the east by the Buryiat Oblast. The Trans-Siberian railroad from Moscow to Vladivostok stops at the city of Irkutsk at the base of the lake.

During this expedition, the five of us slept in a tent, woke at sunrise and had breakfast over the fire before exploring the bird and animal life around the lake. Peter and I jumped in a few times, but the water was really too cold for an extended swim.

At the end of the trip, I told Peter that I was going to wash my shirt and pants in the lake because I had not changed in a week. He blew up at me, saying that I would be participating in the pollution of the lake. My first reaction was that this was the largest lake in the world and I doubted I would damage it. But thinking more about it, I remembered the philosophical injunction: Act as if your example will be followed by everyone. In that light, my small action really could harm the beautiful, clear blue lake.

It was a wonderful week and Peter and I both communicated with our new friends by email for some time. I went off to Ekaterinburg and Peter went back to New York. Unfortunately, shortly thereafter he was disassembling an old wooden shed on his farm in northern New York when some logs tumbled down on him and he passed away.

I went to Peter's funeral in upstate New York and it was a wonderful service with many speakers, including everyone from the police chief to colleagues he worked with throughout his life. I was glad I was able to recount our time together at the Century Foundation and the week we had together at Lake Baikal.

*   *   *

Unhappily, my Russia experience came to an abrupt end in 2012. Bill Browder, a successful Wall Street maverick who went to Russia in the 1990s, made a lot of money in a hedge fund just after the breakup of the Soviet Union. He recounted his experiences in his excellent book, "Red Notice: A True Story of High Finance, Murder, and One Man's Fight for

Justice." It details the governmental corruption he uncovered with the assistance of Sergei Magnitsky, his 37-year-old Russian tax attorney. Browder escaped Russia with his life but Magnitsky stayed on, hoping to expose the fraud he suspected in the Kremlin. He succeeded, uncovering what The Washington Post later called a "dense web of tax fraud and graft involving 23 companies and a total of $230 million linked to the Kremlin and individuals close to the government." Russian authorities imprisoned Magnitsky, who developed acute pancreatitis. They did not treat him for a year and he died, reportedly beaten to death in prison.

Browder felt terrible about this and vowed that the Putin regime would pay for it. He spent over half a decade pushing the U.S. government to punish a list of Russians implicated in the lawyer's death, an effort which culminated in the 2012 Magnitsky Act, which targeted specific Russian officials and businessmen, banning them from the U.S. and its banking systems and seizing any assets they have in this country. Putin responded with a law banning Americans from adopting Russian orphans. He also kicked USAID out after 20 years in Russia as well as any groups which it funded, which included EMEP.

I was in Novosibirsk, in southwest Siberia, when we got the message that we would have to get out in a matter of days. It was a shock given that no one had ever criticized our program. The regional centers appealed the decision but were denied. We packed up and were out of the country within two days. And that was really the end of the line for EMEP. All told, EMEP reached about 10,000 physicians over the seventeen years and was well accepted in the oblasts.

I really loved my twelve years in Russia, even though the transportation by air, rail and road was inordinately difficult to negotiate. The people we worked with were warm and friendly, and it was a real privilege to host them when they came over to the U.S.

Unfortunately, Putin's backlash also disrupted the relationships with colleagues with whom we had spent twelve years working. We would send emails and they wouldn't respond, presumably because they were under pressure not to respond. It was a dispiriting end to a successful and worthwhile program. I never did learn what happened to the Statue of Liberty in the Khabarovsk AIDS clinic.

*   *   *

Holodomor was the Ukrainian famine or death by hunger caused by Joseph Stalin—3.9 million Ukrainian deaths from 1931 to 1933. Stalin wanted the small farms turned into state run collectives and the Ukrainian farmers resisted. He also wanted to punish the independent minded Ukrainians who posted a threat to his totalitarian authority.

Vladimir Putin's war of choice against Ukraine is also punishment for the independent minded Ukrainians who pose a threat to Putin's vision of reestablishing the Soviet Union? Like the Red Famine in the 30s Putin's war is targeting the civilians and children as well as hospitals and centers for the aged.

Putin has been able to do something even Stalin could not do in 1932-33: the unification of international organizations as NATO, which represent over 30 countries and even the partisan divide in the US Congress. For Stalin it took World War II to unify the Western allies.

As of this writing, unlike the Holodomor, the ending of this genocide is not clear.

CHAPTER EIGHTEEN

Mongolia, Romania, Afghanistan, Moldova

Not all of my overseas work for EMEP was Russia-focused. I spent time in Moldova, for example, and had especially interesting trips to one of Russia's eastern neighbors, Mongolia, which is a fascinating country. I had the opportunity to travel there in 2010 and 2011.

Genghis Khan united the various tribes of his region in the late 12th century, founding Mongolia. He achieved the largest contiguous land empire in the world, stretching from present day Poland in the west to Korea in the east and from Russian Siberia in the north to Vietnam in the south. A quarter of the Earth's total population at that time was under his power and Pax Mongolia significantly improved trade and commerce across Asia during its height. His grandson, Kublai Khan reigned over most of present-day China. Genghis was so successful because he had a moving army with extremely skilled horsemen who would go from region to region and brutally conquer the cities. He did not try to change the social structures or plunder their conquered regions but asked only for their allegiance and for free trade. Modern Mongolia has not forgotten its founder and is rife with Genghis Khan banks and Genghis Khan hotels and many other facilities named after him.

One of the most impressive men I met during my work for EMEP was Naranjargal Dashdorj, a medical doctor from Mongolia with a PhD in neuroscience whom I met when he was working at the U.S. National Institutes of Health in D.C. He went on to run the Onom Foundation in Ulaanbaatar, Mongolia, which focuses on improving healthcare and education in that country through President Bush's Millennium Challenge. Naranjargal and I decided to apply for a grant with the George Washington School of Public Health, in Washington, D.C., to work on cardiovascular disease in Mongolia.

The proposal was due in December 2012. George Washington, which would be the primary grantee, had a bureaucratic delay in getting the proposal out and it didn't look like it would get to Mongolia in time. I volunteered to play courier. In a matter of hours, I flew from Washington Dulles international to San Francisco, changed to Korean Air to Beijing and then to a Mongolian airline to Ulaanbaatar. Luckily no VISA was required to enter the country (unlike Russia, from whence I had been unceremoniously turned away once when my visa was out of date).

I handed the proposal in on time and was able to spend a few days in the country. (We did not get the grant, but the following year a reduced version of our program was approved.) Naran's family (he was still in D.C.) was most gracious, warmly celebrating my arrival. The next day I went with Naran's brother to a sheep-herder's yurt on the majestic Mongolian steppe. The herders take care of their sheep flocks, but the winters are often brutal and kill many of the animals. Many herders have had to move to Ulaanbaatar to survive. Unfortunately, they still burn an enormous amount of coal in the country in order to keep warm. When I was there in December the smog was usually so great that the sun did not appear at all. Although it has a high elevation, Ulaanbaatar is in a valley. The smog greatly affects the quality of life.

Naranjargal's family took me out to the Gobi desert which is south of Ulaanbaatar and extends all the way to China. As we drove a figure appeared in the distance. As we got nearer the figure was larger and larger and then when we arrived I saw that it was a huge statue of Genghis Khan on a horse in his army regalia. He was pointing south toward China, the biggest threat to Mongolia.

In the summer of 2020, Naranjargal asked me and my wife Kathy to come to Mongolia in to visit the Altai mountains, and to see the incredible celebrations of horse riding and other sports Mongolians have at their annual Nadam festival. Unfortunately, because of COVID-19 the trip was cancelled. I hope to see Naran again soon, and I told him I expect him to be President of his country!

*   *   *

My last overseas work was in Kabul, Afghanistan in 2015. I went to see the school that an old school friend, Ted Achilles, had helped set up for Afghan girls. Ted and I had been friends since our St. Paul's days. We had competed to be president of the 1954 class. (He won, and I was elected secretary.) He too went on to Yale and then had a successful life in business, and he also served a couple of terms in the Oregon state legislature. We stayed in touch over the years, and he would occasionally reach out to me on matters of public service.

In 1992 Ted had called and asked if I wanted to join him in going to Romania as part of President George H.W. Bush's Thousand Points of Light program. The dictator Nicolae Ceausescu had been overthrown and there was a new democracy in the country and especially in the capital of Bucharest. A new mayor, Crin Halaicu, had been elected there to lead a democratic government and he wanted some help from a former mayor in the United States on how best to work with the public and have a democratic administration.

I gladly accepted. I stayed in a Bucharest hotel where the elevators had been shot up—you could still see bullet holes in places. Nicolae Ceausescu and his wife were terrible rulers for their people, and they were both hung in effigy. Then, after his regime collapsed, they were given a hasty trial and shot by a firing squad.

Not surprisingly, it was a difficult transition for the local and state officials who had governed and served under the Ceausescu regime to suddenly become comfortable with a free press and open government. I worked with the administration to suggest important principles of free speech and press, as well as strategies for how to provide information to the public and answer complaints. Mayor Halaicu was a young guy, around 40 years old, and was enthusiastic about reforming the system and becoming democratic. But neither he nor his aides understood how to manage a budget or deal with a free press. My advice on the latter was to let it all out, but they didn't seem comfortable with that idea. I also advised that he make sure to spend time meeting with regular citizens in unofficial settings—out in the street rather than in his office.

There was only so much we could do during our two-week stay, but it was a satisfying time: It was uplifting, and the people were receptive because it was a new day for their country.

*   *   *

Right after 9/11 Ted declared that he wanted to go to Afghanistan to see what he, as a citizen without any connection to government or any non-profit, could do to help. Afghanistan is a unique country. The English, Russians and now the Americans have all tried to control it, none successfully. There was a telling picture Ted kept in his office showing a lone 19th century British soldier coming back on a horse to town to report grave news. The Mujahideen had annihilated his British squadron. They allowed one person to escape to tell what transpired.

One of the few good things that came from the counterattack to 9/11 was that we initially defeated the Taliban, the religious extremist group which had been ruling Afghanistan. That meant young women and girls could now get an education—the Taliban had denied schooling to girls. If they found out girls were going to school, the parents' and daughters' lives would be in jeopardy.

When Ted got to Afghanistan he quickly decided to focus on education. In 2004 he became head of the Afghan section of the Kennedy-Lugar Youth Exchange and Study Program, a State Department initiative which sends promising high school students to school in the United States for a year. One of the students who went through the program was an industrious young woman named Shabana Basij-Rasikh. They stayed in touch and in 2008 he left the Kennedy-Lugar program and together they founded the School of Leadership Afghanistan, or SOLA ("sola" is a Pashtun word which means peace) for young girls.

I met Shabana on a number of occasions when she was an incredibly talented young woman of about 22. As a child she had cut her hair short so she could appear to be a boy and escort her sister (clad in a burka) through the streets of Kabul to a secret school which still educated girls. Later she would be educated in Middlesex School in Massachusetts and go on to get her college degree from Middlebury College in Vermont (she would later get a master's in public policy from Oxford). She cofounded SOLA with Ted in 2008 when she was still in college.

When I visited in 2015, SOLA had been in operation for a couple of years. Situated in a large rental house on an inconspicuous back street, it educated about 20 young Afghan girls per year who predominantly lived in its upper level. There were classrooms and the eating area on the first floor. Males and females were strictly separated, and any males associated with the school—including Ted—stayed in the basement.

This house was on a dirt road away from the major residences and commercial areas of Kabul, which is a city of 4 million and growing all the time. The people in the rural areas were coming into the city, thinking it was safer than the countryside, where the Taliban were still strong. Of course, basic reading and writing was essential. Most of the young girls were connected with girls in the United States to become friends. Ted was able to attract teachers from the U.S. to rotate through SOLA.

I stayed for a week, giving three or four lectures on American history. Students were bright and very interested in American history, how we dealt with dissenters and the whole concept of democracy—something they didn't have. They were fascinated with President

Barack Obama, about whom they were positive, and wanted to hear about his strengths.

Ted ran a tight ship. When one of the young girls was disrespectful to a volunteer teacher Ted called her and her parents in to see him. He was stern with the girl and her parents, telling them that it was a unique opportunity to have your daughter educated, and she should not throw it away by being rude. The young girl restrained herself from any future infraction.

Ted was also able to place young girls in St. Paul's, Middlesex and other American boarding schools, and many went on to college. He once told me of a student who was educated in the U.S. and went on to become a reporter for a magazine in Virginia. She wrote to her father that she would like to come home and visit him and the family. He wrote back that if she came back he would kill her, but that if she didn't come back he would progressively maim her brother. You can imagine the conflicts in her mind and emotions. From what I know she didn't go back.

Providing the opportunity for young Afghan girls to get an education was perhaps the most important contribution that we made in that country; until the Taliban regained power and reversed these critical opportunities for women and girls.

* * *

Shabana took over at SOLA after Ted left in 2016. Ted had returned to the United States to receive medical treatment for serious side effects from radiation he had received for the prostate cancer he developed in the mid-1990s. He was treated in Anchorage, Alaska, where he was working at the time. The radiation treatment was debilitating, and he had to have multiple surgeries. He had had a total of eight operations. Before the last scheduled operation—he had approval from the surgeon that he could do one more—he told me: "It's just not worth it." Ted passed away in 2018. I went to a memorial service for him at The Fletcher School of Law and Diplomacy at Tufts University in Massachusetts, which his father—a well-known diplomat—had attended. Shabana and many other SOLA graduates spoke movingly of the difference he made in their lives.

SOLA continues with Shabana at the helm. Unfortunately, shortly after I left Afghanistan the school had to move because it became increasingly difficult to continue as it had been. About six months after I left, the foreign couple in the house next door was murdered by terrorists who came into their home. The government, with help from some private interests, built a new boarding school for SOLA with increased security near the center of Kabul. After the Taliban gained authority in Afghanistan in 2021, Shabana had the 250-member school transferred to Rwanda. She burnt the students' records to protect them and their families from the Taliban.

CHAPTER NINETEEN

Public Service For All

Over the course of my life I have always gravitated toward public health over clinical medicine because I am drawn to the responsibilities we have to take care of ourselves, our families and the general public—and I am excited by the many opportunities there are in the field of health care to make things better for people. Happily, over the last 60 years there have been several notable improvements in healthcare programs in the U.S., as well as in the government's role in those programs. JFK focused on mental health and established the U.S. Agency for International Development, which provides funds for health programs in foreign countries. In addition to leading the creation of the pillar programs of Medicare and Medicaid, the Johnson administration recognized the need for public programs that would address heart disease, stroke and cancer, and for community health centers that could administer better out-of-hospital care to people.

The landmark 1964 report by Surgeon General Luther Terry on the ill health effects of smoking started the push for smoking cessation. In the '70s the Nixon administration instituted clean water and air initiatives and established the Environmental Protection Agency—all in response to the need to mitigate the effects of pollution on our health—and launched a "war on cancer." Cancer deaths in this country have been reduced significantly, and the lives of cancer patients have been extended. The Clinton administration paid special attention to improving children's health and the importance of vaccinations, and Mrs. Clinton wrote an influential book, "It Takes a Village," on how a community larger than the immediate family plays an important role in raising kids. The George W. Bush years focused the government on HIV/AIDS prevention and treatment, including through the President's Emergency Program for Aids Relief (PEPFAR) program, which saved the lives of millions of Africans. His administration also doubled the number of community health centers. President Barack Obama continued PEPFAR and established the first comprehensive health insurance program for nearly all Americans, the Affordable Care Act. He prompted the Centers for Disease Control and Prevention to combat national and international epidemics. Since the '60s, ten presidents, with bipartisan support, have increased funding to the National Institutes of Health, leading to advances not only in fields such as human genome research and genetic therapy, but also treatment and control of diseases in the U.S. and around the world.

Unfortunately, President Donald Trump reversed this long trend and devalued public health, to tragic ends during the Covid-19 pandemic. Trump and his administration did not recognize the pandemic in December of 2019 and did not act vigorously in January of 2020. President George W. Bush had developed a pandemic emergency plan after he read about the 1918 pandemic in John M. Barry's book *The Great Influenza*, and the Obama administration had further developed Bush's pandemic emergency plan and had made a point of presenting it to Trump and his incoming administration during the transition period. But tragically, Trump and his administration totally disregarded the pandemic emergency plan, essentially tossing it in the trash.

In addition to failing to recognize the pandemic early on and act vigorously, because of a total lack of appreciation of science, Trump and his administration gave mixed messages and never decided on a consistent course of action. President Trump brought a radiologist he'd seen on FOX NEWS, Scott Atlas, into the White House as his chief COVID advisor. Atlas proceeded to strongly endorse herd immunity by treating only the elderly and allowing millions of others to die. Not only did the administration fail to enlist credible figures to fight the spread of conspiracies and misinformation about the virus, on several occasions it was itself the source of misinformation, as with Trump's promotion of Hydroxychloroquine as an effective anti-Covid-19 drug. He also suggested bleach should be injected. It is no surprise that in the 2020 Presidential race the New England Journal of Medicine and the Scientific American—both over 100 years old—endorsed a presidential candidate (in this case Joe Biden) for the first time.

There were, of course, some aspects of the fight against the Covid-19 epidemic that were handled well in the U.S. The first responders, the medics and nurses in the emergency rooms and other physicians and medical personnel who attended to patients even as hospitals became overloaded were heroic throughout the crisis. The enormous outpouring of volunteers to help people with food and shelter was also heartening. The pharmaceutical companies and the research engine of NIH both should be applauded. The one thing Trump did right—the allocation of $14 billion to develop vaccines to fight the epidemic, a program he called "Operation Warp Speed"—was a triumph of public-private partnership to bring vaccines online as quickly as possible.

Nevertheless, Trump's overall mishandling of the epidemic put an enormous stress on a medical system which was already inadequate. After months of absentee leadership, hollow cheerleading, politicization of science and public health and contradictory and uncertain guidance downplaying the situation, the predictable result was a pandemic that raged out of control, and a U.S. death toll that surpassed 400,000 before Trump left office.

The damages caused by the mishandling of Covid-19 will linger long beyond the end of this pandemic. As Dr. Sherman Bull and I wrote in a letter to our Yale classmates, "Unfortunately there will be more deadly mega viruses after Covid-19 is conquered. The World Health Organization that President Trump withdrew from is the only other international epidemiological body other than CDC and will be needed to identify and prevent future pandemics. Our public health institutions must be guided by data and science to be effective in combating these infectious viruses and maintaining the trust of the American public. The personal politics of President Trump or of any future president should not supersede data driven public health decisions."

Mercifully Trump's chaotic exit—with all the attendant horror of the January 6 siege of the Capitol Building—has allowed reason and science to reign again. President Joe Biden has brought people such as Drs. Anthony Fauci and Francis Collins of NIH back into the public view and has listened to their advice. Biden has been slow to get proper testing protocols for the virus up and running, but he did get the vaccines delivered quickly; he brought tempered optimism to the country and he got the American Rescue Plan passed (without any Republican votes), promoting universal vaccination and addressing the poverty brought on by the pandemic. These actions were badly needed: 8 million people fell into poverty during the outbreak. A lot of workers became unemployed as a result of the virus, and those who continued to work were often in close quarters and thus became infected with Covid-19. As an example, at a Tyson's plant in Amarillo Texas, a whopping 50 percent of the workers contracted the virus.

As we continue out long recovery from COVID, we are facing several other staggering and fundamental challenges as a nation, two of the worse being climate change and racism—our original sin. As Biden guides us through these challenging times, he has an opportunity to try to inspire the country and, not incidentally, start healing the divides which have rent it in recent years.

I believe national public service could be a powerful source of national unity and a social equalizer. It could promote civic education and instill a sense of obligation to safeguard the values of our democracy. A new civilian service corps of all citizens between the ages of 18 and 30 would throw Americans together from all walks of life, exposing them to each other and to parts of the country they would not necessarily see. The private corporate sector, organized labor and private philanthropy could partner with federal, state and local governments on this project. Such a confederation would also provide a ready workforce for dealing with a multitude of national problems. Think of the needs a modern civilian service corps could address, including testing and contact-tracing during a pandemic; educating students about the positive role vaccinations have played historically (including during the Covid-19 pandemic); helping FEMA deal with the results of natural disasters such as hurricanes and forest fires; assisting teachers in overcrowded classrooms; addressing the desperate need for more nurses, whose numbers have plummeted during the pandemic. Such a corps could also be trained for new green jobs, and to assist with the reform of police departments: issues such a domestic disputes, currently handled by police, could be handed over to people who have been specially trained to deal with such situations. History has ample models for civil service programs, from the New Deal's Civilian Conservation Corps and Public Works Administration, to today's Corporation for National and Community Service, VISTA and the Peace Corps.

Retired Gen. Stanley McChrystal, the former head of the U.S. Joint Special Operations Command and later commander of U.S. and NATO forces in Afghanistan, has estimated that a national service plan would cost around $88 billion annually. That may seem like a big number but when you consider that the federal government spends nearly $6.1 trillion every year it doesn't seem that much of a financial burden. In 2021, I co-authored with former Kentucky Representative Mike Ward (and former Associate Director of the Peace Corps under Clinton) an op-end in recognition of the 60th anniversary of the Peace Corps. In it, we said: "Let's spend upfront a fraction of the resources we expend to deal with the result of [our] problems." After all, would a service corps really be that much more expensive than what we now spend to deal with problems such as crime, racial unrest, inadequate education, poor healthcare and climate change? Anticipating these problems and addressing them effectively would help both society and the budget, in addition to increasing job training.

A year or two of national public service with stipend pay for Americans between the ages of 18 and 30 would help our democracy. Such a program would not only provide badly needed jobs, but also would improve its participants. Young people could explore and develop careers in new areas, work off student loans and work alongside people from all kinds of different backgrounds. I know my two years in Appalachia changed the direction of my life. And many who joined the Peace Corps and VISTA as young people now serve in local and national political offices, from former Sen. Chris Dodd of Connecticut to former Rep. Joe Kennedy III of Massachusetts to Tom Wolf, the governor of Pennsylvania.

A national public service corps would, as Oliver Wendell Holmes might have put it, give young people today an unparalleled opportunity to share in the passion and action of their time.

March 2023

As I look back over a life that has now spanned eight and a half decades, I feel unbelievably fortunate on so many fronts, both professional and personal. I was lucky enough to realize early on that medicine and public health were fields in which I could take meaningful action to improve people's lives and feel passionate about the process of doing so. I was equally lucky to have the opportunity to serve in political office, another arena that can deliver the double-barrel rewards of passionate ideas that fuel positive actions. Both fields—medicine and politics—are completely intriguing, have infinite learning curves and are rife with unexpected developments and startling lessons. Who could ask for more?

My work in public health has rebounded on me in a positive way personally; I know that in addition to taking care of others, I have a responsibility to take good care of myself. With the legacy of a father who died of cardiovascular disease at age 58 and a mother who died of cancer of the pancreas at age 63, I am aware of the preciousness of each day and I do everything I can to stay in good shape mentally and physically. The heart is a beautiful organ. For the average person it beats 100,000 times a day; in a lifetime it beats over one billion times. It never rests. Why would anybody consciously damage this precious organ by smoking, having an unhealthy fatty diet, being too sedentary or failing to treat high blood pressure? There were no nutritional courses in medical school when I was a student—a great oversight—but I have come to understand that you really are what you eat, and I try to maintain a diet that is low in fat, sugar and meat. These days I am careful to abide by one of the most important rules for anyone in their 80's: DO NOT FALL!

Physical activity is another important part of my daily routine. As Joe DiMaggio once said, "the legs are what goes first." Over the years I have had two hip replacements (one 32 years ago and another 29 years ago—and they're still working), a shoulder replacement, and two laminectomy surgeries on my back—obviously I have extensive osteoarthritis. But this does not keep me from exercising—swimming, rowing and hiking—seven days a week if possible. I have never smoked, and I try to sleep six to seven hours a night. I have successfully battled a bout of prostate cancer. At age 86 the head and heart appear to be viable. I am blessed to have an intact, healthy and gifted family—a wife of 54 years, three children and four grandchildren. With all this great good fortune, I sometimes feel like singing that famous line Roger Daltrey of The Who delivers in the song "My Generation": "I hope I die before I get old."

I have had an active and passionate relationship with the great outdoors all my life, and just as my professional life has been a largely unplanned venture, so my interactions with Mother Nature and with different places around the world have been largely unplanned and full of unexpected turns and surprising lessons. (I think back, for example, to my sailing voyage in the Carribean.) After a lifetime of annual visits to my family home in La Malbaie in Canada and to

Eternity, the fishing camp on Petite Lac St. Jean, spending time there has become a near religious experience for me—it is a place that recharges me and nourishes my heart and soul. My long relationship with the great state of Kentucky was in many ways an unplanned adventure, but it too has been a profoundly rewarding one. To this day, I believe my most important and proudest contributions in health care have been the establishment of the Park DuValle Community Health Center in Louisville 54 years ago, the establishment of Louisville's first professional emergency medical service 47 years ago, and my work 33 years ago with Jefferson County Board of Health Director Dr. David Allen to open a network of seven health clinics in Jefferson County. I was both touched and honored in 2006 when the University of Kentucky College of Public Health inducted me into their Hall of Fame. Recently my family set up a fund, called the Dr. Harvey I. Sloane Fund, to assist patients at the Park DuValle Community Health Center with uncompensated care and medication expenses.

The friends I made in Kentucky and my colleagues in my various positions there remain among the closest and most important people in my life. The colleagues and friends I gathered during my stints in Washington D.C., Russia and other far-flung places around the globe are equally important to me. I guess one could say that in terms of the body, you are what you eat—but when it comes to nourishing the soul, you are fed by those you meet.

Sadly, at age 86, I have had to watch many good friends pass away. Most of these friends and mentors—Dr. George (Barney) Crile Jr., Sid Lovett Sr., and Jr., Barry Bingham Sr. and his wife Mary, Kay Halle, Arthur Schlesinger, Ed Prichard, Eula Hall, the Reverend Al Shands,

Sally Lyons Brown, Ned Bonnie, John and Nancy Bell, Milton Young, Vernice Hunter, Dora Rice, Lou Byron, Joe Elam, Danny Meyer, Danny Ross, Lovick Miller, and Dr. Edward Burger, have died of natural causes in old age. Others, like Worth Bingham, George Crile III, Bert Combs, Prichard, Ted Achilles, Jamie Houghton and my Century Foundation colleague Peter Berle, were carried off too soon, by accidents or disease. So many dear friends and colleagues are now gone, but while I'm alive they will never be forgotten.

Life continues to be full of serendipity and surprises. One significant new development for me came about indirectly because of a trip Kathy and I made to visit Jay and Sharon Rockefeller in Wyoming in 1972. While we were there, we met Jay's cousin, Laurance (Larry) Rockefeller—an environmentalist and lawyer who worked at the Natural Resources Defense Fund (NRDC). A few years after we met him, Larry started buying land in the Beaverkill Valley in New York's Catskill Mountains, in an effort to keep the valley—which has the legendary trout stream the Beaverkill running through it—from being developed recklessly. Working with his friend and colleague John Adams, a co-founder of NRDC, Larry conducted a quiet and careful experiment about how to develop a wilderness area in a way that preserves its natural beauty. Over time he amassed thousands of acres of land, some of which was then resold in smaller lots with very stringent environmental rules attached. The project was a new and innovative approach for how to protect wilderness and natural resources from harmful development. In 1985 The New York Times chronicled Rockefeller's conservation efforts in an article that started: "Eight years ago, a tall, thin, soft-spoken man who has dedicated his life to conservation causes came here to a beautiful valley that is pierced by the legendary Beaverkill. He fell in love with what he saw, so he bought a stretch of riverbank."

In the mid '80s Kathy began working with Larry as a real estate broker, helping him with his Beaverkill Valley development plan—and she and I began spending more and more time there ourselves. I would never have expected that any other place on earth could evoke such intense and happy feelings as La Malbaie has for me, but the Beaverkill Valley has become just such a place. Today the valley, with about 100,000 acres under strict conservation easements, is protected as a natural resource that will be there for people to enjoy for generations to come. Many families have bought homes in the valley, and a vibrant community has sprung up. The economy of the area has improved significantly, and the land itself is more beautiful and inspiring than ever.

Beaverkill brought deeper relationships. The Rutherfurd-Kernans have had a long history with our family, especially Kathy. Kathy and Mary Rutherfurd (née Kernan) went to Wheaton College together and have been colleagues at Brown Harris Stevens real estate for well over 35 years. Mary is our daughter Abigail's godmother. Her husband, Win is a wonderful friend, a distinguished attorney, and former chairman of the board of St. Pauls School where Abigail, his daughter, Lily and I attended. We have a shared interest in Russia's history and its people, and find there is a lot to discuss about its present day situation. The Kernan sisters Mary, Emily (who is past president of the Metropolitan Museum of Art and served as Chairman of the board of the Federal Reserve Bank of New York) and her husband John who plays a leadership role in the Beaverkill Valley, and Beatrice are also close friends. Beatrice helped me with this memoir.

In a recent conversation I had with John Adams, Adams said that Larry "has been the most important figure for (the Beaverkill) valley in the last hundred years." For me, Larry's project is another brilliant example of what passion and action can accomplish. And I must confess, my admiration for Larry deepened when I learned that in 1966, at age 22, he and a college classmate named Gerry Reese flew a twin engine Beechcraft Baron 33,000 miles around the world in 56 days—neither of them having had much piloting experience beyond getting their flying licenses (in co-pilot Reese's case, it was still a student license). Charles Lindbergh wrote Larry and Gerry a letter of congratulations on their successful flight.

During much of the Covid epidemic, Kathy and I were fortunate enough to be able to base ourselves and work from the Beaverkill Valley. The natural beauty of the surroundings was a great comfort during those stressful times when every day seemed to bring bad news, and our isolation geographically gave me a most precious gift— time to think (and time to write this book). As someone who has dedicated much of his life to trying to improve public health, the question I found myself asking over and over as I watched the horror of the pandemic unfold was this: Will history repeat itself, or will we learn from the great modern pandemic of COVID-19?

We sure didn't seem to learn much from the influenza pandemic of 1918 and 1919. During that pandemic 675,000 Americans and 50 million people worldwide died—more than had died in World War I. Why did we learn so little from such a devastating public health crisis? I never studied the 1918-19 influenza pandemic in medical school— and American historians frequently claim that little has been written about that pandemic. Perhaps one reason was that President Wilson never used the words 'influenza epidemic"—he felt they would make America look weak during the war. (Spain was not in the war, so it was called the Spanish Flu. As it happens, historians now claim that the influenza started in a troop training camp in Kansas.) But during negotiations in Paris for the Treaty of Versailles, President Wilson got the flu himself. Wilson had been fighting against the French Prime Minister George Clemenceau's insistence on severe penalties for Germany, but when he got influenza he was in bed for over a week. Wilson came back to the negotiating table in a weakened state—and gave in to Clemenceau. Who knows, this may have been one reason, however indirectly, that the Second World War occurred.

As I write, the death toll from the COVID-19 virus is over 1 million in the U.S. and 5 million worldwide. And unlike the 1918 pandemic, this time the United States leads all other countries in the world in terms of deaths per thousand population—including much more populous countries like China and India. Long haulers will increase and will require expensive medical care. Many epidemiologists fear thousands more will die in the U.S. before it is over. Why have countries like Korea, Japan, and Australia been able to fight the virus more effectively than the U.S.?

As I noted earlier, a number of critical mistakes with the handling of the Covid-19 pandemic can be traced directly to the White House. But even as I watched this almost surreal series of tragic missteps roll out from the top, it became clearer and clearer that the biggest issue about how the pandemic was mishandled in the U.S. comes from a more systemic problem. Public health simply is not viewed as an essential service in our country, and our public health system is frail and fragmented, with relatively little money put into the system at both the federal and state levels. Dr. Francis S Collins, who in December of 2021 stepped down as the Director of The National Institutes of Health—the nation's medical research agency—has spoken about the unfortunate lag between medical advances that are discovered through scientific research and the public health programs implementation of those advances. Scientists are working hard to develop new tests and new vaccines that will leave Americans less vulnerable to any pathogen that may come our way, but federal and state funding for the public health departments that need to distribute and administer those tests and vaccines is woefully inadequate. And the problem is not just about funding. The fact is, delivering up to date public health efficiently is a more complex challenge than the research and discovery process of pure science, largely because of the human component in public health. The thousands of people who have refused to get vaccinated during this pandemic are one such example; in some cases, the staff at local health departments have even been harassed by anti-vaxxers for just trying to do their jobs. At the national level, the people in charge have little awareness of or appetite for the constantly evolving overhaul of programs and protocol that is needed both to keep up with a constantly evolving virus and to prepare for future pandemics.

There is some positive news here. A conference of the Association of Schools and Programs of Public Health recently found that there is great enthusiasm for careers in public health among the younger generations. This enthusiasm is reflected by a 40% increase in applicants to the 2021 graduate level programs in schools of public health compared to those in March 2020. For that enthusiasm to translate into a stronger public health workforce, however, it must be supported by adequate federal and state funding for schools of public health.

The national political leadership—Republicans and Democrats and Independents—along with private business (for profit and non-profit), labor, foundations, and medical and public health representatives should work together to change this, and to prepare the nation for the next pandemic. We need to carefully assess the failures and successes of our responses to this pandemic in various sectors of our government and society, so that we can make sure such a catastrophe doesn't happen again. A new central Public Health Authority, independent but coordinating with existing authorities such as FEMA and CDC and operating out of the President's office, should be established specifically to handle public health strategies for any future pandemics, as well as all communications related to those pandemics. This reserve team of medical experts could be called upon in times of extreme medical emergencies like the current pandemic, in much the same the way that the National Guard is called upon in times of civic emergencies.

In my opinion all states and localities should follow the directions of this new central Public Health Authority, and the media should have to check every new development with this Authority before broadcasting or printing. Every federal, state, county, and city executive, whether in office or running for office, should know what to do if an epidemic occurs—i.e. who would be in charge of what, how to develop comprehensive testing and contact tracing, and how to translate accurate and crucial information from the central Public Health Authority to the public. Accurate public information is our most important weapon—and it should be shared on a worldwide stage. This is a global problem, and countries need to coordinate.

With more contagious strains of COVID-19 coming from other countries, such as the Delta and Omicron variants, this epidemic is far from over, and epidemiologists and virologists agree that the future will have more pandemics brought on by other viruses. Our country is the most advanced in the world in terms of pharmaceuticals, vaccines and mechanisms of prevention, but this pandemic has left us with more than 1 million dead and in need of 20 percent more doctors, 40 percent more nurses as well as many more public health workers, social workers and other support personnel. It's possible that by the end of the current pandemic the United States will have improved its ranking among the nations of the world, but we have lost so many people because of our inadequate response. We simply cannot let this happen again.

Although the US spends more per a capita on healthcare than any other country, our infant mortality rate is higher than 33 other countries and we rank behind most European and some Asian countries in life expectancy. It has reduced in the US over the past 2 years.

If all of these recommendations about changing our public health system sound like they will involve a lot of work, well, that's because they will. What's more, the complex medical issues the country faces are just one tip of one iceberg in an iceberg-studded sea. Racism, gun control, climate change and income inequality are four more examples of huge and complicated issues that threaten to tear our country apart and keep us from thriving as a nation. So once again, I go back to the clarion call JFK issued on that cold January morning more than a half-century ago:

"Ask not what your country can do for you—ask what you can do for your country."

And so I call out to the younger generations: ASK NOT! Many hands make light the load, and this world is full of exciting opportunities to take meaningful action. Your country needs you. The world needs you. To quote another of our great Presidents, Teddy Roosevelt:

"It is not the critic who counts; not the man who points out how the strong man stumbles, or where the doer of deeds could have done them better. The credit belongs to the man who is actually in the arena…"

In contrast to those high minded comments, I would add a simple quote by my Louisville friend and political colleague, Lou Byron. When I asked him to comment on our first administration, he said "we didn't know what we couldn't do." That was my unconscious attitude in life whether it was climbing Kilimanjaro without any training, hitchhiking and riding the rails looking for jobs, setting up one of the first community health centers in the nation, or leaving a positive experience from years in volunteer and public office. Always strive for something bigger than yourself.

ACKNOWLEDGEMENTS

There were many hands and minds that helped bring this memoir about. First of all the inspiration was given to me by my daughter-in-law, Erin Sloane. I was encouraged and assisted in the dark days by many people but particularly Scott Sullivan, Judy Bross and Cass Harris. Robert Schlesinger was of immense help in structuring the manuscript and bringing my early years and career into focus. The memoir would not have been as well written and refined without the guidance of Leslie Marshall. Leslie and I spent time over six months making the memoir more readable. Many people helped me in gathering information and memories about my experiences over the years, especially: Allen Bryan, Joe Ardery, Sharon Wilbert, Jim Gulick, Ernie Allen, David Tileston, Eva Bright, Mattie Lewis, and Mark Newhouse. My brother-in-law, Mark McNally, helped me better remember various episodes of my time in Louisville; and my daughter, Abigail, helped with final edits.

I am grateful to Peter Hart, the dean of his generation of pollsters and my friend of over 50 years, for helping me launch my life in politics, for his continued support and friendship throughout my adventures in public service, and for his thoughtful foreword to this memoir.

Finally, the knowledge of leaving highlights of my life of public service to my children and grandchildren allowed me to keep laboring over three years. And I could not have accomplished this without the support of my wife and life partner, Kathy.

Printed in the USA
CPSIA information can be obtained
at www.ICGtesting.com
CBHW031649010524
7766CB00003B/94